NATIVE TO THE REPUBLIC

NATIVE TO THE REPUBLIC

Empire, Social Citizenship, and
Everyday Life in Marseille since 1945

Minayo Nasiali

CORNELL UNIVERSITY PRESS   ITHACA AND LONDON

First published 2016 by Cornell University Press

Printed in the United States of America

Library of Congress Cataloging-in-Publication Data

Names: Nasiali, Minayo, 1981– author.
Title: Native to the republic : empire, social citizenship, and everyday life in
    Marseille since 1945 / Minayo Nasiali.
Description: Ithaca : Cornell University Press, 2016. | Includes bibliographical
    references and index.
Identifiers: LCCN 2016015654 | ISBN 9781501704772 (cloth : alk. paper)
Subjects: LCSH: Marseille (France)—History—20th century. | Marseille
    (France)—Social conditions—20th century. | Marseille (France)—Social life and
    customs—20th century. | Marseille (France)—Emigration and immigration—
    History—20th century. | City and town life—France—Marseille—History—20th
    century. | Urban policy—France—Marseille—History—20th century.
Classification: LCC DC801.M37 N37 2016 | DDC 944.9/1208—dc23
LC record available at https://lccn.loc.gov/2016015654

Cornell University Press strives to use environmentally responsible suppliers and materials to the fullest extent possible in the publishing of its books. Such materials include vegetable-based, low-VOC inks and acid-free papers that are recycled, totally chlorine-free, or partly composed of nonwood fibers. For further information, visit our website at www.cornellpress.cornell.edu.

Cloth printing   10 9 8 7 6 5 4 3 2 1

In memory of my grandmother, Rebecca Minayo
Born in Chavakali, Colony and Protectorate of Kenya, 1925.
Died in Chavakali, Kenya, 2009.

Contents

Preface and Acknowledgments

I chose Marseille as my research site on a hunch. I began to think seriously about my research around the same time that cities around France were experiencing a wave of urban insurrection in 2005. As many observers noted, Marseille was an exception in remaining relatively peaceful. Intrigued, I decided, without ever having visited the city, to make the risky choice of focusing my research there. Equipped with the basic question "Why didn't Marseille burn?" I arrived in 2007 and moved into a mosquito-infested apartment in the city's oldest neighborhood, Le Panier. My goal was to study the so-called immigrant question since the 1973 OPEC oil crisis, concentrating especially on local associations and nonprofits dedicated to issues of inclusion and citizenship. It was supposed to be a project about political rights and civil discourse.

Two events dramatically changed my focus. The first was the discovery of a trove of archival documents about squatters and housing shortages in the 1940s and 1950s. After spending time with this material, I realized the project was much bigger than I had previously imagined it would be. It was not just about civil discourse and postcolonial migrants in the last thirty years; it was about the very foundations of the post-1945 French welfare state. It was about how postwar institutions were shaped within a broader imperial context. And, above all, it was about the role that ordinary people—both from the metropole and from the colonies—have played in forging expectations, not just about political but also, importantly, social citizenship.

The second thing that dramatically impacted my research was that I was robbed. I returned home one night to find that the front door of my apartment had been forced open and everything of importance—including my computer with my archival research—was gone. (Luckily I had taken extensive written notes and backed up everything except for a month's-worth of data.) In the days that followed I realized that I had been profoundly unaware of the intricate workings of the neighborhood in which I had chosen to live. First, all the usual avenues of help were fruitless: the police did not seem to care about what happened. When an officer finally arrived nearly twenty-four hours after I had called to report the burglary, his indifferent attempt to dust for fingerprints seemed like a joke.

After a day or two of my feeling helpless, a friend suggested that I consult with one of the *grands frères*, or "big brothers," who lived in the neighborhood. As it turned out, the man who spent most of his time sitting at a table at the local café in the Place de Lenche, whom I saw regularly, was the guy to talk to. "I hear you had some trouble," he said innocently when I approached him, "Let me see what I can do." He stepped outside for a moment and spoke with a few people I recognized who lived on my street before he returned to the café. "Your computer has already been sold," he informed me regretfully, "so unfortunately you can't buy it back. But . . . if you ever have any more trouble, come to *me* first." From that point on, I never did have any more problems during my time living in Le Panier.

I also began to pay much closer attention to the rhythms of everyday life. I noted that the women who sat on my front step chatting most afternoons—who eyed me suspiciously and never budged when I tried to pass—were the mothers or aunts of many of the neighborhood's so-called *grands frères*. Although none of them actually lived in my building, from the vantage point of my front door they could see up and down the length of my street, the rue du Refuge, and down a major side street. I learned that, when the normally bustling neighborhood was quiet and no one was outside, people were probably staying in their homes for a reason. Later, I might hear about some goings-on or a nefarious incident that had taken place. In short, I learned to pay closer attention to the everyday. I determined daily life was an important historical site that demanded investigation and could give me insight into ordinary people's understandings about who did—or did not—belong in their neighborhoods, their towns, and even their nations. From my time living in Le Panier I concluded that the question driving my research was not "Why didn't Marseille burn?" It was "What can looking at the local-level and everyday life tell us about twentieth-century France?" Thus, I owe an incredible debt to my Panier neighbors, including those who passed me on the street, those who shaped my quotidian experiences, and the people whom I came to know and count as friends. They and many others made this book possible.

·   ·   ·

During the many years I have spent on this project, I have benefited immeasurably from the wisdom and encouragement of colleagues, advisers, and friends. I thank Rita Chin, Joshua Cole, and Geoff Eley for their unwavering support and mentorship. I am also incredibly grateful to Tyler Stovall for his guidance and advice. The project has improved and profited immensely from the rich insights of Jennifer Boittin, Catherine Clark, Sheila Crane, Caroline Ford, Amelia Lyons, Andrew Ross, Nicole Rudolph, Lorelle Semley, Miranda Spieler, Pete Soppelsa, Gary Wilder, and Alexia Yates. I extend a special thanks to my friends in the trenches, Danna Agmon, Emma Amador, Sarah Hamilton, and Farzin Vejdani. I am ever grateful to my colleagues and friends at the University of Arizona, Julia Clancy-Smith, Susan Crane, Martha Few, Adam Geary, Kevin Gosner, Benjamin Irvin, Steve Johnstone, Susan Karant-Nunn, Fabio Lanza, Francesca Lopez, Javier Lopez, David Ortiz, and Laura Tabili. For careful reading of all or portions of the manuscript, I am beholden to Danna Agmon, Joshua Cole, Sarah Hamilton, Paul Pasquali, Tyler Stovall, Laura Tabili, and Farzin Vejdani. I extend a very special thanks to the editors and staff at Cornell University Press, especially Jim Lance and Peter Potter, and to the two anonymous reviewers who devoted time to reading and commenting on the manuscript.

Numerous institutions made this book possible. Funding from the Georges Lurcy Charitable and Education Trust helped me immensely during the research and writing stage. A President's Postdoctoral Fellowship at the University of California, Berkeley, supported me during my early efforts to revise the manuscript, and a Rackham Merit Fellowship from the University of Michigan was extremely helpful during my first few years of graduate school. Financial support to complete the final revisions of the manuscript and for the publication of the book has come from the University of Arizona.

I am especially grateful for the conversations with my French colleagues Audrey Celestine, Paul Pasquali, and Sylvain Pattieu. I thank members of *Les populations noires en France* group for the opportunity to participate in an especially fruitful cross-Atlantic dialogue.

I am indebted to the archivists at the Bouches-du-Rhône Departmental Archives, the Center for Contemporary Archives-Fontainebleau, and especially to Isabelle Aillaud at the Marseille Municipal Archives. At the Centre d'urbanisme, Le Musée social, and FASILD in Paris, as well as the Bibliothèque Alacazar in Marseille, numerous librarians and researchers devoted countless hours to help me find rare and extremely helpful materials. Major sections of this book would not have been possible without the generosity of residents and activists in Marseille. I thank Pierre Lezeau from the Mam'Ega association in Marseille's Grand Saint Barthélémy cité who permitted me to consult his organization's archives. I am also indebted to Mbaé Tahamida Soly Mohamed for sharing his many personal documents, photos, and data related to his work as an activist, hip-hop artist, and *animateur*.

I extend my warmest thanks to my French friends who have so generously opened their homes to me during my time in Marseille and Paris. To Sylvian Pattieu, Laureline Uzel, Monsieur Pattieu, and in memory of Madame Pattieu, I will never forget your hospitality and for the night of the *hérisson*. During my visits to Marseille, Arnaud Vassallucci has always made time to show me the calanques, to talk politics, and to help me feel at home in what was at first a strange city.

Finally, I thank my family, especially my parents, Opanyi Nasiali and Kathryn Nasiali, for their unconditional support and love. And I thank Ozan for his grit, his encouragement, and his reverence for no. 34.

• • •

Portions of this book feature revised and expanded discussions of research that appeared in published form in the following articles: Minayo Nasiali, "Citizens, Squatters and Asocials: The Right to Housing and the Politics of Difference in Post-Liberation France," *American Historical Review* 119, no. 2 (April 2014): 434–459; and Minayo Nasiali, "Ordering the Disorderly Slum: 'Standardizing' Quality of Life in Marseille Tenements and Bidonvilles, 1953–1962," *Journal of Urban History* 38, no. 6 (November 2012): 1021–1035.

Note on Terms

Throughout the text I have attempted to draw attention to the socially constructed and highly fluid nature of terms such as "immigrant," "asocial," and "*banlieue*." Even when I do not place them in quotations marks, readers should continue to consider these terms and the concepts they express to be highly fraught, contested, and in need of rigorous interrogation.

NATIVE TO THE REPUBLIC

Introduction

On September 15, 1960, a construction worker named Slimane T. addressed a letter to Gaston Defferre, the mayor of Marseille. "*Monsieur le maire,*" he wrote, "I live in two small rooms . . . without running water, gas, electricity, or a toilet. . . . My wife and I have four children, aged five years, four years, two years and two weeks."[1] Slimane T. explained that before moving to his current apartment he had lived with his family in an abandoned warehouse in another part of the city. For two years, his applications for a new, modern home had been denied, and now he was appealing to the mayor to help him find "a comfortable house . . . or at least one with running water."

Another Marseille resident, Abdallah T., also sent a letter to the mayor in 1960. "I'm married [and on] a pension," he wrote, "and this is the first time, *Monsieur le maire,* that I have asked for your help."[2] Abdallah T. and his wife had lived for years in a rented room on the seventh floor of an old downtown tenement hotel. In his letter he described how his wife had "twice fallen down the stairs" and wrote that he was seeking a more suitable home to accommodate them in their old age. Abdallah T. had migrated to Marseille from one of France's North African colonies twenty years previously, and in his letter he asserted that "since I've lived in Marseille, I have always . . . done my duty like all other good citizens." He also appealed to Gaston Defferre "as the guide and father of the city," to do *his* duty by helping Abdallah T. with his housing request.

Finally, in 1962, the president of a local residents' association, Arnaud R., also wrote to the mayor. He had recently moved to a newly constructed public housing development on the outskirts of Marseille and was concerned about the "danger threatening [his] neighborhood."[3] He wrote that he and his fellow neighbors were alarmed by the numerous "carnival people (*les forains*) and gypsies who [had] permanently occupied" a nearby parking lot. He was also anxious about "the hobos [living] in a nearby abandoned building in ruins." Arnaud R. concluded his letter by declaring, "We residents, conscious of our rights, demand that you . . . evict [these people and] afterwards . . . erase any traces [of them] from the neighborhood."[4]

These letters from ordinary people living in postwar Marseille illustrate three interrelated histories that have defined France in the late twentieth century. The first is the monumental task of post–World War II reconstruction.[5] Following the war, urban planners, technocrats, and other experts considered ways not only to rebuild France's war-damaged infrastructure but also to modernize the nation. Their efforts were deeply influenced by the need to address a serious and persistent housing crisis. Like many others in France, Slimane T. and his young family lived in a run-down, overcrowded tenement, and his situation exemplified the gravity of the housing shortage crippling France in the decades after the war. One major aim of the vast modernization project was to build housing on an unprecedented scale.[6] Importantly, such construction initiatives were not only an attempt to ameliorate the housing crisis but also an effort to find a definitive solution to the social question. Since the nineteenth century, social reformers, public health officials, and others had been broadly concerned about a range of societal problems including poverty, disease, criminality, and urban blight, all of which were assumed to contribute to the degeneration of the populace and the decline of the nation.[7] After World War II, renewed efforts to address the social question focused in large part on the potential for modernization and town planning to improve the everyday lives of citizens, with the ultimate goal of rejuvenating the nation.

Abdallah T.'s and Arnaud R.'s appeals also reflect a second major development in postwar France. These residents not only understood their housing problems in terms of the national crisis, they also saw them in terms of their welfare and rights as citizens. After the war, local and national authorities and ordinary people considered how best to reconstruct the physical space of the nation at the same time they were reimagining what it meant to be French. For Abdallah T. and Arnaud R., postwar reconstruction meant building a new kind of social space, one that would facilitate a reconceptualization of the relationship between citizen and state. More specifically, their letters illuminate how expectations about minimum living standards and decent housing came to be seen as social rights and important elements of a more comprehensive conception of citizenship. Across Europe in the years immediately following the war, policymakers, elected officials, and residents contemplated sweeping social change. Many were drawn to the ideas articulated by a number of reformers that included French civil servant Pierre Laroque and British sociologist T. H. Marshall. Marshall's theory of social citizenship—or the notion that every citizen deserves a certain quality of life—contributed to an evolving consensus about the need to guarantee the social rights of all citizens.[8]

These letters also reveal a third story, namely how the project to build a system of social security in France also entailed defining who *were* and who *were not* social citizens, and that this process was fundamentally shaped by empire. Abdallah T., Slimane T., and Arnaud R. all characterized themselves as dutiful, hardworking members of the polity who had therefore earned the right to modern living. In doing so, they contributed to normative understandings about who deserved access to expanding citizenship rights. Arnaud R. also went a step further by asserting that "undesirables" in his neighborhood were undermining his right to a better quality of life. He drew on the discourse of social rights to argue why others should be excluded. Abdallah T. emphasized that, although he had not been born in metropolitan France, he was nonetheless an upstanding member of what Gary Wilder has called the imperial nation-state. Abdallah T.'s claims about his right to decent housing underscore how people from all parts of the empire helped to define changing expectations about membership in France's postwar social democracy.

These three histories have fundamentally shaped post–World War II understandings about the welfare of citizens. And yet, the central questions at the heart of these stories remains underexplored: namely, how did housing come to be seen, not just as a basic need, but also an essential right of citizens? How did debates about building housing and managing urban space help to restructure the relationship between citizen and state? And how did empire inform this process? This book answers these questions by examining how the right to housing and to a quality of life became important features of the French welfare state and argues that evolving notions of membership were forged at the local-level. Located at the crossroads of metropole and colony, neighborhoods in the port city of Marseille are a dynamic terrain where diverse people made sense of the broader modernizing project and the changing imperial project. Quotidian negotiations between city residents, politicians, technocrats, and social scientists profoundly informed ideas about French citizenship and the built environment. Exploring their negotiations not only provides a more comprehensive history of the making of the postwar welfare state, doing so also helps to contextualize contemporary debates about the so-called immigrant question and the trouble with difference in France.

· · ·

Deliberations about how to institutionalize social citizenship were an important part of the post–World War II settlement in France as well as in Europe more broadly. Emerging from the war, France, West Germany, and most of Western Europe were committed to republicanism, but serious questions remained about precisely what form democratic institutions should take.[9] After the war, Western European nations began to create expansive welfare states at the same time that the nascent United Nations articulated a human rights agenda that included social welfare provisions.[10] While the 1948 Human Rights Charter set forth some theoretical guidelines for social rights, France, Great Britain, and most Western European nations were attempting to put a framework for social welfare into practice.

The post–World War II housing shortage acutely affected the development of nascent welfare institutions in France. In the late 1940s, members of the French provisional government contemplated major reforms that included nationalizing key industries and creating robust pension systems. But many of these long-term initiatives were overshadowed by the immediate and most pressing need to house the people. Around Europe, millions had been displaced from their homes because of wartime damages including the widespread bombardment of cities. In Marseille in 1943, for example, the Germans, in close collaboration with French officials and local speculators, dynamited over half of the city's oldest neighborhood and red-light district, Le Panier, with the goals of cleansing the city of this unruly space and freeing up valuable waterfront real estate. This destruction, combined with allied bombings in other parts of the city, contributed considerably to the postwar problem of homelessness. In Marseille as well as in other parts of France, those not displaced by the war continued to live in dilapidated and overcrowded tenements and slums. For many, the desperately poor state of French housing starkly illustrated how any attempt to modernize the nation would necessitate a fundamental reconceptualization of the meaning of quality of life. Housing—the right to shelter—was not only understood to be a basic human need, it was also increasingly championed as a citizen's right.[11] The housing crisis informed the growing consensus that full membership in the nation necessitated the protection of political, civil, and also—importantly—social citizenship.

In the decades following the war, residents, politicians, central state bureaucrats, local technocrats, and social scientists negotiated ways to institutionalize social citizenship. A primary goal was to facilitate the large-scale construction of housing and extend to all French families the right to a home. From the mid-1950s through the early 1970s, a more comprehensive system of public housing took shape as massive complexes known as *les grands ensembles* were constructed on the outskirts of most major French cities.[12] Many of these developments were hastily assembled out of prefabricated materials, and some families had to finish installing basic amenities such as doors and light fixtures themselves. Nevertheless, these new estates symbolized something important to many families.

Moving to a modern home became a mark of social mobility and an important indication that the welfare state was working. Many families were also willing to go to great lengths to achieve this goal and symbol of "having arrived." Some used their political connections, drawing on historical practices of clientelism and patronage to gain access to a coveted modern home. Others made the case that they had "good" families, that they were dutiful breadwinners or home-makers and therefore deserved to live in comfort. In doing so, housing applicants contributed to normative understandings about domesticity and helped associate the practice of social citizenship with certain kinds of social citizens.

Although many working and middle-class families were ultimately able to move into one of France's many *grands ensembles*, the postwar project to construct housing en masse was uneven at best. As such, it illustrates how understandings of a more expansive form of citizenship also created new spaces for exclusion. Everyday negotiations between experts and ordinary people, and neighbors and strangers, contributed to commonsense perceptions that not every family deserved access to a modern home: not everyone was ready to assume the duties of social citizens and therefore could not yet be extended the full complement of citizenship rights. In the late 1940s and early 1950s, many of these families were labeled "asocial," a catchall term that described everyone from slum dwellers, "gypsies," and drunkards to poor white French families, Italian laborers, and colonial subjects. The term drew on nineteenth-century concerns about the dangerous classes but also increasingly reflected a developing twentieth-century view that associated perceptions of race with assumptions about immutable cultural and social differences. Some asocials were first placed in temporary camps; others were eventually relocated to intermediary shelters known as Reduced Norm Housing where they were expected to adjust, to become more civilized, and therefore more deserving of social rights. Such practices contributed to the formation of a stratified and hierarchical system of housing in France: everyone deserved the right to shelter, but not everyone deserved the right to comfort, to modern living.

Such practices were also developing within and framed by a broader imperial context. Metropolitan debates about the potential for town planning to improve everyday life were shaped in important ways by colonial, and later, by postcolonial migration in the changing empire. The neighborhood-level intersections of modernization and decolonization further underscored how hierarchies of difference became institutionalized within French housing bureaucracies. For example, whereas in the 1940s and 1950s the asocial category referred broadly to France's supposedly undeserving classes, which often included colonial subjects, by the 1960s the term came to refer more exclusively to migrants from France's former colonies in northern and sub-Saharan Africa. In addition, following the so-called end of empire, colonial subjects were ultimately redefined as "immigrants" and included in new ways within welfare regimes. New policies granted these "immigrants" limited welfare services but did not extend to them political membership within the polity. These policies thus helped to decouple the perceived relationship between citizenship and social security by offering limited welfare benefits without political rights.

The economic downturn of the 1970s further called into question the postwar promise of a more expansive notion of citizenship grounded in social rights. During this period, some of the families that had originally moved to *grands ensembles* in the 1950s and 1960s began to move out of their now rapidly deteriorating apartments. And many families from former colonies as well as from France's overseas territories and departments began to move into these complexes in areas referred to as *banlieues*. As the recession persisted into the 1980s, many in France also increasingly imagined immigration to be a problem and associated recent migrants living in run-down public housing with the perceived decline of French welfare institutions more generally. Despite the numerous issues plaguing France's systems of social security, the *banlieue* and its troublesome residents came to symbolize broader concerns about the so-called crisis of the welfare state.

Beginning in the 1970s, efforts to rehabilitate these blighted neighborhoods, as well as the residents who lived there, contributed to evolving ideas that privileged the participation of ordinary people in urban renewal and resulted in new and unexpected understandings about citizenship and the built environment. A major goal of these initiatives was to encourage the formation of a vibrant local public sphere in France's *banlieues*. This emphasis on resident participation was informed by ideas about French republicanism—particularly the notion that abstract, undifferentiated citizens could actively engage in the public sphere—as well as by new trends in urban sociology and theories about social movements. Ultimately, resident involvement in these programs raised important questions about who, precisely, was being included in these projects. During urban planning meetings many residents—including former colonial subjects—argued that the only real way to solve social problems in their neighborhoods was through managing the ethnicity of the local population and by excluding *certain kinds* of neighbors from participating in the local public sphere.

• • •

Although the period following World War II is particularly relevant for exploring the development of welfare states, tensions over the meaning of and access to welfare also reflect a deeper history. During the French Revolution, republicans debated whether citizens had the right to a minimum standard of living and, importantly, if such guarantees should be included among the basic tenets of the universal rights of man. In doing so, they helped to introduce the idea that welfare and individual well-being were potentially human rights. Later, in the nineteenth century, concerns about the social question and the specter of national decline motivated social reformers and other experts to consider new ways of managing the people.[13] Unlike the revolutionaries of the previous century, these reformers imagined welfare to be less an individual right than a means of safeguarding the common good and health of the nation. Also in the nineteenth century, developing measures aimed at protecting workers' social security were seen as a way to guard against risk. Employers and labor organizations from France, Germany, and elsewhere created numerous industry-specific insurance and compensation regimes designed to provide support in case of on-the-job accidents or other work-related calamities. In addition, social Catholic and other private charities helped establish programs to aid needy mothers. Many of these pronatalist initiatives were later taken over and expanded by the state, particularly in France. By the early twentieth century, social security had become increasingly institutionalized as part of the modern European nation-state.[14] In France during World War II, the Vichy regime continued to develop prewar welfare institutions, particularly those programs that especially favored families. After the war, many of the bureaucrats and policymakers who had worked to expand welfare institutions under Vichy remained at their posts. They formed part of a force of technocrats, functionaries, and other experts who helped, in part, to establish France's postwar social democracy, a republic defined especially by its robust welfare state.

Historians have mostly explored the foundations of the modern welfare state in terms of the expansion of social insurance and family allowance programs.[15] Only recently have they begun to examine the large-scale construction of housing in post–World War II France as an important feature of developing welfare regimes. Scholars, notably Kenny Cupers and Nicole Rudolph, have described postwar construction as a process negotiated by networks of central state authorities, architects, and other elite experts.[16] In doing so, such studies mount an important challenge to earlier narratives about post–World War II modernization that have often described modern mass housing as a failed project characterized simply by the top-down efforts of the central state.[17] By contrast, more recent work shows how the cultivation of centralized housing institutions also created new modes of expertise for managing the interiors and exteriors of modern housing.

Such scholarship also takes the burgeoning post–World War II welfare state as a starting point. While these studies show that state officials enacted housing policies with the goal of better guaranteeing the social rights of the populace, curiously they tend not to investigate how social rights—such as the right to housing—came to be seen as so important in the first place. They therefore overlook a vital question: How did fundamental ideas about welfare and social citizenship actually take shape after World War II? More curious still, such works claim that there was no real public discussion about mass housing until after the first *grands ensembles* were constructed beginning in the late 1950s and early 1960s.[18]

In distinction, this study interrogates the rich, and often messy, context in which understandings about welfare and housing came to be understood as essential social rights. It underscores that such ideas were not given, they had to be forged. In doing so, it shows how investigating the evolution of social rights is not only vital to understanding postwar France, it is also important for making sense of the broader history of developing welfare regimes in Europe, North America, and elsewhere. Moreover, this study shows that, in addition to networks comprised of central state officials and other elite experts, municipal authorities and—most importantly—ordinary people played a crucial role in helping to construct social citizenship in the decades following World War II. Residents did not just react and respond to modern housing once they moved into *grands ensembles* beginning in the late 1950s, they were an integral part of the post-liberation dialogue about the meaning of welfare. For example, in the late 1940s homeless families in Marseille helped form a national squatters' movement. They argued that housing was both a human right and a right of citizenship. Their campaign starkly illustrated the monumental task of postwar reconstruction in France and also underscored the need to radically reevaluate what ordinary people could expect in terms of their basic quality of life. Squatters contributed to and helped frame a broader discussion about the necessity for sweeping social change in France, particularly the need to rethink the relationship between citizen and state.

Most studies of post–World War II French housing also tend to take the central state, centralized institutions, and the work of elite functionaries as starting points for their inquiries. I pose a different question and ask: What if we begin our investigation from another perspective? More specifically, how can focusing on the local level rather than the central state offer a more complex picture of postwar modernization? As George Steinmetz and others have argued, "it is impossible to understand the welfare state . . . without attention to the local level."[19] Focusing solely on elite actors and their policies overlooks the diverse local and regional actors that played a vital role in building the modern welfare state. Importantly, as Paul Steege et al. describe, the "local is never solely local" but "involves many 'outside' forces," such as international and national politics and central state and regional bureaucracies.[20] This study thus examines the local level as a dynamic site of interaction and mediation between ordinary people and government authorities from municipal, regional, and national levels. Such a perspective offers an important counterpoint to modernization discourses, which tend to show a linear, unidirectional flow of power from the central state outward.

Finally, most histories of post–World War II modernization and of the welfare state overlook the question of empire.[21] They do so despite the fact that France, as well as other nations, notably Great Britain, etched out comprehensive postwar metropolitan welfare regimes while attempting to redefine their statuses as large colonial powers. These imperial nation-states considered new ways to discipline urban spaces and people as part of the project to reinvigorate the empire and to establish comprehensive social democracies in the metropole. Such efforts thus underscore the centrality of empire and the legacy of imperialism to the late-twentieth-century project to create systems of social citizenship. We cannot begin to adequately examine postwar modernization and welfare without understanding how these processes were inextricably linked with and shaped by empire.

In the case of France, Amelia Lyons has begun the important work of bringing the extensive scholarship on welfare into conversation with empire. By showing how policies and practices aimed at "winning the hearts and minds" of Algerian families were developed as part of the Constantine Plan in Algeria and later transplanted in the metropole, she shows how the civilizing mission did not conclude with the so-called end of empire, but became an important tool for social control in the mainland.[22] Rather than focusing on policies exclusively targeting Algerians, I examine housing projects for both metropolitan French citizens and colonial migrants in a single analytic frame. Doing so permits a more complex and comprehensive look at how housing bureaucracies, and residents themselves, helped to produce inequality. I show how the modern French republic is necessarily shaped by its diverse members and how these members—whether metropolitan citizens, colonial subjects, or postcolonial migrants—have played an integral role in forging a differential system of social citizenship in France since World War II. This book thus shows how tensions over the meaning of and access to welfare were a constitutive element of developing social security regimes in Modern France and that these institutions were fundamentally forged within an imperial context. It builds on the significant contributions of scholars of the new imperial history who have explored how colonial practices have influenced metropolitan institutions.[23] This study, however, pushes beyond the notion that certain approaches were first cultivated in the colonies and then brought to the metropole.[24] Rather than reinforcing the discursive binary between metropole and colony, I show how Marseille's position as a port city suggests a new way of thinking about the space of the imperial nation-state. Rather than a linear site of transmission, Marseille is a hybrid, mediated place where people from all over the empire were part of the post–World War II project to better manage and modernize the populace.

Mapping Marseille

Marseille, like other French cities including Paris, Lyon, and Toulouse, became a vast construction site in the decades following World War II. These cities, like many European metropolises, were important spaces for postwar experimentation. They were places where residents, state officials, and social scientists debated ways to promote individual welfare and to foster the common good of the people. But Marseille's layered spatial history—a history molded by migration, by empire, and by the city's relationship to the central state—uniquely qualifies it as a contested and dynamic space for making sense of postwar reconstruction.[25]

The city's deep history not only frames how residents and state officials negotiated modernization in the late twentieth century, it also draws attention to broader tensions within the developing modern French state. As a port city and the historical gateway to and from the colonies, Marseille is an environment shaped by its position within an imperial and Mediterranean network. Originally called Massilia, the city was founded by Greek sailors from Phocaea in 600 BCE, and by the fourth century had become a major center for Mediterranean trade. Ruled by an oligarchy of wealthy merchants, Marseille maintained its independence as a city-state throughout most of the Middle Ages. In the thirteenth century, the city became nominally part of France when Charles d'Anjou conquered Provence. Despite this loose affiliation with the Gauls to the north, Marseille's leadership of oligarchs continued to prioritize the city's commercial interests in the Mediterranean, maintaining a somewhat rebellious relationship with the French Crown.[26] It was not until the seventeenth century that the increasingly absolutist monarchy definitively made Marseille part of France when, in 1660, Louis XIV quashed a local uprising against the Paris-appointed governor and occupied the city. Marseille subsequently became the leading port and trading center for the French Crown and later republics, as well as the staging point for expanding and defending the French Empire. From the eighteenth through the twentieth centuries, the city's extensive naval and military installations provided an important launching point for colonial offensives in Algeria, Indochina, and other parts of the world.

Marseille was also home to France's largest shipping company, the Messageries Maritimes, which carried goods and people throughout the empire. Exploring Marseille's place as a key node in this imperial system underscores how the city is a significant space of mobility. The city's historically contested and often tense relationship to central state power also draws attention to an important but often overlooked dimension to discussions about modern France, namely that the flow of power between Paris and its provinces was never unidirectional but has always been negotiated, variegated, and complex.

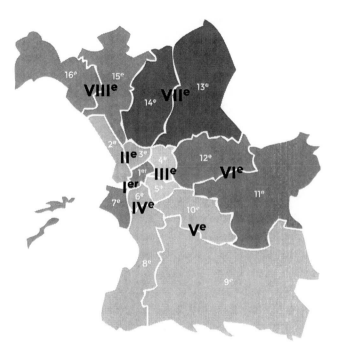

Map of Marseille, its sixteen *arrondissements* and eight sectors.

Source: https://commons.wikimedia.org/wiki/File:Secteurs_Arrondissements_Marseille.svg. Author: Superbenja-
min - Own work. Licensed under CC BY-SA 3.0 via Wikimedia Commons.

Marseille is an environment profoundly shaped by migration. Historically, port commerce brought to town many kinds of people from all parts of the world.[27] Some, including sailors and merchants, only stayed a little while, booz-ing for a few days in dockside bars or carousing in the city's red-light district before shipping out again. Others settled more permanently in the city. Accord-ing to Harlem Renaissance writer Claude McKay, who lived for a time in the city in the 1920s, Marseille was "Europe's best back door ... [with] seamen from Senegal, soldiers from Madagascar ... [and] pimps from everywhere.... The town seemed to proclaim to the world that the grandest thing about modern life was that it was bawdy."[28] In the nineteenth century, Corsicans seeking work on the mainland began settling in Marseille and were joined by Italians in the late nine-teenth and early twentieth centuries. Later, Greeks, Armenians, and Spaniards made homes in the city. People from all parts of the French Empire also traveled through or settled in Marseille. Some came from rural parts of metropolitan France. Others came from France's overseas territories and colonies.

Although colonial subjects had always maintained a presence in Marseille, their numbers increased in the twentieth century. Between the two world wars, a sizable number of decommissioned soldiers from France's colonies in north and sub-Saharan Africa remained in the metropole. After World War II, migration from the colonies increased, in part because of the labor demands generated by the postwar economic boom, but also because of the political upheavals resulting from decolonization. Since the mid-1960s, migrants from former colonies continued to move to the city and were joined by families and workers from France's remaining overseas departments and territories (or the DOM-TOM). Many newcomers initially settled in Marseille's crowded downtown neighborhoods but later moved to large housing developments in the northern and eastern outskirts of the city.

Marseille's history of migration has thus shaped how the city has developed over time, and has also influenced how residents imagine urban space. Much of Marseille's historical development has been oriented around the Vieux Port. When the Phocaeans first settled the area in 600 BCE, they chose the hilly terrain just north of what is now the old port, because the elevation provided an important vantage point from which to watch for intruders and because this was one of the only areas where they found a steady supply of fresh water. Over time, the neighborhoods just north and east of the Vieux Port grew into a labyrinth of closely packed buildings, narrow streets, and steep staircases. These neighborhoods, including Le Panier and Belsunce, have also been the historical destinations of most newcomers to Marseille.

By contrast, the neighborhoods south of the Vieux Port are much newer, dating from the eighteenth and nineteenth centuries, and they are much more open, with airy tree-lined boulevards and roomy traffic circles. The city's historically working-class, migrant neighborhoods extend from the dense city center to the far north of the city, where Marseille's port industries expanded in the nineteenth century, and where most *grands ensembles* were constructed in the late twentieth century. South of the Vieux Port are the more affluent neighborhoods, where luxury villas dot the road along the bay known as the Corniche J. F. K., and where deluxe apartments overlook Marseille's main beach, la plage du Prado. Although neighborhoods in the eastern outskirts of the city also attracted migrants and later became sites for the large-scale construction of housing, many Marseillais nonetheless imagine their city in terms of a north-south divide. Residents' understanding of the space of their city is thus sculpted not only by its physical geography but also by its social and cultural topography.[29]

Local and central state authorities also tend to imagine Marseille in terms of a north-south divide. At various points throughout Marseille's history they have tried to intervene to reshape the city's built environment in the hope that altering its urban space would also affect greater social control over the population. In the seventeenth century, when Louis XIV was trying to bring the city in line

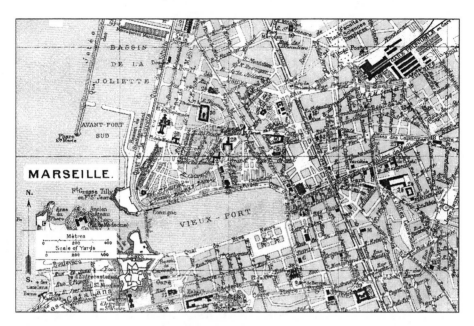

In this early-twentieth-century map of downtown Marseille note the dense, winding nature of the streets in the area known as Le Panier, which is just north of the Vieux Port, and the more gridlike layout of roads south of the Vieux Port.

Source: http://www.tourvideos.com/Images/maps-big/France/France-south-mid/Marseilles-center-France -BlueGuide.jpg.

with the Crown, he commissioned the construction of two military outposts, the Fort Saint Nicholas and the Fort Saint Jean, which guard the entrance to the Vieux Port and were intended as much to keep a watchful eye on the Marseille popu-lace as to protect the town from outside threats. The king also encouraged the development of new neighborhoods south of the Vieux Port with the objective of thinning out the port district neighborhoods. The city's downtown neighborhoods were not only assumed to be spaces of vice and sedition, they were also under-stood to be breeding grounds for such scourges as the plague, which subsequently devastated the city in 1720. In the late nineteenth century, and inspired by Hauss-mann's work in Paris, similar projects were enacted in the *phocéen* city. State authorities brought potable water to new parts of town and also expanded Mar-seille's maritime infrastructure, creating the commercial port La Joliette, which is north of the Vieux Port. But many local authorities ultimately concluded that Haussmannization had been largely ineffective. A major goal of Marseille's rede-velopment efforts was to clear out the city center's dense neighborhoods, construct luxury apartments along the newly widened boulevard, the rue Impériale (now the rue de la République), and to displace the poor and often migrant families who lived there to the outskirts of the city. But port commerce and other maritime-related industries continued to make downtown the most attractive place to live for the city's working residents. As a result, the working-class port-district neighborhoods continued to flourish and few bourgeois families settled downtown. After World War II, the housing crisis, coupled with the influx of displaced persons, migrant workers, and colonial subjects into the city, once again compelled residents and government officials to rethink Marseille's built environment. Following the war, the city scrambled to buttress collapsing buildings in downtown tenements, demolish slums, shelter some homeless families in makeshift detention centers, and move others to new housing. These efforts epitomized the late-twentieth-century undertaking to modernize the nation and its citizens but also reflect a longer, centuries-long concern with disciplining the unruly spaces of French cities.[30]

Marseille's urban history thus offers crucial insights into broader historical efforts to manage city space in modern France. However, Marseille is not simply a stand-in, or a placeholder, merely reflecting national trends. Just as other French cities have their own unique characteristics, there is much that is different about Marseille. Attention to this uniqueness emphasizes why doing history from the perspective of the local level is so important and how such an approach elicits a deeper understanding about the city itself as well as its relationship to the national story.

For example, in the last forty years, discussions about France's troubled neighborhoods often refer to the *banlieues*, or suburbs located just outside major cities such as Paris and Lyon where many *grands ensembles* were built. By contrast, Marseille does not have a *banlieue* in this strict sense of the term. Most of its so-called problem neighborhoods are not in bordering suburbs, they are located *within* the city limits.[31] Instead, references to Marseille's troubled areas usually mention the city's *quartiers nord*. This term refers to the northern, outer *arrondissements* of the city where most *grands ensembles* are located. Like the term *banlieue*, *les quartiers nord* often has a negative connotation. Yet, unlike *banlieue* residents, inhabitants of Marseille' *quartiers nord* are technically part of the political infrastructure of the city: they vote for city council members and they help to elect the mayor. Nevertheless, when talking about problems in France's *grands ensembles*, the media, politicians, and others often conflate Marseille's *quartiers nord* with other cities' *banlieues*. In short, although Marseille's northern neighborhoods and the suburbs of Paris and Lyon have their own distinct histories, they are nevertheless often described in terms of shared pathologies.

As John Merriman, Annie Fourcaut, and others have shown, the fringes of French cities have historically been contested and fraught spaces.[32] In the nineteenth and early twentieth centuries, the term *banlieue* broadly referred to the sparsely populated edges of towns, including those around Marseille. These un-regulated areas attracted working-class families seeking to escape dense, over-crowded city centers.[33] In city outskirts around France, most families built their own single-family homes, dug their own wells, and obtained their own heating sources.[34] Such areas also became sites of concern for public health officials and urban planners who believed these autoconstructed spaces required stricter reg-ulation. In Marseille, many of these areas were ultimately incorporated into the city, whereas in other parts of France they developed into autonomous suburbs. In contemporary discourse, residents of Marseille's *quartiers nord* and other cit-ies' *banlieues* continue to be characterized in terms of their seemingly peripheral relationship to the polity.[35] But as Merriman and others remind us, these marginal spaces of cities—and their residents—had to be invented. The idea of marginality as a constructed space shows how *certain kinds* of residents can be integral parts of their cities at the same time they are perceived to be living on the frontiers of city life. The ways in which Marseille's *quartiers nord* are simultaneously *part of* and *peripheral to* the city starkly illustrate this point.

Making Sense of Everyday Life

Significantly, this idea of marginal space underscores how, as Henri Lefebvre and others have argued, urban space is neither a static nor a neutral category but a social production.[36] Lefebvre has shown how space is dynamic and constructed, and is both experienced and in part produced by people. He and others, notably Michel de Certeau, also explore the relationship between the production of so-cial space and everyday life.[37] According to Certeau, even the mundane daily practice of "walking in the city" is a political act. He argues that the various ways people navigate the city create the potential for the reinterpretation of spatial meanings codified by state governments and other institutions.

Building on this framework, this study takes everyday life as a useful category of analysis and argues that Marseille is an important local-level site for explor-ing the interrelated themes of postwar reconstruction, imperialism, and in-equality. Residents' diverse experiences of living in the city emphasize how everyday life was not only an important realm where politics happened, it was also the space for understanding how social citizenship was institutionalized in postwar France.

Historians of the everyday assert that such a focus underscores how people matter by taking seriously the various ways they interpret, negotiate, shape, and are shaped by their worlds.[38] Yet everyday life has been criticized as an elusive object of study and a parochial method of doing history: it is both everywhere and nowhere;[39] it is hard to pin down. But as Agnes Heller puts it: "everyday life is above all *situated*. It always occurs in relation to a person's immediate locality."[40] It is from this perspective of place that people endeavor to make sense of the contingencies and particularities that compose their daily lives. In postwar Marseille, quotidian patterns—such as going to the bar or gathering with neighbors on the front stoop—gained meaning by becoming ritualized. Such practices informed the stories people told themselves about their neighborhoods and about belonging. They were a way of "making sense," of forming a daily narrative which, Heller argues, "is a fundamental activity of everyday life."[41]

The making of narratives and the ritualization of everyday practices also affect how certain perspectives become normalized or "taken-for-granted." Paul Gilroy has described how this quotidian process of making meaning also produces common sense, which he defines as "storehouse[s] of knowledge which have been gathered together historically."[42] His ideas about taken-for-grantedness are particularly useful for exploring how welfare institutions developed in postwar France. More specifically, commonsensical ideas—which often developed out of the daily experiences of ordinary people—profoundly shaped how knowledge about citizens and state institutions was produced. For example, in the 1950s and 1960s, numerous residents living in rundown Marseille neighborhoods penned letters to the mayor and other government officials complaining about local slums and slum dwellers. Their characterizations of these people as "dirty," "thieving," and "uncivilized," coupled with municipal urban planners' detailed descriptions of the slum problem in Marseille, informed local slum-clearance initiatives, including how best to rehouse the supposedly "unworthy" residents. Importantly, such efforts also illuminate how the making of commonsense narratives is not only shaped by the ritualization of everyday practices but also by conflict. In this case, Marseille residents perceived slum dwellers as disruptive to daily life. Their letters to state officials illustrate how everyday life can be characterized as much by quotidian acts of contestation as by the mundane.

Attention to everyday life helps illustrate how commonsensical ideas have deeply informed France's evolving postwar social democracy. But a focus on the everyday is not limited to an examination of the local level. In Marseille in the 1950s and 1960s, families seeking a more comfortable life not only understood their daily hardships in terms of the struggle to make ends meet but also in terms of national debates about reconstruction and international discussions about guaranteeing basic human needs. Down-and-out families in Marseille ultimately made claims about the best way to improve their daily lives by drawing from and also contributing to broader discourses about citizenship. In this sense, everyday life might focus on a small story, but it also tells a larger story. A careful interrogation of the everyday has the potential to synthesize the study of norms and institutions as well as the activities of ordinary people.[43] Everyday life is the place where contingency and agency overlap.[44]

In order to explore both the practice and the politics of everyday life in postwar Marseille, I have consulted a diverse array of sources including urban planning documents, demographic neighborhood studies, maps, city and regional council meeting minutes, and communications between various departments at municipal, regional, and national levels. Throughout the book I focus on particular neighborhoods in Marseille and how their unique histories tell us something important about social citizenship and inequality in postwar France. But this is not a book about bottom-up contestations of central state power. The focus here is neither purely top-down nor bottom-up. Instead I attempt to draw a much more complex picture of how ideas and institutions crystallize over time and are informed by negotiations at multiple levels. At times I zoom out to show how national debates have informed local politics. In other moments I zoom in to illustrate how local-level issues have played a formative role in shaping national discussions. I have drawn from methods utilized by both social and cultural historians, often reading sources against the grain, or against each other. I have taken seriously the comprehensive quantitative work produced by urban planners, public health officials, and others, but I have also been mindful of the silences such quantitative work can produce and the assumptions on which such work might be based.

As this is a history of the role of ordinary people in shaping postwar understandings of housing and social rights, I have also carefully sought out their voices in a variety of places. I have drawn from archival letters, neighborhood meeting minutes, newspapers, and published interviews as well as my own oral histories with residents and conversations with representatives from local associations. During some of these conversations, several Marseille residents brought to my attention a number of community-run websites that featured video streams of interviews with local people. These resources, coupled with more traditional materials, help to form an archive that showcases a richer picture of neighborhood concerns. They offer a glimpse of local debates that were not always mediated or curated by the state.

Although in large part a history of ordinary people, this is not a study of any specific group—say, "Algerians" or "migrants." It is an exploration of particular spaces and how diverse kinds of people both inhabit and produce meaning about these places. Focusing on neighborhood space allows for a more complex understanding of how categories of difference crystallized and how these notions informed the production of knowledge about citizenship and access to welfare. Moreover, by not focusing exclusively on a specific ethnic group, I have attempted to avoid reifying the very categories I aim to analyze.

This study thus investigates how ordinary people have not only participated but also played a crucial role in constructing the places where they dwell, including the home, the neighborhood, the city, the nation, and the empire. Importantly, such an approach provides a new take on contemporary discussions about the trouble with difference in France. In the last forty years, much debate has focused on whether race and ethnicity should figure as legitimate topics of discussion within the French public sphere. Strict republicanists often claim that, according to the French constitution, citizens appear as abstract individuals without differentiation or particular identification.[45] Republican scholars assert that one participates in the French public sphere "dressed simply and solely in the garb of an individual citizen."[46] In this vein, many French-language studies have characterized postwar migration and the immigrant question in terms of class inequalities, stressing that there are no racial problems in France, only social problems.[47] In the last ten years, however, French scholars—notably in the field of history—have increasingly questioned this line of thinking by demonstrating how perceptions of race and ethnicity have explicitly shaped the imperial nation-state.[48] American scholars of France have also worked to historicize the myth of republican citizenship by showing how understandings about the abstract citizen are not timeless but are themselves products of historical moments.[49] Despite these important interventions, contemporary French discourse still tends to see the abstract citizen, and especially the public sphere, as a priori and essential elements of the republican nation-state. But as scholars of early modern Europe remind us, the public sphere is neither a thing nor an immutable concept.[50] In fact, there can be many different kinds of public spheres, and they can both include and exclude. This study explores the late-twentieth-century process through which the French public sphere came to be seen as taken for granted. It proposes an alternative understanding to ongoing debates about the trouble with difference in France by exploring the public sphere, not as an a priori concept, but as a constructed, historical space. By taking everyday life as an important category of analysis, this study emphasizes how recent debates about difference and the public sphere are above all situated in time and place. In this sense, the public sphere should be seen as a particular kind of constructed site, a built environment profoundly shaped by the postwar effort to define social citizenship within an imperial context.

Chapter Summaries

Chapter 1 focuses on the immediate postwar period as a crucial moment of possibility when new voices participated in a broad discussion about social change.

From the mid-1940s through the early 1950s, homeless families in Marseille helped form a national squatters' movement and argued that housing was both a fundamental human right and a right of citizenship. This campaign for social reform and for a more expansive notion of citizenship also created unexpected opportunities for exclusion as state officials and squatters themselves considered ways to put the right to housing into practice. Chapter 2 examines modernization efforts in Marseille during the Fourth Republic and explores how residents contributed to normative discussions about modern families and urban development, ultimately helping to define both the social citizen and neighborhood space based on commonsense assumptions about difference. Chapter 3 examines slum clearance in Marseille from the end of the Fourth Republic through the beginning of the Fifth and considers the important role of local *techniciens* as mediators between everyday life and central state policies. Their efforts to both categorize and classify slum dwellers coincided with mounting colonial conflicts, particularly the war in Algeria, and these local-level intersections of modernization and decolonization contributed to shifting ideas about who were slum dwellers and who deserved to have access to an increasingly differentiated system of housing. Chapter 4 examines local and national efforts to manage the quantity and the quality of the French populace following the so-called end of empire, and considers how social scientists informed the broader public debate about France's supposed "threshold of tolerance" for migrants. Chapter 5 examines the work of central state institutions, municipal governments, and a New Left generation of sociologists to develop urban rehabilitation programs for France's most distressed neighborhoods, notably several in Marseille. An important goal of these developing policies was to encourage residents to participate in the regeneration of their homes and neighborhoods with the aim of creating a local and vibrant public sphere. Ultimately, resident involvement in these projects raised important questions about who, precisely, was participating in these forums that shaped local understandings about social rights and national belonging. Chapter 6 further explores the themes of urban renewal and resident participation, focusing on the targeted expansion of youth programs from the late 1970s through the 1990s. During this moment, public debate at both local and national levels often characterized youth living in France's *banlieues* as both likely delinquents and potential citizens. Efforts to rehabilitate the built environment included the cultivation of youth programs designed to mold the bodies of teenage boys and girls to encourage the apprenticeship of especially gendered notions of citizenship and civic duty.

Part I

MODERNIZING THE IMPERIAL CITY

On October 14, 1952, the modernist architect and designer Le Corbusier stood in front of a crowd of dignitaries in the port city of Marseille to celebrate the completion of his bold prototype for a new style of housing. In his address to local politicians and central state ministers, he declared: "It is my pride, my honor, and my joy to hand over to you the 'Unité d'habitation,' the first manifestation of an environment suited to modern life. . . . Town planning changes precisely because of . . . the Unité."[1] Located in the southern Marseille neighborhood of Sainte Anne, this rectangular, modular, concrete, twelve-story building—or "vertical village"— is suspended on large pillars and houses over three hundred apartment buildings, as well as a number of shops, a restaurant, medical and sporting facilities, and a theater. While many hailed the Unité, or La cité radieuse as it was also called, as an important template for modern living, others were more critical of the project.[2] Locally, some even called it La Maison du Fada, or the nutter's house.[3] According to one article titled "Corbusier, Should He Be Condemned?" published in the local newspaper, *Le Provençal*: "The apartments in the Cité radieuse are in the fashionable style. But they are also inconvenient."[4] The article quoted Monsieur Vergnolles, president of a Marseille neighborhood housing association, who stated: "The thing that displeases me, it's that the Corbusier building presents itself like an official attempt to direct how we live. . . . The dream of each Frenchman is the villa, with a small garden. Instead of that, they want to contain him in this building."[5] For this Marseille resident, the Unité d'habitation contrasted sharply with his own vision of the good life. Such local debates about the design and construction of the Unité reflect broader post-1945 concerns about modernization and the best way to transform domestic and urban life.

After World War II, living standards rose markedly for many people throughout Western Europe and North America. Labor was in demand, and for the first time some families could afford new amenities and conveniences such as cars, washing machines, refrigerators, and even vacations. But for many other families, the paucity of resources that marked the wartime years continued to shape everyday life well into the postwar moment. Although domestic comforts and better standards of living were by no means ubiquitous after the war, the roughly twenty to thirty years of postwar economic growth have nevertheless been called *les trente glorieuses* (the thirty glorious years) in France, and "the economic miracle" elsewhere. Part I of this book explores modernization initiatives in this moment as an uneven and contested process and shows how the policies, institutions, and even the very ideas central to postwar systems of welfare were fundamentally shaped by the actions—both mundane and organized—of ordinary people in dialogue with local and national officials. Such a focus provides an important counterpoint to the dominant assumption held by many scholars, namely that postwar urbanism was largely directed by the central state and that there was little local-level innovation and public debate about housing and welfare.

1

"WE HAVE THE RIGHT TO A HOME!"

"In Marseille the Squatters Occupy!" read the headline of the *Monde Ouvrier* after six families illegally occupied a vacant house in 1946.[1] Following World War II, France began reconstruction amid a crippling housing shortage. During the housing crisis, homeless families sought shelter in partially destroyed buildings, under bridges, or in rapidly growing shantytowns. Many were from metropolitan France, others were colonial subjects from north and sub-Saharan Africa. Some families had migrated from Italy or Spain before the war, or were displaced persons from central or eastern Europe. As one Marseille squatter remembered, "Families, children, and the elderly lived where they could, in bombed houses, in caves, in public wash-houses . . . and in infectious slums."[2] As the provisional government deliberated over comprehensive plans for postwar reconstruction, many families grew increasingly desperate and began to organize and attend local meetings. Building on their shared experiences of everyday life, a growing movement began to take shape. Although many had begun illegally occupying buildings out of necessity, squatting became a political statement and part of an evolving agenda. Squatters argued that housing was both a human and a citizenship right.

The immediate postwar period was an important moment of possibility for debates about rights and welfare in imperial France. In the metropole, the provisional government considered establishing a robust welfare state that would guarantee the social rights of all citizens. But the postwar housing crisis shaped and gave a sense of urgency to these discussions about the meaning of welfare, and the squatters' movement raised important questions about the relationship between citizen and state. In the colonies, African labor activists also questioned metropolitan discussions about the universality of social rights as Senegalese workers protested about poor wages, calling for "equal pay for equal work."[3] African deputies elected to the French parliament likewise challenged the meaning of membership within the French empire and pushed for new legislation to rework the status of colonial subjects.[4] The 1946 Lamine-Guèye law granted colonized people citizenship status, but it did not give them full access to the rights of metropolitan French citizens. This legislation, coupled with the major campaigns for social reform in both the metropole and colonies, underscores how postwar efforts to define welfare also illuminated persisting hierarchies within the imperial system.[5]

In metropolitan France, squatters advocated for the right to housing using the rhetoric of human rights and citizenship. During the early years of the housing crisis, squatters claimed that housing was a universal human right: everyone deserved to have a roof overhead. In doing so, they invoked human rights to service their own agendas and their efforts show how the language of universalism has been mobilized to serve varying ends at specific historical moments.[6] In the movement's final years, as squatters increasingly partnered with social Catholic and communist organizations, their agenda began to shift. By the early 1950s, they described housing less as a human right than a working-class right that citizens earned by being productive members of the nation. In the mid-1950s, tensions over the meaning of squatting as well as conflicts between Catholics and communists contributed to the disintegration of the movement. Ultimately, squatters used the rhetoric of universal rights to make claims about the particularities of social citizenship within the nation-state.

While squatters largely defended the right to housing by drawing on the rhetoric of class, state officials often classified squatting families in terms of perceived ethnic differences. In the early 1950s, government authorities began to recognize the right to housing by relocating homeless and squatting families to temporary holding camps around France. In the attempt to regulate and rehouse the homeless, local government officials labeled many families—particularly colonial subjects and "gypsies"—as "asocial." The term "asocial" drew on nineteenth-century concerns about the floating poor and dangerous classes in European cities. It also reflected a developing twentieth-century understanding that tied perceptions of race to assumptions about immutable cultural and social differences.[7] Many so-called asocial families lived for many years in what were supposed to be temporary camps. Although many of these families technically had French citizenship because they were part of the empire, they were singled out as distinctly un-French and therefore not fully eligible for the right to housing.

The Housing Crisis and Everyday Life

The post–World War II housing crisis was nearly global in scope. Government authorities in Europe, North America, and parts of Africa and Asia struggled to provide shelter for their populations as demobilized soldiers returned home en masse. In most areas, the postwar crisis stemmed from failed depression-era policies and the stalled global economy of the 1930s. In Europe, the housing shortage was further exacerbated by the staggering numbers of displaced persons who desperately needed homes.

France's housing crisis resulted from wartime damages, but also from fragmented and poorly funded urban planning and public-housing programs dating from the late nineteenth and early twentieth centuries.[8] Prior to World War II, most families undertook new construction themselves, haphazardly adding rooms to existing structures.[9] Many families built homes in the *terrains vagues*—or no-man's-land—that fringed most large French cities.[10] These unregulated areas alarmed public health officials concerned about the so-called degenerative effects of slum living. In France, as well as in other parts of Europe, concerns about inadequate housing prompted state authorities to consider constructing some type of public housing for needy families. In the interwar period, French authorities created the Habitations à bon marché (Low Cost or HBM) system of state-subsidized housing.[11]

Despite these early efforts to construct public housing, the two world wars severely limited hygienists' and urban planners' attempts to combat the slum problem. During World War I, the French government froze rent prices in an attempt to discourage landlords from speculating, but did not systematically unfreeze rents during the sporadic postwar reconstruction.[12] Property owners had little incentive to build new housing or maintain existing buildings, and the housing market stagnated.[13] A 1939 state report noted that France needed an additional 1.5 million new homes to achieve a relative equilibrium between supply and demand.[14] However, during World War II, an additional two million houses and apartment buildings were destroyed, which exacerbated an already critical situation.[15]

In the first years following the war, French authorities struggled to implement an effective housing construction policy. In 1948, fewer than 40,000 houses were constructed in all of France, and only 55,000 were built in 1949.[16] Many of these new homes were too expensive for most working-class families to afford. As a result, houses with high rents stood empty, while overcrowding became endemic in the old tenements and homelessness increased.[17]

Between 1945 and 1946, approximately 32,000 families remained homeless in Marseille alone, and slums and shantytowns mushroomed around the city.[18] As one resident remembered, "Children were the most susceptible to disease. . . .

Families shared a single 'room,' parents and children together. Rats ran through these shacks, over the blankets of families sleeping on the bare earth."[19] In addition to seeking refuge in slums or under bridges, Marseille families also began to take shelter illegally in abandoned buildings.[20]

Concerned authorities searched for some kind of short-term solution to the crisis. Confronted with widespread homelessness, the provisional government passed the ordinance of October 11, 1945, which granted homeless families the right to apply to requisition unoccupied buildings. Although intended to help families circumvent outdated housing bureaucracies, in practice the ordinance required cities to establish a new bureaucracy out of older, stagnant, and often corrupt housing offices. Most often, municipal housing offices were simply swamped with requisition requests, and extreme understaffing led to hopeless backups. In Marseille, out of the more than 10,000 requisition requests filed at the local housing office, 7,500 were refused. Very few of the 2,500 families whose applications were approved were actually able to move into requisitioned housing due to legal protests by landlords.[21]

The Squatters' Movement and the Human Right to Housing

As the housing crisis escalated, Marseille families began to organize meetings. Many met regularly with Henri Bernus, a former resistance leader, who petitioned the prefect to streamline the requisition process. By 1946, several other organizations began to participate in Henri Bernus's gatherings, including members of the Marseille branch of the Mouvement populaire des familles (the Popular Movement for Families, or MPF), a social Catholic organization.[22]

Initially, this loose affiliation of Marseille groups attempted to work within the local bureaucracy, but with little success. Marius Apostolo, secretary of the Marseille MPF, described the growing frustration among homeless families as discussions with authorities stalled: "During our meetings with the prefect, he would make notes of some addresses and promise to act within the week. The days passed, and despite our formal reminders, nothing happened."[23] As a result, these organizations began to debate alternative approaches to the problem. As Apostolo recounted: "After a meeting on September 29, 1946, we decided on the need for direct action. . . . we had heard of a British news item about an Englishman who tried to occupy Buckingham Palace illegally. The idea hit us like lightning: squatting!"[24] These Marseille groups joined to form the Comité d'entente de squatters (The Committee for the Alliance of Squatters). While many homeless families were already illegally occupying buildings out of necessity, these activists began to view squatting as a political strategy.

In October 1946, the Marseille-based Comité occupied their first strategically chosen squats, which included a brothel, a mansion, and an unused portion of a monastery. As one activist described moving into the monastery: "The Brother Superior couldn't believe his eyes. Here we came, a caravan of old trucks, with women (what scandal!) and children, setting up house next to the poor retired monks."[25] By August 1947, the Comité claimed to have established five hundred squats around Marseille.[26] The movement also began to take root in other French cities, including nearby Aix-en-Provence and Anger, Arles, Lyon, Nice, and Lille.[27]

As the movement in France gained momentum, authorities grew increasingly anxious about squatters. They were especially concerned about the movement's seeming disregard for public order and private property. In an attempt to curb the wave of squatter occupations, the Ministry of the Interior began ordering police raids to expel families from unlawfully occupied properties. Authorities also began to repeatedly arrest and fine leaders of the movement.[28]

The government's heavy-handed approach to the growing squatters' movement stemmed in part from postwar concerns about reestablishing order. In the months following the Liberation, *comités de libération* sprang up around France, many calling for *autogestion*, or workplace autonomy.[29] Other *comités* formed soviet-style councils and agitated for a new political system privileging local political participation. In all, such groups offered a multiplicity of visions of the postwar order.[30] Government officials, particularly Charles de Gaulle, viewed these impulsive expressions of direct democracy as anarchic threats to the still fragile provisional government. And they viewed squatters' disregard for private property as part of this alarming trend. Though authorities understood that major social and political reform was necessary, many also believed that these efforts should be managed by the central state in Paris. The concerns of French officials reflected the postwar anxieties of many Western European governments. As officials in France, West Germany, and Britain contemplated the scope and scale of reform they also questioned the potential roles of the state and its citizens to define and develop systems of welfare.[31]

By the late 1940s, squatting had become a national problem in France, and concerned state officials continued to order police raids and violent evictions in an attempt to suppress the squatters' movement. The Marseille-based Comité d'entente des squatters vehemently protested against these forced evictions. In a 1947 letter to the Bouches-du-Rhône prefect, Henri Bernus condemned one such police raid of the Chateau Fallet, a mansion occupied by several families: "Monsieur le Préfet . . . eight families were thrown out into the street by police methods that can be called neither French nor even humane: one does not chase families out of their homes at night, one does not throw their furniture out of the windows, or refuse a blanket to a pregnant woman, who, denied the right to shelter herself in an empty chateau, was forced, along with the other homeless, to shiver in the night."[32] By condemning such police tactics, Bernus evoked recent memories of the occupation and the role the police and other authorities played in rounding up, persecuting, and expelling Jews and other "undesirables" from Marseille neighborhoods.[33] The letter also criticized housing authorities' insufficient efforts: "If the public-housing authorities would do their jobs, the homeless would have no reason to squat."[34] Most important, the Comité began to use the language of rights to justify squatting: "[Squatters] take no pleasure in creating public disorder and simply desire to live in more humane conditions. *It's their right*, even if they don't possess the deed."[35]

Squatters began to argue that families had the human right to occupy vacant buildings even if they did not have the legal right to the property. As one housing activist wrote in a newspaper editorial: "The right to a life . . . surpasses the right to possessions and belongings."[36] Squatters even invoked the Declaration of the Rights of Man to justify illegally occupying buildings: "If squatters are outside the law in terms of written, legal text, their actions are completely justified in terms of the meaning of the law in regard to *les droits de l'homme . . .* these women and men oppose these violations of human rights."[37] They argued that housing was a natural right that should be guaranteed prior to any legal claim to private property.

Squatters thus attempted to invest their movement with legitimacy by claiming that housing was a universal right.[38] In doing so, they contributed to a broader international debate about the postwar future of human rights—especially questions about which rights should constitute human rights. Historians have shown how allied leaders heralded the protection of universal rights as one of the major justifications for fighting the war, but that serious questions remained about whether a human rights regime should focus on civil liberties or address, as Mark Mazower puts it, "the social demands generated by [World War II]."[39] Such work has also cautioned against essentializing rights discourses by showing how the language of universal rights functioned as part of the war effort at the same time that such rhetoric opened up questions about how to define an international rights regime.[40] French squatters similarly utilized the rhetoric of universal rights as a tool in their struggle for housing. By illegally occupying privately owned buildings, they presented an alternative view to a liberal defense of rights by privileging human welfare over private property. They also made the case that housing—very much a particular concern in the postwar moment—was a natural, timeless, and therefore essential human right.

If an important postwar debate was about which rights should constitute human rights, another key question pertained to who had human rights. Historians have examined how twentieth-century human rights ideas and regimes have been a product of empire. For example, studies have shown how the United Nations, and the League of Nations before it, were initially conceived—in part—to carry on the work of civilizing others by maintaining a "differential system" with the goal of encouraging human progress in line with Western ideals.[41] Such work has raised important questions about the "degree" to which diverse peoples are able to have human rights.

As French housing activists emphasized the universality of their claims, their accounts of the everyday lives of squatters and the homeless also described the diversity of these families. For example, as one activist recalled, "Life wasn't easy. . . . We lived in a wooden shanty in one of the poor neighborhoods populated by Italians, Belgians . . . Algerian workers [and people] from Africa."[42] Another activist described the residents living in one of the earliest organized squats in Marseille: "eight nationalities lived together, which often strained mutual understanding. . . . A Russian family, the wife an aristocrat and painter, the husband an ex-legionnaire alcoholic, lived next door to a Corsican shepherd."[43] Several leaders of the movement were also the children of recent migrants. Marius Apostolo, the secretary of the local branch of the MPF and a rising leader in the movement, was born in Marseille in 1924 to parents who had recently emigrated from Greece. Apostolo's parents were part of a wave of interwar migration to France that included Armenians escaping the genocide in Turkey and refugees displaced by the Spanish Civil War. This population of recent arrivals also grew as colonial subjects came to metropolitan France in increasing numbers. Many settled in Marseille's dank, downtown neighborhoods, which were particularly affected by the destruction of World War II.

Did housing activists claim to represent all homeless or squatting families in their campaign for the human right to housing? Who made up the "we" in "we the squatters?" Apostolo and other activists referred to the various ethnic backgrounds of homeless families. However, as they sought to legitimize their movement, the Comité did not defend squatting and homeless families in terms of their differences but in terms of their universality. In the early years of the movement, housing activists claimed to speak for all destitute families. In doing so they argued that social rights—such as the need for shelter—were basic and thus universal.

A Place in the Sun: Working-Class Families and the Right to a Home

As the squatters' movement continued to spread throughout French cities, activists' agenda gradually shifted from a defense of the human right to housing, to a claim that housing was an important citizenship right. This important distinction ultimately raised new questions about who was eligible for the right to housing and who, precisely, should be considered a French citizen. Squatters were increasingly influenced by the national Mouvement populaire des familles, which began to play a larger role in the growing movement. According to internal correspondence from the Ministry of the Interior: "The Mouvement populaire des familles, whose goal, in general, is to provide moral and material aid to families, has created a special branch of its organization devoted to the issue of 'squatters.' "[44] According to this report, leadership among housing activists also began to shift as Henri Bernus was increasingly marginalized, while others—particularly Marius Apostolo—began to participate in the national MPF organization. The movement also began to garner support from the communist affiliated Confédération générale du travail (or CGT). These changes reflected a larger trend as political Catholics and communists briefly cooperated after the war, helping to shape ideas about social democracy throughout Europe.

Created in 1939, the MPF was initially part of the Catholic social reform movement and promoted charitable organization against problems like poverty.[45] Founded on the defense and promotion of the family, the MPF's vision fit in with Vichy policies, and it was able to operate relatively freely under the regime. Both during and after the war, the MPF was concerned broadly with the welfare of poor and working-class families. For the national MPF, the housing crisis and plight of displaced families became key issues in the postwar settlement.

Initially, the MPF contributed to squatter arguments about the human right to housing. For example, in a 1947 pamphlet entitled *Housing for the People*, the MPF asserted that the right to housing was "human and natural."[46] Elsewhere, in an op-ed for the *Monde Ouvrier*, an activist justified the right to shelter in terms of the fundamental importance of "respect for the human person" and for human needs.[47]

Although the MPF claimed that the right to shelter was "human and natural," in the same pamphlet, *Housing for the People*, it also stated that "all men who work deserve the right to a roof overhead."[48] The MPF thus claimed that housing was both a universal need and a particular citizenship right of the working classes. In doing so, it exploited a central paradox of human rights discourses—specifically, the question of whether rights can be guaranteed outside or within the nation.[49] The ways in which the MPF blurred the distinction between human rights and citizenship rights reveal how squatters invoked the human right to housing in a universal sense, but did so with the aim of entreating the French state to engage in actual social reform.

By the late 1940s and early 1950s, activists' understanding of who squatters were began to narrow, particularly along class lines. As the MPF asserted in one publication, "the right to property is one of the first rights demanded by the working class. . . . They want their place in the sun. They want their own home."[50] French activists began to argue that the state had a responsibility to provide for its citizens, but citizens had a duty to be productive and working members of the polity. As the movement continued to gain momentum in France, activists increasingly claimed that housing was less a human right and more one of the important tenets of a postwar vision of social citizenship.

In addition to the growing role of the MPF in the movement, communist syndicates also began to support French squatters. Members of the CGT began to participate in squatter meetings and joined protests in several French cities including Anger, Caen, and Lyon.[51] The CGT began supporting the squatters' movement at a time when the French Communist Party (PCF) had emerged as the dominant political party after the Liberation.[52] As a result of the pivotal role communists had played in resistance movements around Europe, communist parties were at their most popular following the war.[53] In France, PCF leaders acknowledged their mainstream role in the government by expressing their support for national reconstruction and by taking up the theme of citizenship and responsibility. In several 1945 speeches, for example, PCF leader Maurice Thorez asserted that "the recovery of France [must] be the task of the whole nation" and that "to produce," to be working members of the polity, was the "highest form of class duty."[54]

The participation of both the CGT and the MPF in the squatters' movement reflected a brief moment of cooperation between Catholics and communists in the 1940s.[55] In the interwar period, many Catholic groups had outrightly condemned communism, and some had supported right-wing forms of national socialism as the better "third-way option."[56] During the war, communists and those Catholics who were disillusioned with fascism formed an uneasy alliance within resistance movements around occupied Europe.[57] For a brief time during the war and into the postwar moment, left-leaning Catholics and communists shelved interwar hostilities in order to work together on national reconstruction. In France, Catholics and communists found common ground in the squatters' cause and helped to make claims about the working class right to housing.

The popularity of the PCF and the role played by communist and Catholic groups in the squatters' movement contributed to a wave of populist sympathy for squatters.[58] As a result, state authorities became increasingly concerned about public opinion. Government correspondence reveals internal deliberations about "the problem of evictions . . . which [are] very delicate."[59] As one Marseille official wrote: "pure and simple eviction is problematic. It fans the hostility of public opinion and risks serious trouble."[60] State officials also recognized that the "reason why public opinion and the press in particular condemn the eviction of squatters

is because those often evicted—or affected by the problem of run-down housing—
are often working-class families."[61]

Correspondence between the Bouches-du-Rhône prefect and the Ministry of
the Interior demonstrate that not only were state officials concerned about managing public opinion, they were also—to a certain degree—sympathetic to the squatters' situation: "In the particular case of squatters, eviction from illegally occupied
buildings further compromises their interests because they are prevented from
definitively resolving their unstable situation by finding permanent housing.
Chased from their houses, the only other option for these homeless families is to
find another squat."[62] Although the central Ministry of the Interior pursued an
official no-tolerance position on squatting, between 1946 and 1950 local and national authorities increasingly questioned the effectiveness of these policies in
internal correspondence.

Such communications between various levels of the administration contributed to a slowly emerging consensus about the right to housing. As early as 1947,
local officials began to discuss the need to rehouse squatting and homeless
families.[63] From 1949, reports from the Bouches-du-Rhône prefect's office began
to emphasize that any eviction for unlawful occupation must be accompanied
by rehousing: "Evictions must be more humane and the possibility of rehousing
must be offered to a displaced family."[64] By 1950, officials at the central Ministry
of the Interior began to acknowledge that "roughly evicting squatters will do
nothing to solve the problem."[65] Local and national authorities understood that
the housing crisis could no longer be ameliorated through mass evictions: "The
only real and efficacious solution lies in . . . the construction of new buildings."[66]
In acknowledging the construction of housing as the only lasting solution to the
crisis, state authorities also began to recognize the legitimacy of squatters' claims.
This was reflected in a report sent to the prefect of the Bouches-du-Rhône that
openly stated, "The leaders of the squatters movements have been advocating for
this kind of solution."[67]

From 1946 to 1950, about 20,000 people—or 5,000 families—found shelter
by participating in the squatters' movement around France.[68] In the early years
of the movement, housing activists were generally concerned with the issue of displaced and diverse homeless families. They participated in postwar debates about
what constituted a human right by claiming that squatters had the right to housing by virtue of their basic humanity. As the movement gained momentum,
Catholic and communist groups played a growing role in squatter campaigns
and activists increasingly invoked housing as a basic citizenship right.[69] In doing
so, they show how postwar debates about the right to housing ultimately contained the idea of the universal human within the social citizen.

Implementing the Right to Housing

The housing question was integral to postwar discussions about national renewal and managing the built environment, and squatters contributed to these debates by emphasizing the duties and social responsibilities of citizens and the state. While activists were able to house some families, the bulk of responsibility for constructing housing ultimately fell on the French government. In 1944, the provisional government created the Ministry of Reconstruction and Urbanism (MRU).[70] The mandate of the MRU was not just to reconstruct war-damaged buildings and resolve the housing crisis but also to modernize cities.[71] As Raul Dautry, the first head of the MRU, wrote: "It's necessary to conceive of and realize the modern organization of life . . . the time has come to 'rationalize' the city."[72] In addition to the serious problems caused by the housing shortage, the majority of French homes lacked indoor plumbing and other amenities.[73] Urban planning officials believed that new plans for large-scale housing construction would resolve the housing crisis as well as create a new, efficient domestic lifestyle.[74] Such plans were designed to give substance to the developing consensus that all deserved a right to a certain quality of life and standard of living.

The MRU's far-reaching plans reflected the ambitions of urban planners and architects on both sides of the Atlantic. In the interwar and post–World War II periods, civic reformers considered novel ways to reshape the built environment.[75] Many civic reformers were influenced by the work of designers such as Walter Gropius and Le Corbusier and believed that architecture could transform and improve everyday life.[76] For postwar urban planners, reconstruction meant putting modernist theories into practice and at the service of the nation. For some in Europe, reconstruction also heralded a break with the past. In France, the politics of reconstruction often emphasized the rebirth of the nation.[77] MRU head Dautry, for example, described his vision for comprehensive urban planning as an "essential part of France's renaissance."[78] Despite such rhetoric emphasizing 1945 as a watershed moment, many of the officials who had worked under the Vichy regime remained at their posts after the war.[79] And many of the bureaucracies established in the 1930s and 1940s continued to play key roles in the postwar reconstruction process.[80] In establishing the MRU, for example, Charles de Gaulle and the provisional government stressed that the institution would play a key role in planning for France's future, but the ministry itself was created by combining two housing and planning institutions established during Vichy. Moreover, although Dautry had distanced himself from Pétain during the war and was thus deemed a suitable candidate to head the new ministry, he nonetheless retained many of the bureaucrats and urban planners who had been active during Vichy.

Although housing construction was a top priority in most of Europe, many housing institutions struggled to fulfill their mandates in the years after the war. In France, the stagnant postwar housing market and the rapid succession of Fourth Republic ministers and governments stalled MRU efforts to solve the housing problem.[81] Moreover, as Danièle Voldman has explained, in those years, central state officials, though concerned about housing, tended to prioritize the reconstruction of France's industrial infrastructure.[82] Although French housing authorities were developing comprehensive construction plans, any significant increase in housing was still years away.[83] Officials still had to resolve the problem of homeless and squatting families. If families could not illegally occupy private properties but were also entitled to the right to housing, how could authorities address their immediate needs?

In the late 1940s, French authorities considered establishing temporary camps to house squatting and displaced families.[84] According to a report submitted to René Paira, prefect of the Bouches-du-Rhône department: "The only thing we can do while we await real construction is to put families in camps."[85] The MRU, in cooperation with the Marseille municipality, chose sites for two squatter camps: Grand Arenas, in the south of the city, and Grande Bastide, in the north.[86]

Initially called the Baumette Prison, Grand Arenas had been constructed as a penitentiary in the 1930s. However, the prison never kept inmates. Instead, during World War II, French and German officials used Grand Arenas as a detention camp for captured Jews and members of the resistance prior to their deportation to concentration and death camps.[87] After the war, French officials housed colonial soldiers and workers in Grand Arenas as well as in its sister camp, Grande Bastide.[88] Displaced persons of all origins passed through Grand Arenas, including released POWs and Jews on the way to Palestine. Following the independence of Syria and Lebanon in 1946, exiles from this first wave of decolonization also landed in Grand Arenas.[89] In the 1950s, officials further expanded the function of the camp to house squatting families. Camps such as Grand Arenas were intended to be temporary holding centers until the MRU could move families into newly constructed housing.

Recent studies have examined the multiple uses of detention and concentration camps following World War II.[90] Such scholarship has underscored important continuities across the so-called zero hour of 1945, as well as emphasized how camps became part of the postwar settlement.[91] In France, camps such as Grand Arenas became important sites for imagining the meaning of reconstruction, particularly the process for articulating what the nation should look like, and who belonged to it.

In the early 1950s, municipal and regional authorities began relocating families from Marseille squats to the Grand Arenas camp. For those who had never before experienced life in a provisional camp, first impressions were often incredulous. As one former Grand Arenas resident recalled: "There was the first shock with the shanties. . . . It was hideous."[92] Most families were housed in sheet-metal, shanty-like barracks.[93] A typical barrack was divided into sections and shared by about thirty-five people.[94] As another resident remembered: "We lived in barrack 89; it was shaped like a half-barrel. The room was cut in two and there were two bedrooms. We put ten children in one bedroom, the parents in another, and there remained a common room we shared."[95] There was no running water in the barracks; showers and toilets were collective and outdoors.[96] According to one resident: "[T]here was no real sewer, only a kind of sewage pit which was a fiefdom for the rats."[97] Conditions were poor in these makeshift shelters, and exacerbated by bad weather: "There were terrible moments of flooding. . . . When there were enormous thunderstorms there were always people who lost their barracks."[98] Rain transformed the earth around the barracks into swampland, or the Mistral—the strong, dry, north wind—kicked up great clouds of dust. In the summer, the extreme heat was oppressive, as most barracks were constructed out of sheet metal and tar. Camp conditions also took their toll on residents' health. Skin diseases like impetigo were rampant, and the most common contagious diseases were tuberculosis and trachoma.

As squatting families were relocated to Grand Arenas or Grande Bastide, residents' accounts of camp living conditions began to trickle out to the press and to the MPF. The MPF initially responded vociferously: "It's a scandal!" wrote one activist in the *Monde Ouvrier*: "Here is how, in the twentieth century, the families of workers 'live.' "[99] Another activist called the camps "an attack on our dignity" and an "easy way out" of the housing crisis.[100]

Why were activists so up in arms over government attempts to ameliorate the housing crisis? State authorities were, after all, doing what squatters had initially asked for: supplying homeless families with "a roof overhead." The outcry over the camps reflected housing activists' shifting claims. In the early days of the movement, the Marseille-based Comité d'entente des squatters had originally framed the housing crisis in terms of the need to shelter all destitute families. As the movement gained momentum, as well as support from the national MPF and communist syndicates, housing activists no longer argued for the need for housing, but the right to a home. Squatters asserted that a proper home was "the ideal that permits the family to thrive . . . [and] assures national progress."[101] They specified that, in addition to a "roof overhead," a working-class home should include: "a kitchen . . . a living room, a minimum of three bedrooms . . . and a bathroom."[102] Such an idealized description of domestic space drew a sharp contrast with the overcrowded barracks and unsanitary conditions in Grand Arenas. Squatter protests thus underscored the growing importance of the relationship between class and the housing question for French activists. Drawing on communist and progressive Catholic ideas, activists argued that the working classes were central to the rebirth of the nation, and that reconstruction should—for the good of the nation—provide families with their own homes.

Despite housing activists' condemnation of the camps, French officials reasoned that rehousing squatters was the best way to suppress the movement, and that the camps were the best means at their disposal. As a Marseille city official wrote: "The social trouble constituted by the squatter movement must disappear. These camps are the only solution that might actually obtain this result."[103]

After the initial protests by the MPF, newspaper reports about camp housing conditions did indeed begin to dwindle. By the mid-1950s, the squatters' movement had also effectively broken apart. Fissures within the movement had appeared as early as 1949, as some activists remained committed to Christian-inspired work but distanced themselves from the growing participation of communists in squatter campaigns. Henri Bernus, who had been increasingly marginalized within the movement, ultimately left the Comité allied with the MPF to join the Castors, a group of workers and worker priests committed to self-help and the construction of small, cooperative communities around France.[104] Others chose communism over political Catholicism. In the mid-1950s, Marius Apostolo left the MPF to join the PCF and became heavily involved in the labor movement.[105]

The disintegration of the French squatters' movement in the 1950s encapsulates, in part, growing tensions between political Catholics, communists, and socialists, and highlights developing competing ideas about the best ways to cultivate postwar social democracies around Europe. As Cold War lines hardened, the moment of cooperation between communists and social Catholics drew to a close. In Western Europe, nascent Christian Democratic parties developed large followings, articulating a democratic vision that stressed broad interconfessional unity among citizens—and the necessity of an explicitly anti-communist agenda.[106] By the late 1940s, the communist party was banned in West Germany and Greece, and marginalized in France and other parts of Western Europe.[107] In 1947, Paul Ramadier—the first prime minister of the French Fourth Republic—purged the communists from his cabinet, thus ending the coalition between the Catholic Popular Republican Movement (MRP), the French Section of the Workers' International (SFIO), and the PCF.

Although short-lived, the French squatters' movement highlights how left-leaning Catholics and communists helped to imagine and define the social citizen as a productive, respectable member of the national community. The initial universalism of squatters' claims—that housing was a natural right—became more particular as activists increasingly drew on the rhetoric of class to make their case.

Squatters and "Asocials"

Activists helped to define a much narrower conception of squatters as social citizens and, in doing so, raised more questions about which families were fully eligible for the right to housing. Although the French squatters' movement began to disintegrate in the mid-1950s, numerous families continued to move to and live in the Grand Arenas camp. They did so at a time when Marseille had become one battleground for Cold War conflicts between the CIA, French anticommunists, and local communist worker unions.[108] Marseille was also the staging point for the movement of soldiers and colonial subjects as France engaged in costly colonial wars in Indochina, and later, in Algeria. Within this broader context, local and national officials tried to initiate comprehensive plans to modernize Marseille as well as confront pressing issues such as poor living conditions in Grand Arenas.

In January 1956, Grand Arenas' sewage system flooded, which threatened camp residents as well as a nearby canal that brought potable water to Marseille.[109] Several months later, in July 1956, the director of the municipal bureau of hygiene attributed the deaths of two infants in the camp "to toxic contamination."[110] This public health official also noted that other young children in the camp were "covered in open sores"[111] and, in a memo, "insisted that the municipality (1) improve water mains and (2) impose a regular trash service."[112]

Despite such warnings about camp conditions, government officials struggled to make significant improvements to the camp. One explanation stemmed from the multiple bureaucracies that disputed their jurisdiction over Grand Arenas. For example, the camp was initially managed with funds from the central Ministry of Reconstruction and Urbanism before the city of Marseille took over in the early 1950s. Camp management changed hands again in the mid-1950s when the regional branch of the MRU took charge. It was therefore often unclear who was actually responsible for Camp Grand Arenas. For example, in a 1956 letter to Mayor Gaston Defferre, prefect Raymond Hass-Picard asserted "that no part of Grand Arenas is under my jurisdiction."[113] Gaston Defferre likewise denied any municipal administrative responsibility for the camp.

Out of these disputes, local and regional officials gradually came to a consensus about the "real" source of the problem. In response to a number of critical letters from the Bureau of Hygiene, R. Calloud, the director of Sanitary Services, argued that "the number of trash cans is sufficient for the population and we pass by three times a week to collect the garbage."[114] The real problem, Calloud wrote, was that "damages are due to poor use. . . . The principal origin of these issues is due to the negligence of a large number of camp users who dump their garbage around their barracks."[115] According to this official, the sanitation problems in

Grand Arenas were not caused by poor infrastructure, overcrowding, and mismanagement, but by the residents themselves.

By the mid-1950s, local-level correspondence about sanitation problems in Grand Arenas had shifted from the camp to the residents. As one official from the prefect's office wrote: "There exists in Marseille, without doubt, an extremely colorful and cosmopolitan population, a minority of asocial nomads and vandals."[116] According to this official, many had been squatting in Marseille prior to moving to Camp Grand Arenas, and "it [was] precisely these asocials who cause[d] the most amount of worry."[117]

What did the term "asocial" mean to French officials?[118] In their descriptions of asocials, government officials evoked historical anxieties about the floating poor. As studies of nineteenth-century Europe have shown, concerns about the so-called dangerous classes and their concentration in urban slums contributed to state initiatives to better classify and categorize the populace in an effort to solve the "social question."[119] With the rise of the international eugenics movement in the early twentieth century, social fitness became increasingly associated with biological characteristics. Eugenicists contributed to an emerging scientific imagination which claimed that degenerative behavior could be marked and measured on the body. Following World War II, French officials continued to utilize the term "asocial" to describe an urban populace deemed unfit. Their understanding of the asocial category thus attests to the pervasiveness of racialized thinking in the twentieth century and how it remained central to state officials' postwar concerns about the social question.[120]

Government officials also understood "asocials" to be distinctly foreign. As an engineer for the city of Marseille described them: "These [Camp Arenas] residents have many different nationalities . . . and they don't make use of the eight garbage dumpsters."[121] Authorities thus associated foreignness with un-French and therefore socially unfit behavior. According to R. Calloud: "It is important to note that the behavior of many of the camp residents conforms to habits imported from their countries of origin."[122] The ways in which Marseille officials described "asocials" reflected older perceptions of social class and anxieties about the floating urban poor. But such descriptions also explicitly reflected assumptions about racial and ethnic difference. More specifically, when identifying Marseille's "asocial" residents, officials also described this local "foreign" population in ethnic terms, as "North Africans" or "gypsies."[123] According to an official at the Bouches-du-Rhône prefect's office, asocials were: "nomads as well as people from all parts of North Africa."[124] Government officials' tendency to describe North Africans as foreigners is particularly curious, as most were technically part of the French empire.[125] Moreover, after 1946, colonial peoples also technically had French citizenship.

Although state officials understood "asocials" as part of the squatter category, they differentiated between working-class families who deserved a roof overhead, and this other "undesirable" subgroup. For the population of working-class squatters, the camps were a temporary solution to the housing problem. It was understood that these families would eventually move into better, modern homes once they were constructed. For the other population of squatters, the timeline for their stay in camps such as Grand Arenas was less definite. As one official wrote, this "mobile and poorly defined population" needed to be "fixed" in place.[126] Authorities reasoned that "gathering and containing this population" of asocials would better allow for the project of national reconstruction.[127]

By the mid-1950s, although Grand Arenas was still labeled "provisional," it began to house more permanent populations. While many squatting families cycled through the camp in the early 1950s—eventually moving to newly constructed HLM apartments—by mid-decade, many "asocial" families had formed a permanent presence in the camp. By 1961, 40,592 residents were still registered in Grand Arenas.[128] As one former resident remembered: "My parents had a bakery in Oran. Our family told us to come to France because there was work. We squatted for two years in Marseille before we landed in camp Grand Arenas. I was young, but I understood then that the camp was supposed to be temporary and we wouldn't be staying there for long. Even so, we stayed there seven or eight years."[129]

Sanitation and management problems also persisted in the camp. After a 1959 visit to Grand Arenas, Marseille city council member Jean Fraissinet described camp conditions in a scathing letter to the regional and national branches of the MRU: "One could believe that this is a concentration camp . . . garbage was being scattered by the wind and dogs. . . . I don't know how it could be designed like this but I saw a tall sewage tank, very odorous, built exactly in front of a barrack, occupied by the family A.!"[130] Over time, and after multiple appeals by camp residents as well as city council members, regional MRU officials did make some improvements to the barrack-shanties. In the mid-1960s, authorities built more permanent housing out of prefabricated materials. By the 1970s, families were still living in Grand Arenas when the state began efforts to close the camp for good.

• • •

The debates and issues surrounding the Grand Arenas camp illustrate the complicated and unexpected ways that the right to housing was put into practice. In the early days of the squatters' movement, the local Comité defined squatters in general terms, as families in need of housing. Although activists recognized the diverse ethnic and cultural backgrounds of these families, they defended housing as a universal right. In doing so, they revealed one of the key tensions in human rights discourses—specifically, how universal claims are often inextricably tangled with the particularities of nation-states and perceptions of national belonging.[131] However, by the early 1950s, as the MPF and labor organizations became more involved in the movement, activists narrowed their claims. They increasingly defined squatters as working-class citizens who deserved the right to a home.

As government officials began to implement the right to housing by moving families into temporary holding camps, they understood squatters, neither in general terms—as just humans—nor solely as working-class citizens. Government officials understood squatters as a differentiated category that included working-class families as well as another group, whom they called "asocials." Although state authorities perpetuated nineteenth-century anxieties about the "dangerous classes" in their descriptions of asocials, they also identified some in this group in ethnic terms—most often as "North Africans" or "gypsies." According to state officials, asocials needed to be set aside from the general citizenry in order for the nation to undertake the project of postwar reconstruction. The concentration of asocials in camps such as Grand Arenas thus demonstrates how notions of Frenchness were being reinscribed in a time when such ideas were seemingly up for debate.

As the subsequent chapters explore, in the decades following World War II, French officials and ordinary people reconsidered the republican pact to include an expanded notion of social rights, such as the right to housing. In implementing these presumably universal rights, attempts to rehouse and concentrate populations deemed "undesirable" contributed to the development of a stratified and hierarchical system of housing in late-twentieth-century France.

"WE HAVE THE RIGHT TO COMFORT!"

In a 1953 interview, newly elected socialist mayor Gaston Defferre declared: "We must modernize and develop this city that we love, to ameliorate the standards of living of our residents."[1] In his first years in office, Defferre worked with the municipal council to "transform the visage" of Marseille by balancing the budget, renovating the potable water and sewage infrastructures, and redeveloping key areas of downtown.[2] With help from the central government and funds from the Marshall Plan, the city also improved roadways, constructed a tunnel under the port, and built the Corniche John F. Kennedy, the highway that replaced the old road around the bay.[3] Politicians and local businesspeople also worked to bolster the port economy with the goal of maintaining Marseille's position as an important junction between Europe and Africa. After the war, most of the port's hangars and docks were rebuilt or retrofitted to accommodate larger cargo ships and other advances in shipping technology. In addition to increased port traffic, the city's growing naval and oil-refining industries also helped to form the industrial backbone of this "second city of France."[4] According to Mayor Gaston Defferre, he and his administration wanted to make Marseille and the surrounding region into "the California of Europe." Although several of these projects built on plans introduced during the interwar period, they were nonetheless characterized as something new and were intended to revolutionize and rationalize city space.[5]

Marseille's postwar development projects are often seen as local extensions of the comprehensive national project to modernize France. For example, under the guidance of Jean Monnet, the national Commissariat général du plan implemented a program for postwar reconstruction and initiated policies aimed at fortifying France's long-term economic strength. The commissariat oversaw the national-ization of key industries and prioritized the production of industrial goods deemed vital to national interest. Jean Monnet and members of the commissariat also believed that the future health and stability of the nation depended on reestab-lishing France's place within the larger international community, which entailed both strengthening colonial ties and encouraging a more economically interde-pendent Europe. These comprehensive and ambitious projects were laid out in a series of five-year plans. As part of these national initiatives, Marseille and most of France's larger cities also drafted their own municipal five-year plans, which included major projects to improve local infrastructure and to construct housing.[6]

Scholars have situated these post–World War II modernization efforts within France's historical tradition of centralization. Indeed, most historians of mod-ern France tend to make Paris and its institutions the dominant foci of their studies. For example, scholars have discussed how elite technocrats and other nonelected, central state officials formed a cadre of actors who played a key role in forging postwar modernization initiatives. Such work has underscored the apolitical nature of their efforts to produce new forms of knowledge and modes of expertise.[7] In distinction, this chapter shows how focusing on Paris and the efforts of nonelected experts only reveals part of the modernization story. Only by looking at the local level can we gain a fuller picture of the project to revitalize the nation. There was not a single, monolithic development plan for France, but rather a multiplicity of visions.[8] Ordinary people, in particular, helped to imag-ine and forge the meaning of modernization, and it was thus shaped by and fil-tered through local practices and culture. Moreover, this chapter argues that modernization was a highly political affair. In Marseille, residents formed associa-tions to protest about pollution caused by nearby factories and petitioned city hall to improve their neighborhood infrastructures. They also engaged in pa-tronage politics by promising to vote for local socialist and communist politi-cians in exchange for access to new housing. In doing so, residents—including colonial subjects—contributed to broader normative discussions about modern-ization and the modern family. They helped to define social citizens in gendered terms as breadwinners and homemakers.[9] Perceptions of class and ethnicity also shaped residents' understandings about neighborhood space as well as their ex-perience of urban development. Commonsense assumptions about difference informed how residents from diverse backgrounds imagined who was "from" their neighborhood and who therefore deserved the right to modern living.

The Right to Comfort

In the 1950s, the local lifestyle periodical *Marseille Magazine* published several feature articles exploring resident expectations about the modern home. One article, entitled "The Apartment of an Intelligent Couple," featured an interview with two young newlyweds and focused especially on their understanding of postwar domesticity.[10] "Every apartment," the wife stated, "must have a refrigerator and a washing machine."[11] "Next," the husband exclaimed, "we shall have a machine in the kitchen that will do everything, peel everything!"[12] The wife concluded the interview by asserting, "We have the right to comfort."[13] The article showcased how postwar understandings of welfare were framed by evolving expectations about comfort. In particular, access to a well-equipped home was understood to be an attainable right rather than a mere privilege. As Nicole Rudolph has shown, "comfort" was a "domestic ideal that celebrated the modern home as ground zero for individual happiness and family unity."[14]

A series of surveys conducted by the city of Marseille and the regional branch of the Institut national de la statistique et des études économiques (INSEE) further illuminates changing understandings about modern domesticity in the 1950s and 1960s. In one 1960 study, four hundred residents living in both new and old houses around Marseille were asked to respond to a series of questions: "Do you consider yourself poorly housed?" The survey asked, "Do you have a kitchen? Do you want a new house for your family?"[15] According to the results of this study, 77 percent of the families surveyed did indeed desire a new modern home.[16] Researchers also compared the results of this 1960 survey to one conducted five years earlier, in 1955. In both studies, residents were asked: "How many rooms [does your home] have? How many rooms do you want?" In 1955, most families of four "wanted at least three rooms."[17] However, according to the 1960 survey, a family of four now wanted a larger home with "between four and five rooms."[18] Moreover, even those families surveyed in 1960 who believed their existing "homes were an appropriate size and not too overcrowded, still wanted to move to a larger house."[19] These studies suggest that desire for more domestic space was increasingly part of residents' understandings about the right to comfort.

Residents' expectations about modern amenities and appliances were also shifting. In another study, residents were asked if they wished to own a washing machine and a refrigerator. Most residents overwhelmingly responded that they did indeed want to own these appliances. The same survey also asked if their existing homes had enough space to accommodate these machines.[20] Although many responded that they did *not* have room enough for either appliance, most asserted that they nonetheless wanted to have both in their homes.

Such surveys attempted to illuminate how residents conceptualized what they believed were the essential features of a modern, comfortable life. Such surveys also reflect how minimum expectations for "basic needs" changed dramatically in the fifteen years following World War II. In 1946, hardly any homes in France had running water, let alone refrigerators or washing machines. Although many homes still lacked basic amenities in 1960, Marseille residents nonetheless expressed extreme dissatisfaction if their apartments could not accommodate truly modern appliances. As Victoria de Grazia explains: "To acknowledge that a 'minimum existence' was a right . . . marked a big step forward. If nothing else, it opened the way for a new consensus, namely that everybody could disagree about the specific sets of goods and services that added up to an adequate 'minimum.'"[21] By the 1950s, the issue was not if France should modernize, but how and when.

Despite the prevailing consensus that modernization was not only inevitable but that such progress was inherently good, serious questions remained about the best way to improve everyday life. Such varied understandings about the purpose of modernization were on display at a 1959 meeting of the Marseille city council when a number of residents complained that industrial pollution was compromising their right to comfort. According to the meeting minutes, residents from the Saint Louis neighborhood in northern Marseille were deeply concerned about a nearby petroleum oil refinery. As one resident explained to the council: "The Antonin Roux oil factory expels dust and debris that the wind carries to our adjacent neighborhood. The roads as well as the plants in the garden are covered with this ash; you can't even tell the color of the flowers. In apartments, the floor and furniture are covered with a layer of powder; the drinking water is discolored; food is inevitably covered with a powder the color of chocolate . . . and breathing is obviously difficult."[22] In response to this complaint, Mayor Gaston Defferre explained: "We are a great industrial city, the second city of France. We are also the first oil refinery port of France, maybe even of Europe. . . . I know that the residents of this neighborhood suffer on certain days when the wind is right . . . and we have taken measures to ameliorate these smells. . . . Alas! If Marseille is going to remain an industrial city, the reality is that some of our residents will suffer inconveniences . . . if we close our factories, Marseille will become a city of tourism and she won't know the activity that we have now!"[23]

Saint Louis residents argued that pollution in their neighborhood undermined their right to cultivate a quality of life. In contrast, Defferre argued that if Marseille was going to be a modern industrial powerhouse, residents would have to accept certain, as he put it, inconveniences. Many municipal officials, including Defferre, viewed industrial expansion as the primary way to improve the city's overall welfare. They believed that attracting big business was central to making the Marseille metropolitan area into the "California of Europe." The questions raised in this city council meeting point to key tensions at the heart of the debate about modernization, particularly how concepts like "public good" and "social welfare" were differently imagined and articulated.

New Homes for Modern Families

Although residents' expectations about domestic comfort and basic living standards changed dramatically after World War II, for many, *actual* housing conditions remained dismal. In letters to housing officials, Marseille residents described cramped quarters, moldy walls, and the general paucity of decent housing. Many of these families lived in the city's oldest neighborhoods near downtown.[24] Ongoing shortages and poor conditions in the Marseille housing market epitomized the larger, national state of housing in France. In the late 1940s, the squatters' movement had focused national attention on France's grave housing problems and also spurred a broader debate about the meaning of welfare. Despite squatters' contribution to important discussions about social rights, the housing crisis persisted. During the winter of 1953–1954 the nation again fixated on the housing question when two Parisians froze to death after being evicted from their homes, sparking public outcry. Following these deaths, Abbé Pierre, a priest and social Catholic activist, emerged as a vocal critic of the unrelenting housing shortage. His campaign galvanized mass public support and became part of a sustained national critique about the lack of proper housing in France.

Since the late 1940s, the Ministry of Housing and Reconstruction (MRU) had struggled to construct housing on a large scale. After World War II, the MRU engaged in a period of experimentation as the institution considered multiple solutions to the crisis.[25] In a major 1952 policy change, one of the first directors of the MRU, Eugène Claudius-Petit, modified the prewar Habitations à bon marché (HBM) public housing system to create the Habitations à loyer modéré (or HLM) housing system. While the interwar HBM model was aimed specifically at housing France's poorest families, the postwar HLM model targeted both working- and middle-class families. The new system was intended to encourage more social mobility and to allow greater numbers of families to move into state-funded housing. Some of the new HLM apartments were available for purchase; others were set aside for the rental market. But the pace at which new HLM apartments were constructed was still far outpaced by housing demands. HLMs were also expensive to build.

Pierre Courant's brief tenure as the head of the MRU in 1953 marked a major turning point for housing construction in France. Courant sought a cheaper and quicker solution to the ongoing housing crisis, and he initiated a plan he hoped would definitively solve the nation's housing problems and hasten the arrival of a new era of comfort for all. His *logement million*—or Million Housing project—was the first comprehensive plan that succeeded in building mass quantities of housing at a relatively quick pace. According to the plan, the construction of each individual apartment building was supposed to cost no more than one million francs. To realize this goal, the Courant Plan, as it was also called, took its cue from housing campaigns in other parts of Europe. In Sweden, for example, town planning officials similarly faced a serious housing shortage and ultimately developed their own mass-construction project they called the "million programme."[26] And, like many council housing estates in Great Britain, French *logement million* often relied heavily on prefabricated materials.[27]

In France, between 1953 and 1962 nearly 500,000 housing units were built as part of the *million* initiative, and for the first time families began to ascend into the public housing system in fairly large numbers.[28] In Marseille, 4,000 *million* housing units were constructed between 1954 and 1960. Like the other HLM developments, Million Project housing often consisted of large, multistoried apartment complexes, and these clusters of buildings came to be known as a *grand ensemble*. Unlike HLM apartments, however, *logement million*—or *logécos*—were often smaller and more hastily constructed. In 1958, the MRU was renamed the Ministry of Construction (MC), and it initiated another program aimed at further streamlining and accelerating the construction process. The new *zones à urbaniser par priorité* (or ZUPs) identified key development areas around France and placed a single urban planning team in charge of building each new *grand ensemble*.[29] Both Million Housing and ZUPs reflected government efforts to balance the need for large-scale construction with rising expectations about modern living and domestic comfort.

Although such construction projects helped to increase the supply of new homes around France, demand for better housing still remained dauntingly high. As new apartments became available, families applied to move into these homes located in developments that were often located on the edges of French cities. For many families, moving to a new HLM, or even a Million apartment, was a symbol of having "made it," and a fulfillment of the postwar promise of social citizenship.[30] Families seeking to move out of their old, decrepit homes had to submit detailed packets to several different housing offices in a protracted application process that often took years to complete and regularly ended in failure. In Marseille, families made the case for why they should be granted a new, much coveted apartment by appealing to housing authorities and utilizing a common set of strategies. Residents often emphasized the general state of disrepair of their existing homes and how such poor conditions posed serious health risks to their families. For example, in letters, they stated that their apartments had "no natural sunlight, and no toilets."[31] They described crumbling staircases, crowded conditions, and sagging walls. As one resident wrote in a letter to an official at the Marseille Municipal Housing Office: "I am the father of two children, aged nineteen months and four months. I live in a hotel and I have a tiny room which is too small for four people. We cook on a camping stove (*un réchaud à alcool*) and we don't have heating. You see the situation we're in . . . I am desperate."[32]

Most housing applicants recurringly used two key adjectives to characterize the poor conditions of their homes, describing them as "humid" and "damp." In doing so they capitalized on the anxieties of local officials about urban blight and social degeneration. Humidity, for example, was a grave concern for public health and urban planning officials because it was believed to contribute to diseases such as tuberculosis, a common illness afflicting residents of urban tenements. In some housing applications, residents described how family members, particularly children, had already been hospitalized for various lung ailments. They also included doctors' notes in their application packet in the hopes that such medical documentation might aid their appeals.

Residents made the case that they deserved new housing because they had "good" families. Applicants began their letters by stating how long they had been married and by detailing the names and ages of their children. These applications were most often written by men who presented themselves as the central breadwinners for their families. For example, in his 1960 letter to the Municipal Housing Office, Slimane T. emphasized that he was a "construction worker" who worked six days a week and was therefore a good earner and provider for his family.[33] He explained that he had "four children: five years, four years, two years, [and] two weeks."[34] He described the dismal state of his home and the toll it was taking on the health of his family: "I live in two small rooms on the fourth floor of the building and there is no running water, no gas, no electricity, and no toilet."[35] He also asserted that his wife was a dutiful homemaker, but explained how she "must go a hundred meters down the street to get water that is always dirty and salty," thereby implying that their decrepit living conditions required his wife to work harder in order to adequately perform her duties as a spouse and mother.[36]

Slimane T. also appealed to housing authorities by invoking the historical importance of families to national interests. Since the late nineteenth century, anxieties about France's low birthrate led to the creation of maternalist welfare institutions that privileged and supported women's roles as childbearers and child rearers. During the Vichy regime, pro-family policies buttressed the efforts of earlier institutions by continuing to incentivize maternalism, as well as by underscoring how, as Paul Ginsborg explains, "the husband [was the] moral and material head of the family . . . [who] had the right to make all the most important decisions regarding the destiny of the family, including choice of abode and the welfare of his children."[37] Following World War II, many of these late-nineteenth- and early-twentieth-century policies remained in place and were bolstered by a system of family allowances that especially benefited large families with stay-at-home moms.[38] In housing applications, residents helped define and reinforce these postwar notions about what made for a good family by emphasizing how husbands and fathers were responsible breadwinners and how wives and mothers were capable homemakers.[39] Residents made the case that they had good, moral families in order to underscore that they were also productive members of the nation. In this sense, resident applications drew a causal link between their duty to propagate the nation and the state's responsibility to help families be constructive citizens by granting them access to modern housing.

For state officials, however, large families did not always make "good" families. Housing authorities were interested in awarding homes not only to growing families but also to healthy ones. A historical concern of health officials and social reformers was that overcrowded living conditions also bred disease and led to social problems like degenerate families. For many officials, a healthy family was also a moral family. Officials tended to prioritize new housing for families that fit a certain nuclear model. They discouraged grandparents, aunts, uncles, and other so-called vestigial family members from living within a single housing unit. Moreover, single-parent families—particularly unmarried mothers—divorced families, or unmarried couples were often completely discounted by housing officials.

In some cases, housing applicants attempted to turn their problematic familial situation into a potential boon for their case. In one application, a single father named Alexis G. explained that he and his children lived with his parents and he was applying for a new home so he could move his family out of his parents' house. He especially emphasized that the reason he wanted a new home for his children was so they could better achieve the ideal of the nuclear family: "I have worked for the city for several years. . . . I live with my parents and my two daughters and my son in a two-room apartment . . . my children are growing and it is more and more difficult for six to live in two rooms."[40] By specifying the genders of his children and by hinting that they were nearing adolescence, Alexis G. further brought attention to another concern of public health officials—that children of opposite sexes should not share bedrooms, and that no child, under any circumstances, should ever share a bedroom with parents or other older family members. The rhetoric of Alexis G.'s letter played nicely into general concerns that overcrowding led to potentially incestuous social situations.

In addition to metropolitan French citizens, colonial subjects also helped to define social citizenship by emphasizing that they were valuable members of the

French imperial nation-state. In a letter to Mayor Defferre, Abdallah T. wrote: "I have lived in Marseille for twenty-one years, and. . . . I've always conducted myself well and I have done my duty like all citizens."[41] Abdallah T. was an elderly retired laborer who lived with his wife in a furnished hotel in downtown Marseille. He was requesting a new home because his wife had twice fallen down the stairs of their rundown hotel. Abdallah T. wrote how he had been a working, responsible citizen of Marseille and entreated Mayor Defferre to do his duty: "You are, *monsieur le maire,* our guide and our father in this city. It's to you, therefore, that I address this letter as I ask you for an apartment."[42] Abdallah T. thus framed himself as a productive member of the city and, by extension, the nation. He also implicitly drew attention to the 1946 Lamine-Guèye law, which abolished the subject status of colonial peoples and granted all members of the empire French citizenship. Abdallah T. entreated Defferre to extend to him and to his wife the full benefits of social citizenship by granting them access to better housing.

In making claims about social citizenship, colonial migrants living in the metropole also called attention to their military service. For example, when in 1960 Mohamed B. wrote to Mayor Defferre requesting a better home for his family, he noted that he had served both in World War II and in Algeria and was forced to leave Algeria around 1958 because of what he called "military reasons."[43] He also noted that he had been decorated with numerous medals for his service in both wars.[44] In 1960, Mademoiselle D. A., an unmarried mother of five children, wrote the Marseille Housing Office requesting an HLM apartment. She cited her father's military service in both World War I and World War II, adding that, "after being mobilized in 1939 . . . he died for France at Bonne."[45] Finally, in another letter Abdelkader R., who lived in a blockhouse in the southeastern part of the city, similarly cited his military service in a terse letter to the mayor: "Dear Mr. Mayor, I have made several requests and I have received no response. I am French and I repeat to you that I have done my military service like everyone else, I was mobilized like everyone else and I even stayed in the military . . . [attaining] the rank of corporal."[46] In this letter, Abdelkader R. not only underscores his service to the nation, but states outright that he is French and therefore deserving, like everyone else, of decent housing.

The letters and other correspondence of colonial subjects in the late 1950s and early 1960s demonstrates how they too participated in the important and formative discussions about social rights. Their contribution to evolving housing allocation institutions during the *trente glorieuses* is especially notable because it challenges the dominant narrative that colonial and postcolonial migrants only began to figure prominently in the housing question in the 1970s and with the so-called decline of the welfare state.

Their efforts form part of a broader set of strategies Marseille residents utilized in their attempts to acquire better housing. All noted the severe dilapidation of their existing homes. Many pointed out that they had neat, nuclear families and that they were husbands and wives appropriately fulfilling their respective roles as breadwinners and homemakers. Others emphasized their military service to France. In all of these requests, residents made appeals for new housing by drawing direct connections between modernization and citizenship. They understood that access to a modern apartment was a citizen's right. Unfortunately, of all the previously cited applications, all were refused a new apartment. In fact, of most of the letters I poured through in the archive, most applications were denied. Although the city was constructing more housing, there was still much more demand than supply. These letters and applications are nonetheless important because they formed part of an evolving discourse about social rights, one that was fundamentally shaped by the everyday experiences of ordinary people.

A Wink and a Nod: Clientelism and Modernization

Although many Marseillais struggled to acquire a new, modern home, residents still had another way to appeal to authorities for housing. They relied on patronage politics to gain access to new apartments. According to Philippe Sanmarco, patronage politics—or clientelism—is a "personal and personalized allegiance . . . [and] a phenomenon established for the most part at the local level. . . . The heart of clientelism is linked to the electoral campaign. In its most simple form it consists of a classic offer: 'At the moment of the election, you (*tu*) vote for me. . . . and I will hire you, or your son, or your daughter.'"[47] In post–World War II Marseille, housing allocation became an increasingly important part of "the currency of clientelism," and this particular form of patronage politics intersected with modernization efforts in compelling ways.[48] Marseille residents often expressed their desire to live a "modern life" as justification for why they deserved new housing. But they often turned to local leaders to ensure that their housing applications were read by the right people. Patronage politics has been a notorious historical practice in Marseille, and the way modernization discourses filtered through and were shaped by clientelism demonstrates how the local level is an important site for illuminating the messiness and inconsistencies of the modernization project.

In addition to the offer of jobs and housing, clientelism took many other forms. In early-twentieth-century Marseille, for example, local politicians drummed up new votes by arranging for speedy naturalizations for recent migrants from Italy, Spain, and Greece. Politicians pulled strings to issue medical exemptions from military service. They granted or delayed granting commercial permits. They bought rounds of drinks. They accepted rounds of drinks. They also set up and paid for rendezvous between prostitutes and businessmen. In the interwar period, Marseille's finances were in a shambles due in large part to clientelism and the general misappropriation of funds. For example, each newly elected mayor often went on a hiring spree, rewarding constituents with city jobs and pensions. In 1930, then city council member Simon Sabiani proclaimed that "there were a thousand superfluous employees in the Hotel de Ville," but when he was temporarily elected mayor in 1931, he promptly hired nearly a thousand more people.[49] Within a five-year period in the 1930s, as Paul Jankowski explains, "the street-cleaning force doubled [yet] the rubbish remained."[50] Many of the city's tax collectors were also conveniently illiterate.[51] Although Marseille is infamous for such practices, the custom of exchanging favor for support is not unique to the *phocéen* city. In the late nineteenth and early twentieth centuries, clientelism was integral to developing forms of mass and popular politics on both sides of the Atlantic, including such big cities as New York, Philadelphia, and Chicago.[52] Patronage was also an important feature of daily and political life in old regime France.[53]

In twentieth-century Marseille, residents most often appealed to politicians and local officials who represented the two dominant political blocs in the city—the socialists on one side, and the communists on the other. In the 1930s, the Communist Party [PCF] had been a major force in Marseille politics, and most working-class neighborhoods tended to vote overwhelmingly for communist city council members. The communists continued to be the dominant party in Marseille immediately after World War II, when Jean Cristofol, a PCF leader, was elected mayor. However, following the 1947 expulsion of communists from high-level national posts, Marseille politicians—particularly the staunch socialist and anti-PCF Gaston Defferre—looked for ways to marginalize the communists locally. The major turning point for Marseille communists came with the 1953 municipal elections. Until then the Marseille PCF was supported by the majority of the voting public. During the 1953 election, however, Gaston Defferre was able to secure a voting majority in the city council by forming a coalition between the socialist and center-right parties.[54] Defferre's coalition succeeded in reducing the communists to a minority with limited voting power in the council.[55] Defferre remained the elected mayor of Marseille from 1953 until his death in 1986. He maintained this anticommunist coalition throughout most of his thirty-year tenure in office.

Gaston Defferre's socialist coalition was widely known for using housing allocation to drum up support among constituents. Housing allocation was supposed to be handled by nonpartisan state institutions called Les offices publiques des habitations à loyer modéré (OPHLMs). These institutions were charged with evaluating new housing candidates and placing them on waiting lists for the next available apartment. In Marseille, however, the OPHLM was closely linked with Gaston Defferre's socialist coalition and was typically staffed by up-and-coming leaders of the Socialist Party. The housing office was a training ground for aspiring local politicians who needed to build their constituencies.[56]

Communist city council members vociferously denounced the clientelistic practices of the socialists. They complained that "the housing attribution process remains a mystery" and that the socialist OPHLM bureaucracy was hopelessly corrupt.[57] But they too had their own means of attributing housing. In his memoir, former docker, union leader, and communist city council member Alfred Pacini recalls how he made use of patronage. In the early 1950s, Pacini desperately needed a new home for his family. They had been living in a run-down ground-floor apartment, and his wife and two children were sick with tuberculosis and other lung infections. Pacini was able to acquire a new home through his political connection to Jean Cristofol, the former communist mayor of Marseille, who still controlled a block of newer apartment buildings in the city. In 1953, Pacini himself was elected to the city council, and he used his new authority to help many constituents and fellow dockers get new housing. "I helped out dockers whenever I could," Pacini recalled. "I made several interventions. I found an apartment for one guy who worked on the docks and lived in two small, damp rooms with his seven children. I went to see him and said, 'Go to place Sadi Carnot, here, take the keys, you have a house.'"[58]

Like the socialists, the local communist party also controlled their own, albeit much smaller, housing allocation institution. In 1953, communist city council members, including Alfred Pacini, proposed an alternative to the socialist-controlled OPHLM and ultimately created a new housing commission.[59] This commission—which included mostly communist city council members—was supposed to create more transparency in the housing allocation process by holding public meetings and allocating housing on a case-by-case basis. The committee also went so far as to create an elaborate and supposedly objective point system that ranked families in terms of the condition of their existing housing as well as the number of children and length of couples' marriages.[60] Yet, the manner in which communists introduced family case files during committee sessions suggests that the applications were evaluated less according to these supposedly "objective" criteria than according to political interest. For example, in four 1953 commission meetings, all the families that communist members "recommended for housing" whose files represented "interesting cases that merited attention" lived in working-class and historically communist neighborhoods in Marseille.[61]

Despite such goings-on, both local socialist and communist politicians publicly denied indulging in patronage politics. In a 1959 city council meeting, for example, Mayor Defferre defended himself against charges of clientelism: "I am very aware that I pass my time responding to those who demand housing and I indicate that I cannot intervene because of my elected position as Mayor of Marseille. They ask my friends, they solicit elected officials to intervene on their behalf. I tell them that I cannot do anything, that there are rules for which I cannot make exceptions."[62] In his memoir, Pacini is similarly emphatic that he never even "accepted a coffee" from a constituent, let alone a vote in exchange for housing.[63] He asserted that he was "too afraid to compromise" himself.[64] In Marseille's "wink and nod" system of politics, to acknowledge the existence of clientelism would undermine the very mechanism of the practice.[65] Although the allocation of new HLM or *logement million* apartments was supposed to help families most in need of a modern home, clientelism was an important way that a connected family could receive new housing. In housing applications and letters to Marseille politicians, residents expressed their desire for a new home alongside declarations of their continued commitment to their city council members and political party.[66] The relationship between clientelism and housing allocation in postwar Marseille shows how evolving housing institutions were not just formed by policies meted out by the central state; modernization was a highly politicized process that was fundamentally shaped by local practices and culture.

The Saint Lazare Disaster

Neighborhoods were important sites where residents, politicians, and other officials engaged in sometimes vociferous debates about social citizenship. In 1960, the collapse of a neglected apartment building in one of Marseille's working-class and predominately communist neighborhoods ignited a fierce local dispute between residents, socialists, and communists about the meaning of modernization and—most important—who deserved access to modern living. The Saint Lazare disaster became a rallying point for members of the Marseille PCF, who argued that Defferre's vision of modernization excluded Marseille's working classes.

On June 26, 1960, at 6:10 p.m. the *commissaire de police* received an urgent phone call notifying him that a building had collapsed on the rue du Caire in the Saint Lazare neighborhood. Saint Lazare is in Marseille's 3rd *arrondissement*, north and slightly east of the Vieux Port.[67]

Saint Lazare is in Marseille's 3rd *arrondissement*.

Source: https://commons.wikimedia.org/wiki/File:Marseille_Arrdt_3.svg#/media/File:Marseille_Arrdt_3.svg.
Author: Superbenjamin - Own work. Licensed under CC BY-SA 3.0 via Wikimedia Commons.

Once on the scene, the *commissaire*, along with police officers and firefighters, pulled three victims from the rubble: an infant twenty days old; a single mother, Madame C.; and a mother of four children, Madame M. The infant and Madame C. were already dead, but Madame M. was rushed to the hospital in critical condition, where she later died of her injuries.[68] The police and firefighters then rushed to evacuate the eighty-five families who lived in the surrounding buildings, which were also in danger of falling down.[69] In the next few hours and in the following days, the city moved quickly to tear down these structurally unsound buildings to prevent squatters from moving in. Most of the evacuated families did not have the chance to retrieve their belongings and lost their furniture and other domestic items, which were bulldozed along with the buildings.[70]

The Saint Lazare collapse took most city officials by surprise. In the hasty investigation that followed, officials determined that its cause was a rotted supporting wall that had simply given way. In a memo to the mayor's office, the head municipal architect, Albert Villard, struggled to explain why his department had "left many buildings throughout the city," including the ones in Saint Lazare, in such "a state of abandonment."[71] Villard claimed that his department had been aware of the decayed state of the supporting wall in Saint Lazare and his workers *had* made a number of repairs on this wall as well as others within the neighborhood. But families displaced by the disaster contradicted Villard's story, asserting that few or no repairs had ever been made in their neighborhood. They argued that municipal neglect was the root cause of the collapsed building and that they had been excluded from city efforts to modernize Marseille. Villard's troubles were further compounded by the fact that the city actually owned and was the de facto landlord of the collapsed building in question.

Despite resident claims, technically the neighborhood was not excluded from the municipality's development plans. Many of the buildings there had been acquired by the city through eminent domain in the 1940s. The creation of a highway network was a major part of Marseille's modernization plan, and much of the Saint Lazare neighborhood was scheduled to be razed to make way for a new freeway, the Autoroute Nord. This freeway was to be an important addition to the transportation infrastructure that would increase the flow of goods in and out of Marseille, thus boosting the local economy. However, the highway expansion was still in the planning stages, and in the meantime many of the buildings owned by the city had fallen into disrepair. In an attempt to defend himself and his department, Villard wrote to the mayor's office, asserting: "You know that the mentality of many of the inhabitants of these neighborhoods are influenced by a certain propaganda, and I must indicate to you that the residents . . . are the first to proclaim that absolutely no work has been done in the area for years, despite our evidence to the contrary."[72] Villard claimed that communist influence in Saint Lazare led residents to exaggerate the degree of municipal neglect of their neighborhood. It was the communists—not his department's incompetence, he insisted—who were the real source of trouble in Saint Lazare.

Following the collapse, Marseille communist leaders pounced on the opportunity to galvanize their constituency. Over the next few weeks, they entered into a public relations battle with Gaston Defferre and his socialist-led coalition. Both the socialists and the communists relied on local newspapers to broadcast their messages. The daily newspaper *La Marseillaise* was the mouthpiece of the local communists and was widely circulated in Marseille's working-class neighborhoods such as Saint Lazare. It was also an important counterpoint to the city's other main news source, *Le Provençal*, which was owned and operated by Gaston Defferre. In the week after the disaster both *Le Provençal* and *La Marseillaise* featured a series of front-page articles and editorials about the collapse. While *Le Provençal* focused on damage control after the disaster, *La Marseillaise* launched an all-out assault on Gaston Defferre and his failure to deliver on the postwar promise of social citizenship for all.

On June 28, 1960, two days after the collapse, the front page of *Le Provençal* read: "Evacuated residents have received good shelter in hotels, with meals included. . . . They will receive new housing within the week."[73] On the same day *La Marseillaise* reported: "After the tragic accident, ninety families lost everything, the others no longer have a roof over their heads. . . . Most desperately seek shelter. . . . The municipality has offered to rehouse the homeless of Saint Lazare but we'll see if they keep their promise."[74] Over the next few days, Louis Gazagnaire, a communist city council member, penned a series of editorials criticizing the Defferre administration for excluding working-class residents from the opportunity for modern living. Gazagnaire argued that the mayor had forsaken his "social duty" to Marseille residents.[75]

However, most displaced families did receive new housing as promised. Many were relocated to a newly completed *grand ensemble* called Saint Barthélémy, which was located in the northern outskirts of the city. Saint Barthélémy was Marseille's first major project completed under the national ZUP initiative. Like many other *grands ensembles* around France, a portion of the Saint Barthélémy apartments was set aside for the city to distribute, while the others were allocated by the socialist-controlled OPHLM. According to Marseille's secretary-general, Jean Poggioli, after a temporary stay in hotels or gymnasiums, families began moving to Saint Barthélémy on July 2, 1960, just six days after the disaster. He specified that families also received funds to purchase new "bedding, cooking utensils, tables, [and] chairs," as well as a one-time "emergency donation of 20,000 francs to cover the most urgent purchases."[76]

In a *Marseillaise* op-ed, communist city council member Gazagnaire acknowledged that most victims of the collapse were relocated, but he nonetheless criticized the state of the new housing in Saint Barthélémy. "They will be rehoused," he wrote, "but let's see how."[77] Despite local officials' assertions that Saint Barthélémy was fully constructed, Gazagnaire claimed that the new residents moved in to find their apartments unfinished: "Residents were obliged to undertake and pay for more construction as many apartments lacked doors . . . lights were not installed or wired."[78] Saint Lazare victims also had to pay to have the electricity and gas installed in their apartments. While most of these families had relied on portable butane stoves in their old tenements, in these new apartments, such stoves violated building codes and were not permitted.

Gazagnaire and other communist leaders also criticized the cost of this new housing and focused especially on the issue of high rents. Although public housing was supposed to be subsidized, the state partly financed construction by charging more. In one op-ed, Gazagnaire described those victims of the Saint Lazare disaster who could not afford the higher costs in Saint Barthélémy, quoting one displaced resident who complained: "The municipality offers us new housing . . . but in apartments too expensive for us!"[79] Gazagnaire reported that out of roughly eighty-five families evacuated from Saint Lazare about thirty could not afford the higher rents. He explained how one evacuee, a Monsieur Tiran, was offered an apartment in Saint Barthélémy, but prior to moving he was asked to pay a 31,400 franc deposit and was also informed that his rent would be 15,000 francs per month. Monsieur Tiran explained: "What would you do? With my salary? I am a pipe fitter, I can't afford these expenses. Why accept this apartment and not be able to pay the rents and the extra charges?"[80] Gazagnaire described the local communists' perception of the central problem for working-class families: "the most distressing dilemma: to live in a slum and have almost enough to eat, or to live in comfort and tighten the belt."[81] He also noted that in addition to high rents, residents in new housing developments also had to pay additional fees such as compulsory renters' insurance.[82]

The outcry generated by the Saint Lazare disaster reflected the larger debate about the problem of housing in France. In Marseille, it also epitomized local-level tensions between socialists and communists. Pierre Courant's Million Project and the ZUP initiative that followed were supposed to allow more families to enter into the public housing system, and many French families did benefit from these programs. However, working-class Marseille residents, particularly those affiliated with the PCF, argued that they could not afford even the subsidized rents of these new apartments. They argued that the very program that aimed to help working-class families acquire a new, modern home—and ascend into the ranks of the burgeoning middle class—only succeeded in further marginalizing them.[83]

The Village in the City: Who Belongs to the Neighborhood?

Saint Lazare is one of many distinct neighborhoods in Marseille and the larger metropolis is often described as a "plural city."[84] Marseille's sixteen *arrondissements* contain a total of 111 neighborhoods, and residents, politicians, and the media refer to them as *petits villages*. Resident understandings of modernization were shaped both by the physical spaces of their *petit village* and by commonsense perceptions about who belonged there. Based on these understandings of neighborhood space and community, many Marseille residents formed associations called Les comités d'intérêt de quartier (neighborhood interest committees, or CIQs). CIQs became another way for residents to participate in modernization debates and to contribute to evolving concepts of welfare.

CIQs were established in Marseille in the early twentieth century and often grew out of older informal groups formed in the city's historic neighborhoods, fishing villages, and Marseille's growing northern and eastern districts. Formed under the auspices of the national 1901 law of associations, CIQs are important because they point to new developments in associational life in Marseille as well as in France more broadly. In the late nineteenth and early twentieth centuries, most neighborhood associations were centered around religious affiliations, the communist party, and labor organizations.[85] CIQs represented a new and different form of associational life, one premised less on the church or syndicalism—although these certainly remained important—and more on the role of residents gathering together to modernize their neighborhood spaces. For example, in the early twentieth century, the northern and eastern outskirts of the city attracted working- and middle-class families, but these areas also lacked basic infrastructure.[86] Marseille's new *banlieuesards* began to form CIQs to petition city officials to install sewers, roads, and gas lines.[87]

By the mid-twentieth century, Marseille CIQs had become a more formalized part of local politics as these organizations cultivated close ties with elected officials, particularly the city council member who represented their borough.[88] By the 1960s and 1970s, many CIQs had become an important cog in the Defferre political machine.[89] Most were (and still remain) an integral part of the local culture of clientelism in Marseille. Importantly, the city's CIQs also reflect the particular concerns of many neighborhoods, and membership is often diverse. Some CIQs were formed by residents in predominately working-class, communist neighborhoods; others by residents whose families originally came from Italy or Corsica. Although CIQs are unique, in many ways, to Marseille, other French towns—including Lyon and Toulon—have similar networks of neighborhood associations.[90]

In the 1950s, residents of the Sainte Marthe neighborhood, located in the 14th *arrondissement* in the northern outskirts of Marseille, formed a CIQ with the goal of working with city hall to undertake several modernization projects in their neighborhood. Many CIQ members had moved to Sainte Marthe from downtown because of the cheap land and, over time, the neighborhood had grown into a sizable community. Between 1952 and 1962, this association repeatedly petitioned the city to construct sewer lines, roads, and schools.[91] In letters to the mayor, residents asserted that they paid city taxes but received little benefit because of their distance from downtown. They even tried to secede from the city of Marseille and form their own municipal government. By the mid-1960s, the municipal administration began to work with Sainte Marthe residents, ultimately installing sewers and building roads and a post office. By this time, the neighborhood had also become prime real estate for the construction of large public housing projects, which necessitated further infrastructure development in the area.

Neighborhood resident associations like the Sainte Marthe CIQ are one way to make sense of how residents understood modernization. Whom they excluded also reveals local notions about who belonged to the neighborhood and who merited access to modern living. For example, resident associations often mobilized against the problem of squatters, petitioning local officials to evict illegal occupants from buildings or abandoned fields. In 1956, a CIQ from the Calade-Bernabo neighborhood in northern Marseille complained to the mayor about "a clandestine village . . . occupied by numerous gypsies" that had sprung up in an abandoned factory.[92] Elsewhere, in a petition signed by forty-one residents of the La Renaude public housing complex, the president of the association included a letter complaining "about new inhabitants—dirty, flea-infested gypsies—who insult us" and were living in several unoccupied apartments.[93] Finally, in another letter, Arnaud R., president of the Saint Charles housing association, stated: "We, the residents, conscious of our needs and rights, demand the eviction of the nomads."[94]

In 1963, the Belle-de-Mai Neighborhood Association (CIQ) wrote several letters to city hall expressing concern about squatting families. Like Saint Lazaire, Belle-de-Mai is also in Marseille's 3rd *arrondissement*. According to the Belle-de-Mai CIQ, families had been squatting in an old industrial building that was scheduled to be torn down to make way for new public housing. Unexpectedly, the association did not ask city officials to evict all the squatters. Instead, the CIQ asked the city to find permanent housing for *some* of the squatters in Belle-de-Mai.[95] The association, however, distinguished between the twelve families they hoped could remain in the neighborhood and the "problem of the four squatting gypsy families" who also lived in the abandoned warehouse.[96] While the Belle-de-Mai CIQ advocated for some of the squatting families, the association asked city officials to evict the "gypsy families," stating that they "camped without right" in the outdoor courtyard of the building.[97] In a letter responding to these petitions, the mayor's office stated that they would attempt to rehouse the twelve families in the Belle-de-Mai neighborhood but that the "gypsies" would be evacuated from the area. According to municipal reports, once the "gypsies" were evicted they were not rehoused.[98]

Why did the Belle-de-Mai CIQ try to help some of the squatting families but not the others? The organization's efforts to rehouse some—but not all—of these families suggests that twelve of the squatting families were integrated into the local fabric in ways the others were not. One of Marseille's most sizable Italian communities lived in Belle-de-Mai, and municipal reports suggest that those squatting families—whom the CIQ wanted to remain in the neighborhood—had

Italian-sounding last names. Residents' perceptions of ethnicity and cultural identity help to explain their differing attitudes to these squatters. Their understanding of such differences was also profoundly shaped by the ways in which residents both experienced and helped to construct neighborhood spaces.

Many Italians had migrated to Marseille in the late nineteenth and early twentieth centuries. Although initially the victims of extreme xenophobia in Marseille and other parts of France, by the 1950s Italians were an established community in the region. They owned shops; they held important positions within local trade unions; and they had begun—as evidenced by Alfred Pacini—to run for local office. In his memoir, Pacini described growing up in Belle-de-Mai and living among "all the other Pacinis."[99] He also described the diverse regional affiliations of Marseille's Italians. Many had originally come from Piedmont, Italy's northern region bordering France. Others were from Sardinia, the second largest Italian island in the Mediterranean after Sicily. Despite the regional diversity of the Italian community in Marseille, most, according to Pacini, shared the common experience of migrating to and settling in southern France and of making a living in Marseille. Perhaps Belle-de-Mai residents' perception that they were already part of a diverse Italian community enabled them to embrace the twelve Italian squatting families as natural members of their neighborhood.

While many Belle-de-Mai Italians imagined their own community to be notably heterogeneous, they often spoke of outsiders in homogeneous terms. For example, in letters to city council members, the Belle-de-Mai CIQ distinguished the twelve Italian squatter families from the four "gypsy" families. To do so, they drew on commonsense assumptions about Roma, describing them as uniformly "thieving" and "dirty."[100]

The actual physical space of Belle-de-Mai and residents' experience of living in the neighborhood also shed light on how and why members of the CIQ perceived differences between Italian and "gypsy" squatters. The Italian squatting families belonged to the neighborhood not only because of a shared perception of cultural and ethnic ties, but also because they seemed to share in and help construct the physical spaces of the neighborhood. For example, the Belle-de-Mai CIQ distinguished between the Italian families who "lived" in the abandoned building and the gypsies who "camped" there. Former Belle-de-Mai resident Pacini further illuminated the importance of spatial relationships in the neighborhood. He recalled the shops he frequented near his home, including "Bruni, the grocer who took credit" and whose shop was next door to "Madame Janotti's notions shop." Near these establishments was "the bar called Paul" owned and run by an Italian.[101] For Pacini and other Belle-de-Mai residents, the grocer, the bar, the street, and other such public spaces became important points of convergence in their everyday lives. These were meaningful sites that helped produce a local understanding of belonging.

Belle-de-Mai's Italian residents thus imagined their local community in terms of a shared sense of space. Interestingly, their notion of belonging was also informed by a plural sense of Italian-ness.[102] As such, they illuminate how perceptions of diversity—rather than sameness—shaped a local sense of community. Just as Marseille is noted for its diverse neighborhoods, so too did residents of neighborhoods like Belle-de-Mai understand their "little villages" in terms of their heterogeneity. Conversely, assumptions about the homogeneous characteristics of other groups informed residents' commonsense ideas about who were outsiders. Neighborhood-level discussions about belonging and "strangeness" thus point to unexpected ways that residents—and CIQs—informed evolving discourses about who deserved access to a certain quality of life.

•   •   •

Beginning in the mid-1950s and during his early tenure in office, Mayor Gaston Defferre helped to spearhead a comprehensive city modernization project. These local efforts were part of the national postwar project to not just reconstruct France but also refashion the nation. Modernization was pursued in the name of republicanism, with the aim of guaranteeing the equality of all citizens through improving their standard of living. Attention to neighborhood debates in postwar Marseille offers a more complicated and nuanced sense of this project by showing how a local politics of difference played an important role in shaping this national endeavor. It also shows how new forms of associational life helped to reconfigure the relationship between citizen and state, and how street-level politics influenced urban redevelopment efforts.

Marseille citizens participated in the modernization project by petitioning city officials to make changes in their neighborhoods and by articulating their own expectations for modern living. Many Marseillais—particularly families from the French colonies—justified their right to comfort in terms of their service to the imperial nation-state. They also helped shape normative understandings of family domesticity and belonging by helping to define social citizens in gendered terms as breadwinners and homemakers. Perceptions of class affiliation and ethnic identity also informed how modernization was understood and carried out at the local level. While many city officials believed that working-class residents were unduly influenced by communist propaganda, working-class residents argued that they were excluded from the full benefits of modernization because of their social status and political affiliations. Finally, resident notions about ethnic differences further shaped their understanding of who belonged in their neighborhood and who deserved the right to the full complement of social citizenship.

ORDERING THE DISORDERLY SLUM

In 1954, *Marseille Magazine* published an exposé of a slum that was located in downtown Marseille and known as Peysonnel. Referring to it as one of "the most flea-ridden of flea-infested places," the article described Peysonnel as a "leper at the heart of the city . . . [and] the domicile of the tribes of Mohammed and Santiago."[1] Peysonnel was a few blocks east of the Vieux Port and just north of the main boulevard, La Canebière, and had been built up gradually by its residents since at least the late nineteenth century. Because of its proximity to both the old port and the commercial port, La Joliette, it was a convenient residential site for families who hawked wares along the waterfront and for laborers who worked at the nearby docks. After part of Le Panier was dynamited during World War II, Peysonnel also became a refuge for families displaced from their homes. According to the article in *Marseille Magazine*, Peysonnel residents constructed haphazard shelters out of sheet metal and cardboard, children played near open sewers, and rag pickers pushed dilapidated carts through narrow, refuse-encrusted alleys. In a 1951 memo, the head of the municipal bureau of hygiene, Dr. Girbal, denounced the slum as a "veritable foyer of degeneration," which he said was inhabited by North Africans, black Africans, gypsies, drunkards, pickpockets, and down-and-out French families.[2]

Despite historical efforts to sanitize cities, sites like Peysonnel remained a common feature of the urban landscape in twentieth-century France. Some of these areas—often referred to as *taudis*—were vast shantytowns on the outskirts of French cities. Others, also known as *îlots insalubres*, were run-down and overcrowded tenements in working-class and poor neighborhoods. Some—including

Peysonnel—had sprouted up in the middle of French towns and were of particular concern to urban planners. In addition to the large-scale construction of
housing, slum clearance was also an important part of the postwar project to modernize the nation.

In the mid-1950s, Mayor Gaston Defferre, in partnership with private enterprise and with the help of the central state, created a master plan to redevelop
downtown Marseille. The central aim of the project was to turn the area just east
of the old port and north of La Canebière into a major commercial hub dubbed
Centre Bourse. The project included plans to construct high-rise apartment buildings, office space, and a large, modern shopping mall that, once finished, would
neighbor Marseille's historic Chambre de commerce. But before construction
could begin, the old eyesore, the Peysonnel slum—and its unruly inhabitants—
needed to be cleaned out.

In order to begin the tasks of modernizing cities and ridding the urban
landscape of so-called scourges like Peysonnel, an army of local experts—or
techniciens—fanned out in cities around postwar France, descending into *taudis*
with the object of meticulously mapping these problematic sites as well as analyzing the people who lived in them. Local *techniciens* were technocratic experts,
including urban planners and public health officials, who were tasked with
classifying particular people and places and weighing their findings against supposedly universal expectations for modern living. These experts used rigorous
techniques—such as statistical or demographic analysis—to quantify quality of
life. Local *techniciens* were mediators between everyday life and state redevelopment policies, and their methods helped shape a stratified and hierarchical rehousing system. After these experts had completed their studies of slums and slum
dwellers, they labeled some families "normal" enough to relocate to HLM or *logement million* housing. Other families were classified as "subnormal" and needed
to be both quarantined and resocialized in a second-tier form of public housing
they called "reduced norm housing."

This chapter examines local *techniciens*' central role in shaping slum clearance
and rehousing practices from the 1950s through the early 1960s. In Marseille, for
example, they examined the living conditions of Peysonnel families to determine
whether they were too "asocial" to be rehoused in HLM or *logement million* apartments. Their efforts in Peysonnel and other Marseille slums showcase a more
general shift in understandings of the category "asocial," which was widely utilized by state officials involved in modernization projects around France. In the
early to mid-1950s, local *techniciens* had a hierarchical understanding of the term
"asocial" that was based in part on perceptions of class and partly on commonsense understandings of ethnic difference. Families that local *techniciens* labeled
"asocial" included poor, working-class French families, Italian migrants, "gypsies,"

and families from French colonies. "North African" or "gypsy" families were often categorized as more asocial than poor French families, and Italian and other European families were placed somewhere in the middle of this taxonomy of "asocial-ness."

But by the early to mid-1960s, local *techniciens*' understanding of the asocial category had narrowed. Local modernization efforts had been occurring within the broader context of decolonization, particularly the escalating war in Algeria.[3] By the early 1960s, colonial institutions began to play a greater role in slum clearance and rehousing programs in the metropole. Employees of these institutions, particularly SONACOTRAL and ATOM, began to work more closely with local *techniciens*, and, together, their collaborations further shaped racialized understandings of the term "asocial." More specifically, as local *techniciens* began to partner with colonial administrators, they started to imagine and label slum-dwelling families more narrowly as "Algerian." This shift in perception was also reflected in the terminology local *techniciens* used to describe blighted urban space. Rather than labeling slums *îlots insalubres* or *taudis*, metropolitan urbanists and public health officials began to call these areas bidonvilles.

Solving the Social Problem: Technocracy and *Techniciens*

Since the nineteenth century, urban planners, social reformers, and other experts had been developing new social-scientific methods to better classify people and places with the aim of putting the populace in order.[4] They believed they could provide technical solutions to social problems such as overcrowding, poverty, delinquency, and promiscuity. After World War II, debates about a new and better relationship between citizen and state similarly focused on the need for a more systematic approach to the management of social welfare. The Ministry of Reconstruction and Urbanism (renamed the Ministry of Construction after 1954) was one of the state institutions charged with tackling the broad array of social problems associated with urban life. MRU officials were confident that their plans to modernize France would be the culmination of the earlier efforts of nineteenth-century social reformers.[5] They believed they could provide a definitive solution to the social question.

Technical expertise played a central role in MRU and other state officials' vision for fashioning a modern France, and the technocrat emerged as a key actor in the organization and definition of social welfare. Scholars have defined a technocrat as "any expert or high-level bureaucrat involved in state administration"[6] who is "a technician of general ideas."[7] Recent studies have also introduced the French term *techniciens*, referring to a cadre of individuals from top schools including the Ecole Polytechnique and other elite institutions such as the engineering corps, Ponts et Chaussées.[8] Such work has been useful for considering the development of what Paul Rabinow calls certain "practices of reason" or faith in quantitative methods in the construction of systems of social security.[9]

Techniciens contributed to the evolving notion that human need and the public good were not simply ideals contemplated by humanists but concepts with empirical value that could be precisely measured and calculated. Moreover, they believed that such a calculus of social welfare could be universally applied to everyone. *Techniciens* at the MRU, for example, concluded they could accurately determine the basic domestic needs of all French families. As they developed and began to implement plans for the large-scale construction of housing, they calculated the precise square footage that an average family of four would need to live comfortably in a typical HLM apartment. In addition to determining the appropriate physical size of the modern home, they also introduced new standard requirements in all new construction. After 1950, all new homes were supposed to include indoor plumbing, among other amenities, and all new construction to accommodate urbanist Robert Auzelle's universal "Tableau of Habitants' Needs."

While most studies have explored the role of central-state *techniciens*, few have considered the importance of local *techniciens*. These experts were municipal and departmental employees who participated in larger national debates about technology and social security but were outside the elite corps of individuals forming the top ranks of state institutions. Though local *techniciens* were not part of this cadre of high functionaries, they nonetheless similarly characterized their work in terms of the welfare of the nation. Often trained at local universities, or perhaps having earned a certificate in demography or cartography, they cultivated a firm faith in the efficiency of rational method for the management of everyday life. Local *techniciens* were in a unique position: they were government officials charged with the task of carrying out centralized policies, but they also interpreted national standards at the local level. Because they mediated between everyday life and the central state, they were confronted—in their daily work—with the paradox of applying universal standards of need to a diverse population.

Local *techniciens* played an important role in the national project to build housing. In order to make room for new construction, they worked to clear out slums and tenements. Experts from local urban planning and public health departments collaborated to assess the integrity of buildings and general living conditions in specific neighborhoods.[10] If these local officials decided an area was indeed a slum, or *taudi*, this cluster of blighted buildings was officially marked for redevelopment.

Beginning in the late 1940s, officially labeling a slum an *ilot insalubre* began the legal process through which it could be appropriated by the city, the residents evicted or rehoused, and the site redeveloped. In Marseille, Peysonnel was designated an *ilot insalubre* in 1949, and in the 1950s local *techniciens* began to work in earnest to analyze the site and its inhabitants.

Slumming

By the mid-1950s, Peysonnel was getting a lot of attention from the regional press. In 1954, the local lifestyle periodical *Marseille Magazine* gave an especially colorful and alarming account of life in the *taudi*. The article described Peysonnel as the "court of miracles of all the derelicts of Marseille," alluding to the seventeenth- and eighteenth-century Parisian slums romanticized in Victor Hugo's *The Hunchback of Notre Dame*. The article also described the slum as a haven for criminals and the transient, destitute poor: "Only honest men are in danger here. This underworld does not only shelter witch doctors and she-sorcerers, but also criminals seeking asylum."[11]

Marseille Magazine invited its readers to tour the slum safely from the comfort of their own homes. The article characterized Peysonnel as a dirty and disorderly no-man's-land, where residents "live[d] in conditions that defy the laws of hygiene and the rules of morality."[12] Prior to touring the area, the authors of the article recounted how they protected themselves: "Before entering the *ilot*, our guide extracted a small box of powder from his pocket and conscientiously sprinkled this powder on his shoes, his socks, the bottom of his pants. . . . He took off his hat and sprinkled it too. . . . Then he handed us the box and said, 'It works, DDT.' "[13] In order to guard against perceived slum pathogens, these reporters believed they needed to liberally sprinkle themselves with the toxic pesticide.

The article also explored the supposedly foreign origins of Peysonnel residents, describing the slum as bursting with "poor blacks, poor Arabs, [and] poor gypsies." Detailing the so-called exotic practices of these slum dwellers, the article explained how "at night, the strum of guitars and husky voices of flamenco waft over the shanties, undercut by the insistent throbbing of African tam-tams." Full of "Negro huts, Arab hovels, and bohemian caravans," the slum was like a casbah, but at the heart of the French metropole.[14]

The *Marseille Magazine* article drew on a number of historical tropes to describe Peysonnel. By underscoring the foreignness of the slum and its residents, the article both exoticized and orientalized Peysonnel. The slum became a place to explore—a space of colonial adventure—where Marseille residents could "plunge into the wild" without having to leave France. Peysonnel was like an un-

"This old Bedouin Woman . . ."

Source: Marseille Magazine, *no. 28 (1954): 22. Archives Municipales de Marseille 439 W 25.*

ruly, unregulated—and therefore more exciting—colonial exhibition where diverse groups of "natives" roamed freely, on display for whoever was brave enough to venture into this local heart of darkness.[15]

In one photograph featured in the article, a robed woman with her head covered is shown walking away from a shanty. She holds an empty tub in one hand and her body casts a shadow that leads the eye toward a small child seated in the dirt. The caption below the photo reads: "Although settled in Marseille for many years, this old Bedouin woman has changed nothing of her traditional costume, she doesn't want to smile for the camera." While the photo captures the woman in motion, walking away from a rude shack, the caption attempts to fix her in time: she has been in Marseille for many years, but because she lives in Peysonnel and still dresses in a "traditional costume," she has remained unchanged and un-assimilated, and is thus perfectly suited for display.

By emphasizing the slum as chaotic and dangerous, and by playing on fears about the floating and dangerous classes, the authors also made a case for bull-dozing Peysonnel. They saw it to be particularly threatening because its borders were porous and ever-shifting as residents built lean-tos and makeshift shelters that encroached—gradually but steadily—into the surrounding city.

Another photograph in the article shows a crowded scene. In the image, laun-dry and rugs form a canopy over a narrow alley packed with men and women. A barefoot, shirtless child forms the centerpiece of the image, as a gaunt man in an oversized suit—but with coiffed hair—lurks in the bottom lefthand corner of the image and gazes back into the crowd. The caption below describes the scene as "A Gypsy alley . . . less than one kilometer from the Canebière."[16] Although par-tially obscured by hanging clothing and the throng of people, the buildings ap-pear to be haphazardly constructed and seem to lean into the alley. In fact, the image is so dense and so dynamic that it literally seems to burst from the page, to overflow even the boundaries of the photograph. The photo thus reinforced the perception that Peysonnel was not easily contained.

According to the authors, Peysonnel was a leprous outcast that should be ex-pelled. The slum's proximity to the city center was dangerous because it was like a cancer threatening to eat away the heart of the city. The article drew on medi-calized discourses from the late nineteenth and early twentieth centuries to char-acterize the slum and its residents as contagious. Peysonnel was a breeding ground for disease, and special measures were necessary to protect Marseille's surround-ing citizenry.

Concerns about slums like Peysonnel were not only articulated by the Marseille press but were also voiced by state authorities at both local and national levels. Officials at the central MRU similarly described slums as diseased urban tissue. In one pamphlet, entitled "The Struggle against Slums" (La lutte contre les taudis), the MRU linked the dangers of slum living to the degeneration of city and family life: "Slums sterilize our city centers . . . and there is a direct correlation between mortality rates and the nature of habitat: dark and humid rooms, over-population, crumbling walls . . . are detrimental to the physical and moral health of the occupants. . . . The degradation of family life contributes equally to the augmentation of the number of alcoholics, insane, juvenile delinquents, prosti-tutes, and asocials who are simultaneously the charges of, and dangers to, the collectivity."[17] According to MRU officials, the solution to France's slum prob-lem was a meticulous and quantitative assessment of slum living. The pamphlet described the need for "doctors, economists, administrators, journalists, lawyers,

"Less than one kilometer from the Canebière."

Source: Marseille Magazine, no. 28 (1954): 23. Archives Municipales de Marseille 439 W 25.

urbanists, and politicians, to study defective habitat from within their respective disciplines in order to cure our civilization of this scourge."[18] The MRU detailed a method of assessment involving "systematic analysis of the territory in its entirety . . . these studies are not only of the buildings, but also the inhabitants, detailing: familial composition, financial means, occupation, house-keeping methods, etc."[19]

At the local level, *techniciens* echoed the positions and policies outlined by the MRU. In a 1952 report, the departmental head of the architecture and urbanism department, André Hardy, mused: "What is the cure for this disease which afflicts our cities? How do we rehabilitate the urban tissue?"[20] While he described slums in pathological terms, he outlined a technocratic solution to the problem. For Hardy, these "wounds [could] be healed by: (1)statistical analysis; (2) the examination of these statistical results using demographic, material, and financial analysis; (3) developing construction programs."[21] According to him, these "meticulous and detailed studies [were] necessary" to solve the social question.[22] For central state and local authorities, solving the slum problem required a detailed examination both of the dilapidated state of buildings and also, importantly, of slum residents.

A 1952 memo from the MRU to the Bouches-du-Rhônes urban planning office outlined the methods local *techniciens* were supposed to use for evaluating *taudis*. Drawing largely on the procedures developed by the top MRU official and urbanist Robert Auzelle, the memo called for a "summary inventory of the specific local problems" of slums and slum dwellers.[23] In particular, the MRU directed local *techniciens* to work closely with municipalities to conduct local studies. These studies were supposed to evaluate "the composition of families, their means of existence, and their sociability and the state of habitability of the buildings they occupy."[24]

So-called slums such as Peysonnel may have faced condemnation by state officials and the wider public, but they were also communities in their own right. For most Peysonnel residents, shanty life was undesirable, but it was also home, even if only temporarily. In addition to hastily constructed shacks and other dwellings, Peysonnel had its own local economy featuring several stores where residents purchased groceries and other goods. The community bar was not just an important meeting place for Peysonnel residents, it was also the de facto administrative seat of the *taudi*. Any mail or other documents sent to Peysonnel residents was addressed to the fictional "1 rue Peysonnel" and was delivered to the bar. The proprietor then took over the mail carrier's duties, seeing to it that mail was delivered to the correct resident. "Slums" like Peysonnel thus illustrate how *taudis* were vibrant ecosystems unto themselves and, because they benefited from some services like the post, were also tacitly legitimated as established—albeit troublesome—residential spaces within cities. For urban planners and local officials, however, these areas were nonetheless vexing reminders of the scope and scale of the modernizing project.

Quantifying Quality of Life in Peysonnel

In 1951, the director of the Municipal Bureau of Hygiene visited Peysonnel and described its living conditions: "Most buildings are constructed from chance materials like plywood and sheet metal, and these huts shelter seven or eight members of a family in a single, drafty room with a low ceiling. The floor is typically bare earth, and ventilation comes from the open door. There are often no beds, and even less often bedding; just mattresses thrown on the bare earth, and rags for blankets."[25] The director also described the lack of running water and a sewer system, as waste drained directly onto the narrow streets and collected in pools around the shanties. He concluded that "[t]here is absolutely no possibility to ameliorate these *taudis* in order to render them habitable. The only rational solution is to bulldoze all these completely insalubrious dwellings."[26]

After this preliminary report, local *techniciens* from the urban planning department began a comprehensive quantitative assessment of Peysonnel. While the report from the director of the Municipal Bureau of Hygiene assumed there was a causal link between the deplorable material conditions in the slum and the moral decay of the residents, local *techniciens* sought to demonstrate this connection empirically. A team of *techniciens* from the city's Direction des services techniques division of the Bureau central d'études began to walk the paths and alleyways of the *taudi*. Whereas *Marseille Magazine* had characterized Peysonnel as a mysterious, elusive underworld, local *techniciens* sought to demystify the site. They sought to produce a body of knowledge about the slum and its inhabitants.

Local *techniciens*, led by a city employee named Feracci, began to meticulously map Peysonnel. According to the maps drawn by Feracci, the *ilot insalubre* was shaped like a pentagon and bounded by the rue Clary, the avenue Roger Salengro, and the rue Peysonnel.[27]

In addition to documenting the precise perimeter of Peysonnel, Feracci also mapped the locations of all residences and other constructions within the slum. He numbered each dwelling, no matter its state, described what it was constructed out of, and who owned it, if anybody. For example, for the building Feracci labeled Number Ten, he described it as part old stone hangar, part lean-to. He also noted that over the years "many of its occupants had added haphazardly" to the original building.[28] Another building that Feracci numbered seven was made of "very dilapidated brick." According to his report, the city of Marseille was the original owner of this building but it had been occupied for some time by a

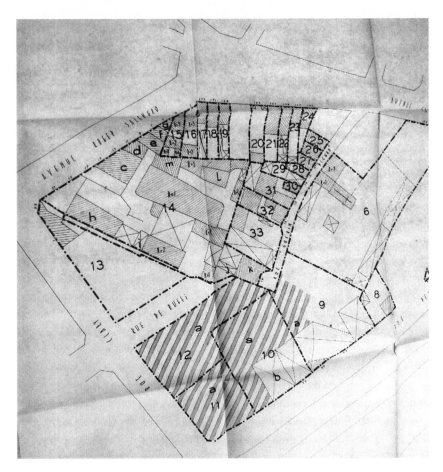

Feracci's map of a section of Peysonnel.

Source: *Archives Municipales de Marseille 439 W 25.*

non-rent-paying "vegetable merchant."[29] In all, Feracci and his team counted at least 122 dwellings and 34 shops in the slum. While Feracci conceded that it was difficult to ascertain the exact number of people living in Peysonnel, he determined that between 700 and 900 residents lived in the *taudi*.[30]

After mapping the exteriors and locations of all buildings in Peysonnel, Feracci and his team also analyzed the interiors of these dwellings. To do so, they entered each of the homes they encountered and once inside also examined the people who lived there. They used a form titled "Les enquêtes sur l'habitat" to assess the material condition of each dwelling as well as the moral condition of each family. The form was issued by the central MRU and reflected urbanist Robert Auzelle's directions for evaluating French living standards. It had two main categories: *salubrité* and sociability. The French term *salubrité* translates rather awkwardly to "salubriousness"—meaning quality of hygiene—but it also has a strong connotation of moral purity. Local *techniciens* utilized this standardized form to analyze the particularities of Peysonnel residents and their dwellings.

For *salubrité*, local *techniciens* examined the interior state of the building, including air circulation, light, access to water and toilets, and number of rooms. They also assessed the proximity of the building to neighboring houses, garbage, or sewage. While the *salubrité* category checked for the physical integrity of the building, the sociability portion of the form judged the domestic and moral state of the family.

The sociability portion of the form was divided into four subcategories: profession, housekeeping, furnishings, and manner of living. Except in the case of a single mother, the "profession" subcategory documented the employment status of the male head of the family (the *chef de famille*).

Aside from profession, most of the criteria used to determine the sociability of a family evaluated the role of the wife and mother. Under the second subcategory— housekeeping—the investigator inspected for bad odors, dirty dishes, unclean windowpanes, unswept floors, and cluttered tables. Under furnishings, the third subcategory, the investigator checked for the presence of a kitchen stove, dining table, beds and bedding, bathroom commodities, and even a parlor. The fourth subcategory, "manner of living," assessed the presence of a laundry line, cooking fuel, trash bins, and decorating style.

For each violation of any of these categories, the family received one demerit point. The more points a household had, the more "insalubrious" or "asocial" the family. A score between 0 and 2 meant that the family was normal. A score between 2 and 2.5 indicated that the family had average sociability. If the family received above a 2.5, they were "asocial." By analyzing sociability and *salubrité* as discrete categories local *techniciens* meant to separate the material condition of the house from the family. However, in the final tabulation the scores overwhelmingly reflected the moral condition of the family. The *salubrité*—or condition—of the house was based on the way in which a family lived in it.[31]

Interestingly, Feracci added a new category to the individual household studies that was not part of the original standardized form provided by the central state—namely, "nationality."[32] He documented four main nationalities in Peysonnel: French, Spanish, Italian, and North African. For most of the 126 families living in the slum, Feracci wrote "French" under the nationality category. Italians formed the next largest group, followed by Spanish and, finally, North Africans. So, although several municipal memos and local newspaper articles characterized Peysonnel as a "court of miracles" inhabited by foreigners, Feracci's empirical work showed that most residents of the slum were actually French. The picture of the Peysonnel population that emerges from Feracci's quantitative work differs markedly from the image constructed by the local media and other municipal reports.

It is unclear how Feracci arrived at his documentation of nationality, whether he asked to see official identification papers or simply made assumptions about nationality based on residents' appearance and language skills. He did, however, note the city where residents were born. Many of the residents labeled "North African" were born in Algiers or Tunis. However, several of the other families labeled "North African" were from Beirut. Curiously, Feracci classified "North African" as a distinct category of nationality although he used it to label families who were not only from Algeria or other parts of North Africa but also from the Middle East.[33] Moreover, many of these residents were technically French, because they were part of the imperial nation-state. As Cliff Rosenberg has noted, colonial subjects have historically maintained a unique position as "not quite French" but "not foreign."[34] The work of local *technicien* Feracci reflected this ambivalent position of colonial subjects within Greater France.

Why might Feracci have added the nationality category to his individual household studies in the first place? Since the late nineteenth century, nationality had emerged as a key marker of difference. For example, during the interwar period, nationality became an important category in the developing system for immigration control. As France pursued a relatively open-door policy, officials also developed stringent practices for the surveillance and documentation of newcomers to the metropole, including colonial migrants.[35] Such efforts to manage migrants were shaped, in part, by notions of race and ethnicity. It is possible that Feracci and other local *techniciens* in postwar France were influenced by these older practices of documenting difference.

Feracci's understanding of the category "Spanish" further illuminates how the nationality category did not refer simply to legal country of origin but also to perceptions of race. Although many of the Peysonnel residents that Feracci labeled "Spanish" were actually born in Marseille, he also noted that they were of "nomadic origin." For Feracci, and for most municipal officials at this moment, the term "nomadic" was another way of saying that these residents were Roma, often referred to as "gypsies." Although some were relative newcomers to the region, many had also lived in southern France for generations. According to Shannon Fogg, in the early twentieth century all "gypsies" were subject to additional classification measures.[36] Beginning in 1912, they had to "carry anthropomorphic identity cards documenting their physical characteristics."[37] At the time, these measures reflected new developments in the "science" of eugenics that linked biological perceptions of race to concerns about criminal behavior. Although such studies of race, biology, and criminality were supposedly discredited after World

War II, the ways that Roma continued to be marked as distinctly foreign in post-war France shows the persistent influence of such ideas. For groups like the Roma, their "nationality" or "foreignness" was often associated with the perception that they were "asocial."

Although Feracci decided to add the "nationality" category to his studies of Peysonnel, he did not do this for all of the slums he assessed around Marseille. In addition to Peysonnel, Feracci conducted individual household studies of most of the *îlots insalubres* in the city in the 1950s. During much of this decade, and because of the push to construct new housing, he evaluated multiple sites around Marseille simultaneously. In 1955, for example, he conducted individual household studies of an *îlot insalubre* near the avenue Joseph Vidal in the south of Marseille, but in this instance, he did not deviate from the standardized form. The same is true for assessments of other blighted areas in the southern part of the city where he did not document the nationality of slum dwellers.[38] But for his assessments of several other slums, Feracci *did* add the nationality category to his studies. For example, in his 1955 study of a *taudi* on the boulevard du Capitaine Gèze, which was just north of the Vieux Port and near the docks, Feracci noted a number of "North African," French, and "gypsy" families and laborers living in abandoned barracks or in trailers.[39]

Why did Feracci add the nationality category to some of his household studies but not to others? The geographical location of *îlots insalubres* within Marseille may have influenced his actions. Feracci evaluated slums in many parts of the city, including the northern and southern outskirts of Marseille as well as downtown. For *îlots insalubres* located in the southern part of Marseille, he did *not* tend to document the nationality of residents. However, for *îlots insalubres* in the city center or north of downtown, he *did* document nationality. As Mary Lewis has shown, Marseille residents considered the city center and port districts blighted, dangerous, and foreign spaces.[40] Moreover, Marseille's northern neighborhoods were associated with poor, working-class, and foreign families, while the south of Marseille was understood to be more affluent, and supposedly more French. Feracci's inconsistent application of the nationality category maps rather neatly onto those parts of the city historically imagined to be home to foreigners and the urban poor.[41]

In their efforts to document and classify slums and slum dwellers, local *techniciens* sometimes deviated from central state policies by adding the category "nationality" to their demographic studies. While their application of the nationality category was not especially new, their use of the category in the service of modernization programs had a marked effect on postwar slum clearance. Local *techniciens* understood nationality less as a legal category than as a racial one. Moreover, nationality was not only a marker of familial origin, it was also a measure of a family's "associability." Local *techniciens* understood slum-dwelling families in terms of a taxonomy of "asocialness." They often classified metropolitan French families as least asocial, followed by Italians, with "gypsy" and "North African" families bringing up the rear as the most asocial.

From Peysonnel to La Paternelle

The "struggle against slums" and the system of classifying families and their homes was part of France's rehousing and construction program. From 1953 to1962, local *techniciens* assessed 25 slums and *îlots insalubres* around Marseille. They examined 2,285 housing units (including apartments, shacks, and tenements) and conducted individual household studies for 2,317 families.[42] As local and national authorities continued to quantify family norms and practices, concerns arose over rehousing. Should families previously living in slums be allowed to move directly into new HLMs? Could people with low sociability scores manage living in modern apartments alongside other, seemingly more respectable families?

In a letter to the minister of reconstruction and urbanism, Marseille mayor Gaston Defferre expressed concern about rehousing families who had previously lived in slums: "We have difficulties rehousing a category of the population, at once unadapted and without sufficient resources."[43] In enacting its slum-clearance program the city had to relocate displaced families. Officials worried that if these families were not rehoused, they would simply move to another slum. Many municipal officials also believed that these families were too "asocial" to live in normal housing: "It is neither possible nor desirable to rehouse these occupants in normal housing right away."[44] Debates about so-called unadapted families continued throughout the 1950s, and three cities, Marseille, Lille, and Lyon, took the initiative in addressing the problem of where to put asocial families. Their solution was to construct "reduced-norm housing."[45]

Reduced-norm housing would house families deemed not sociable enough for normal housing. These buildings literally had reduced norms. For example, these apartments did not have hot water or central heating. Rather than the "universal" norm of a toilet per household, many of these buildings had only one toilet per floor. At work behind the concept of reduced-norm housing was a logic of gradualism: certain families were not yet ready for modern housing. Following this logic, these families would not know how to conduct themselves and would misuse modern amenities. Therefore, they had to be schooled in proper domestic practices by being exposed to modern living gradually.

In early 1959, Marseille constructed the city's first reduced-norm housing development approximately five miles north of downtown.[46] The new residence was named La Paternelle (The Paternal). La Paternelle was supposed to be an intermediary step between slum and normal housing where "unadapted" families could be trained in modern domestic norms and practices. Over time, such families might qualify to move into normal housing.[47]

According to the report describing the construction project: "This housing will be for residents as yet little adapted to modern construction and collective life. All materials must be robust, and all important drainage should be located on the exterior of the building for easy access for repairs. Combustible materials should be reduced to a minimum."[48] Each housing unit had two rooms—one main room and one bedroom. While each apartment had access to running water, there was no hot water and no heating source aside from the gas stove in the kitchenette.[49] The plans for La Paternelle also designated the use of inexpensive construction materials: "As the goal is to keep costs as reduced as possible, the contractors will use materials at hand in their warehouses."[50]

La Paternelle was a cheap and quick solution to the problem of where to house "asocial" families. As its name suggests, it was also supposed to resocialize families to French ways of life. Municipal urban planners and architects designed Paternelle to reorder and discipline disorderly families through standardizing their living spaces. Paradoxically, one key way in which families were to be resocialized was not through access to new modern modes of living (such as central heating), but through exposure to reduced norms as a half-step toward modern life.

By the middle of 1959, city contractors had finished building La Paternelle, and housing officials were ready to move residents into this reduced-norm housing. Many families living in Peysonnel, as well as in other slums around Marseille, were ultimately relocated to La Paternelle. Of the families living in Peysonnel, several that Feracci had labeled "French" were moved to "normal" housing, while most of the families he had labeled "North African" or "gypsy" were sent to La Paternelle. Curiously, many of the "French" families that were ultimately moved to normal housing had actually received *salubrité* and sociability scores that were *lower* than most of the "North African" families. Although the individual household studies were supposed to rank families empirically and objectively in terms of their social condition, when it came to determining where to rehouse them, local *techniciens* seemed to make decisions in terms of commonsense and subjective perceptions of racial difference.

As residents began to move to La Paternelle, city officials were keen to monitor the domestic practices of these families. They were especially concerned that Paternelle's new residents might fall back into their old ways: "We don't want things to deteriorate in such a short time to a new slum. It's important to take draconian measures to police this group of residents. It is necessary, notably, to forbid occupants from constructing this-and-that outside their apartments (animal cages, various kinds of huts). Considering these conditions, a guardianship must be set up . . . and the guardian must be helped by frequent police rounds."[51]

Despite efforts to police La Paternelle, however, municipal officials remained concerned that the new development was deteriorating. For example, in late 1959 and early 1960, in the months after the residents moved to the new reduced-norm housing complex, reports began to circulate about the seemingly abnormal practices that residents had "imported" from their old ways of life.[52] A report from Pouchot, a local *technicien* in the urban planning department, detailed the problems at Paternelle: "the electrical wiring appears to be malfunctioning, and the water and sewage lines are clogged or leaking . . . these problems are due to resident misuse, including throwing large objects down drains and toilets."[53] Other reports described "a group of gypsies living in La Paternelle [who] have begun a kind of nightly orchestra. They are exceptionally noisy and are menacing to their neighbors."[54] Based on these reports, officials concluded that La Paternelle was "rapidly transforming into a new slum."[55]

While municipal officials had imagined Peysonnel to be full of "foreign North Africans and gypsies" they ultimately moved mostly "North African" and "gypsy" families to La Paternelle. Moreover, despite the shoddy construction of Paternelle, municipal authorities tended to cite resident misuse and disruptive behavior as the main reasons why Paternelle was falling into disrepair. City officials and local *techniciens* had created in La Paternelle the slum they had imagined in Peysonnel.

From the perspective of municipal authorities, the Paternelle experiment was not working as well as hoped. They began to consider new methods for resocializing Paternelle residents. However, they were restricted by a shortage of money: the Marseille municipality had funded Paternelle largely from the city budget comprised, in part, of taxes paid by residents. As Marseille continued to look for a solution to its slum problems, new colonial institutions offered possibilities for increased funding.

From Asocial to Algerian Families

From the mid-1950s through the early 1960s, local slum-clearance efforts were occurring within the larger context of decolonization. At this time many colonies in French West Africa became independent and France was deeply involved with the Algerian War of Independence. As the conflict in Algeria escalated, the French government was increasingly concerned about the population of Algerians living in the metropole, as well as the threat of attacks by the Front de libération nationale (FLN) and the l'Organisation de l'armée secrète (OAS).

In 1958, the government of the Fourth Republic dissolved amid the crisis of the Algerian war and terrorist threats in the metropole. Charles de Gaulle reassumed the presidency but set a number of preconditions for his return, including the drafting of a new constitution that bestowed more power on the executive branch of government. Once the constitution establishing the Fifth Republic was ratified, de Gaulle worked to bolster the French presence in Algeria. The 1959 Constantine plan was the signature component of the new government's efforts to keep Algeria French. The plan was intended to counter the influence of the FLN through social welfare and infrastructure programs for Algerian workers and families in both Algeria and France.

Several institutions were mandated under the Constantine Plan to provide welfare services and promote social education in French ways of life. As Amelia Lyons has shown, two institutions, the Fonds d'action social (FAS) and the Societé nationale de construction de logements pour les travailleurs algeriens en métropole (SONACOTRAL), received special funding to provide social services and benefits for Algerian single-male workers, but especially for Algerian families.[56] Under the Constantine Plan, the main objectives of the FAS and SONACOTRAL were "to eliminate terrorism, to promote cultural and psychological social education for migrants and their families, to act to promote public opinion and separate agitators from the mass of migrants that can be welcomed comprehensively and fraternally."[57] The FAS worked in concert with the SONACOTRAL to become the "instruments of the Constantine Plan" and the "organisms specializing in slum clearance."[58]

A significant element of the SONACOTRAL's mandate was to construct housing for Algerian workers and families in the metropole and to foster "the amelioration of the living conditions of Algerians and facilitate the accession of families to modern habitat."[59] Many SONACOTRAL employees were *techniciens* who had previously established careers as urban planners, security officers, or bureaucrats in French colonies. Moreover, the new head of SONACOTRAL was none other than Eugène Claudius-Petit, the former head of the Ministry of Reconstruction and Urbanism, who had built his career by promoting slum-clearance and urban hygiene and by standardizing domestic norms in the immediate postwar period. Claudius-Petit's faith that modern life could be socially constructed, and SONACOTRAL's roots in colonial management contributed to the institution's special mission to clear slums, rehouse Algerian families and workers, and suppress the rebellious elements assumed to be thriving in hot spots around France. Most important, SONACOTRAL worked to resocialize Algerian families to embrace French ways of life through the control of domestic spaces and practices.[60]

The FAS and SONACOTRAL worked with local organizations to promote social welfare services for Algerians. For example, the FAS funded the Association des travailleurs d'outre mer (or ATOM) in Marseille, the Association for Housing and Social Promotion in Paris, and the Foyer Notre Dame des sans-abris in Lyon. SONACOTRAL also began to fund the construction of dormitories for single-male workers and reduced-norm housing for families in Marseille and throughout France. From 1959 until the end of the Algerian War of Independence in 1962, these associations received ample financial support from the central government.

As municipal authorities searched for additional means to continue slum-clearance programs, associations like FAS and SONACOTRAL became attractive sources of funding. As a result, local modernization efforts became increasingly tied to Constantine Plan funds. As municipalities rehoused families in facilities such as La Paternelle, they needed more money. In a memo to local housing and urban-planning departments, Marseille mayor Gaston Defferre outlined the particular difficulties of financing reduced-norm housing and the potential role of the FAS and SONACOTRAL in ameliorating the problem: "In order to realize our goal of clearing slums and tenements, the municipality must be in a position to build and allocate housing. . . . SONACOTRAL is specially charged with constructing housing for North Africans, and the organization benefits from special funding from the Fonds d'action social. As there could be anywhere from five to six hundred North African families in our *îlots insalubres*, there should be a way to reconcile these different desires among these organizations."[61] In other words, although Marseille officials and local *techniciens* were concerned with the war against slums and the reeducation of *asocial* families, the FAS, SONACOTRAL, and ATOM were preoccupied with the war against *Algerian* slums and the reeducation of *Algerian* families. In the interest of Marseille's redevelopment plans, the mayor suggested that there must be a way to reconcile Marseille's goals with the FAS/SONACOTRAL/ATOM mandate.

By the early 1960s, municipal authorities and local *techniciens* in search of government funding began to employ a different kind of vocabulary. Rather than discussing the slum problem in terms of "asocial" or "unadapted families," they began to describe it exclusively in terms of "North African," especially "Algerian" families.[62] Several letters from Mayor Gaston Defferre to the MRU trace this shift. In an earlier memo, Defferre described a diverse population of "Africans" and "gypsies" living in shantytowns: "[our] problems concern demolishing *îlots insalubres* and rehousing the population that includes North Africans, Roma, and nomads in the slums, North Africans and black Africans in the tenements."[63] But in a 1961 memo, Defferre discussed the population exclusively in terms of "North Africans in bidonvilles."[64] In another example, a letter to the prefect from the mayor's secretary-general described "the presence in a field of about thirty Algerian families . . . the problem in this bidonville is more than just a question of urbanism, it is a question of security."[65]

Officials also ceased to refer to slums as *îlots insalubres* and *taudis*, but increasingly called these areas bidonvilles. The term "bidonville" first appeared in Morocco in the late 1920s in reference to the haphazard dwellings that colonial subjects constructed in Casablanca. These shantytowns began to pop up following the migration of Europeans to the city. As local industries grew to accommodate this new population, they attracted colonial subjects in search of employment. As David Hauw outlines, few provisions were made for *indigènes* who came to work in European factories, and they began to construct make-shift homes out of the discarded remnants of industry.[66] They used sheet metal, boxes, and *bidons* (or cans or large drums) to construct what came to be known as bidonvilles. Over time, the term was most often used to refer to the shantytowns of colonial subjects living in North African cities, and it took on both spatial and racialized characteristics. By the mid-1960s, the term "bidonvilles" was being widely utilized by local *techniciens* in Marseille and also gained widespread currency among other state officials and the general public in France. While North Africans were assumed to be *part* of the social problem in the early 1950s, by the early 1960s they were considered to *be* the social problem. In the early 1950s, local *techniciens* identified "North African" families living in slums to be part of an asocial group that included poor working-class French families as well as "gypsies" and migrants from Italy. After ATOM and SONACOTRAL became more involved in local slum-clearance efforts, local *techniciens* and municipal officials began to single out North Africans exclusively as slum dwellers. More specifically, North Africans became Algerians.

How can we explain this shift from concerns about asocial families living in *îlots insalubres* to Algerian families living in bidonvilles? Increased funding from the Constantine Plan is one part of the explanation. Municipal officials and local *techniciens* began to approach ATOM and FAS, especially if they had a slum or tenement with a particularly high concentration of North Africans. ATOM officials and local *techniciens* also began to work in tandem to assess families living in bidonvilles. Local *techniciens* often did the initial leg work, mapping the slum and identifying where Algerian families lived, but they let ATOM conduct the individual household studies for these families.

Other explanations have to do with the escalation of the Algerian War of Independence and Marseille's position as an imperial city. As a Mediterranean port, Marseille is the closest major French city to Algeria and was an important staging point for shipping troops and supplies. Because of its location, Marseille was also particularly vulnerable to attacks. As the war escalated, city officials were concerned about terrorist attacks from the FLN as well those *pieds noirs* (white settlers in Algeria) who opposed Algerian independence and carried out their own attacks in the metropole. For example, during this period, several large factory fires—linked to either the FLN or OAS—raged through the city's port district, causing widespread destruction. City hall also received frequent bomb threats, and Mayor Gaston Defferre employed a detail of bodyguards for constant protection.[67]

Lastly, the shift from evaluating slum-dwelling asocial families to singling out Algerians living in bidonvilles reflects how perceptions of race shaped local *techniciens'* understanding of modernization. For local *techniciens*, ethnic difference was part of what they saw in everyday life, but they struggled to find a way to classify families. They were constrained by a state model that made recognizing difference problematic. In the 1950s, their solution was to label families by nationality, but even this category did not really fit, as local *techniciens* used a legal paradigm of formal citizenship to describe their own perceptions of ethnic differences.

Colonial institutions like SONACOTRAL helped to make these racial hierarchies more explicit. During decolonization and the Algerian War of Independence, colonial institutions began to play a greater role in local slum-clearance projects. Examining this evolving relationship between SONACOTRAL and FAS employees and local *techniciens* in Marseille helps shed new light on the Constantine Plan. It was not simply a linear effort unilaterally applied across France and Algeria, it was merged with and reflected through local development plans and concerns. As employees of SONACOTRAL and the FAS began to work more closely with municipal officials, local *techniciens* began to appropriate the vocabularies utilized by former colonial functionaries. Other groups that had been considered part of the population of *îlots insalubres*—including "gypsies" and poor French— became increasingly invisible as Algerians came to stand out in the public imagination as the principal residents of bidonvilles.

Part II
THE WELFARE CITY IN DECLINE?

On the "hot, oppressive" Saturday afternoon of August 25, 1973, reported the front page of *Le Provençal,* a man later described as "a North African type" boarded crowded Bus 72, the line that traveled from downtown Marseille to the city's main public beach, La Plage du prado.[1] It was nearly 2:30 p.m., and "as several passengers dozed due to the heat, others tried to open a bus window for the hint of a breath of fresh air."[2] During the summer months, this line was especially popular with schoolchildren and residents seeking to escape the heat of the city, and for "all Marseillais, the number 72 [was known as] the bus to the beach."[3] On this afternoon, so the *Provençal* reported, "it was a day like any other."[4] After the "North African" had boarded the bus, he and the driver quibbled briefly over the fare. After this exchange, the man, who was later identified as Salah Bougrine, originally from Algeria, sat quietly for a few seconds as the bus began to rumble away from the stop. Suddenly, however, he sprang from his seat, pulled a knife out from the folds of his clothes, and began to attack the bus driver and nearby passengers. The bus driver was stabbed "several dozen times" and seven passengers were injured: "It was a veritable massacre. Blood on the windows, blood on the seats, blood everywhere."[5] The bus plowed out of control through traffic, hitting cars and zigzagging across the street before crashing to a halt.

Bougrine continued to brandish his knife wildly until he was overpowered by Gracieux Lamperti, who was later described in the Marseille papers as "a former boxing champion, and now a hero."[6] As the bloody passengers began to pour out of the bus, Lamperti and a few others wrestled with Bougrine. They finally wrenched him out of the bus and into the gathering crowd. In the chaos someone shouted that Bougrine should be lynched, and the crowd prepared to string him up. Before the police arrived on the scene, the bus driver died from loss of blood and Bougrine was beaten into a coma. In the following days, and as the police began their investigation, they learned that Bougrine had suffered a severe head injury in 1969 while working in a factory in Nice but had never received proper treatment. Once he regained consciousness and the police were able to question him, they also determined that he was mentally ill.

Three days later, Marseille held a massive and public memorial for the slain bus driver. *Le Provençal* featured extensive coverage of the event. Under a photo of a large crowd of mourners slowly making their way down La Canebière, the main boulevard in downtown Marseille, the caption read: "Adieu from an entire city."[7] For the next week, every regional newspaper—the socialist-affiliated *Le Provençal*, the communist *La Marseillaise*, and the conservative *Le Meridional*—capitalized on the story, devoting the front page and several additional pages of articles to what they were calling the "Massacre on Bus 72." According to *Le Provençal*: "after the tragedy . . . the public [is] beginning to feel a diffuse and widespread fear. What used to be a commonplace thing—riding on the bus—[now] provokes anxiety and heated emotions in all milieux of Marseillais."[8] The "massacre on Bus 72" was committed by a solitary individual with a history of mental illness. But as *Le Provençal* reported: "Salah Bougrine is North African, and the generalization is quickly made."[9] The press, Marseille residents, and local officials began to discuss the incident, not as an isolated and violent crime, but in terms of the broader "immigrant problem."

The conservative Marseille newspaper, *Le Meridional*, was particularly volatile in its reporting on the "Massacre on Bus 72." The day after the attack, the owner of the paper, Gabriel Domenech, published an editorial titled "Enough! Enough! Enough!" which condemned the crime as an attack on the nation as a whole:

> Enough of these stealing Algerians, enough of these thieving Algerians, enough of these swaggering Algerians, enough of these troublemaking Algerians, enough of these syphilitic Algerians, enough of these raping Algerians, enough of these pimping Algerians, enough of these insane Algerians, enough of these murdering Algerians.

> We have had enough of this rampant immigration that brings to our country all of the scum of the Mediterranean who mix with honest and brave Frenchmen who work to earn a living for themselves and their families.

Yesterday, it was a poor bus driver who was the victim of the beastly, wicked deed. Next a worker is attacked . . . or the defenseless elderly, or young girls, or women. Until when? What are we waiting for before we act?[10]

The *Meridional* also began to publish editorials from nascent extreme rightist organizations who called for action against the immigrant threat. In one editorial, the Committee for the Defense of the Republic demanded the death penalty for Salah Bougrine.[11] In another article, a group calling itself the National Front demanded the "legitimate defense" of France and "invite[d] all French" to join with them.[12]

In the weeks following the incident on Bus 72, there was a dramatic surge in "worrisome attacks against immigrants" in Marseille as well as in surrounding towns, including Perreux, Puyricard, and Aix-en-Provence.[13] In most instances, solitary young men—including a sixteen-year-old boy—were attacked and severely beaten, and almost all of them were beaten to death, or later died from severe injuries.[14] Most political leaders and the mainstream press were alarmed by this wave of violence against migrants. In a special editorial in *Le Provençal*, Mayor Gaston Defferre roundly condemned the wave of killings and appealed to his constituents to stop the violence. But he also went a step further in his characterization of the attacks. According to Defferre, the recent violence was proof that the nation was reaching its tipping point because of "the high accumulation of foreigners" in France.[15] Defferre's comments illuminate how immigration was increasingly imagined to be a national threat and how the idea that France had reached its so-called threshold of tolerance for migrants began to gain currency among politicians, policymakers, and ordinary people.

Part II of this book explores shifting notions of social citizenship from the 1960s through the early 1990s in terms of the anxieties generated by two "ends": the end of the economic miracle and the so-called end of empire. Although the economy showed signs of trouble as early as the 1960s, by the early 1970s most people were feeling the effects of what would be a prolonged period of decline. In Marseille, many of the city's established naval and oil refining industries were suffering, and unemployment levels rose dramatically. For many in France as well as in Europe more broadly, the recession was the first fundamental test of the welfare state, as people questioned whether postwar social democracies could actually deliver on the promise of full citizenship. Moreover, many in Europe increasingly viewed immigration as one of the main factors fueling the presumed crisis of the welfare state. In France and Great Britain, migrants from former colonies, as well as citizens from remaining overseas departments and territories, continued to settle in the mainland. In Germany, guest workers and their families, many of them from Turkey, formed an important population of newcomers. The economic downturn not only exacerbated historical anxieties about immigration but also raised important questions about the future viability of the welfare state.

MANAGING THE QUALITY AND QUANTITY OF THE POPULATION

After World War II, an important aim of the reconstruction project was to include social rights within a more comprehensive notion of citizenship, and this process was fundamentally shaped by empire. Although most French colonies had gained independence by 1962, the legacy of imperialism nevertheless continued to inform evolving ideas about welfare in mainland France. The end of the Algerian War of Independence marked an important turning point for metropolitan welfare policies. In 1962, nearly a million people fled Algeria for France in the wake of the war, and as Marseille and central state authorities debated how best to accommodate these newcomers, their negotiations influenced new directions for social security and housing institutions. More specifically, after 1962, colonial subjects were redefined as immigrants and included in new ways within welfare regimes. Policies granted migrants limited welfare services, such as access to shelter, but did not offer them political membership within the polity. Such policies helped to call into question—and to decouple—the perceived relationship between citizenship and welfare.

As part of this restructuring of welfare services, state officials also tried to define migration in exclusively economic terms by focusing resources on the construction of dormitories for single male migrant workers. But despite such efforts, local and national authorities still had to contend with a large and growing number of families, many from former colonies, who had come to France for economic *and* political reasons. As officials renewed efforts to clear bidonvilles and deliver on the postwar promise of comprehensive town planning, they placed many postcolonial migrant families in temporary housing developments called *les cités de transit.* Such efforts underscored how these families were seen as transient and mobile. It was assumed that one day they would return to their countries of origin. However, these temporary homes suggested family mobility in a double sense. Most *cités de transit* were managed by former colonial institutions that also required residents to enroll in social education and other domestic training programs. Not only were migrant families expected to leave France eventually, they were also supposed to evolve, to assimilate, to become *more* French during their stay in the metropole. The migrant social welfare programs of the 1960s thus underscored the ambiguous status of postcolonial migrants in France and reflected state officials' attempts to regulate the "quality" or "Frenchness" of the population in the metropole.

By the early 1970s, and as the French economy slipped into recession, government officials were not only concerned about managing the quality of the migrant population, they were also especially anxious to limit its quantity.[1] Migration to France was increasingly imagined to be a problem and one of the causes of the so-called crisis of the welfare state. In 1974, President Giscard d'Estaing approved a measure intended to ban future immigration to France and thus attempted to end a period marked by relatively laissez-faire migration policies. The ban was justified in large part by a developing consensus that France had reached its *seuil de tolérance* or "threshold of tolerance" and could not absorb any more newcomers without threatening the nation and its cultural heritage.

While scholars have discussed at length the largely ineffective 1974 immigration ban as well as social education efforts within *les cités de transit,* few have placed these particular issues within the broader history of the politics of population management. More specifically, late-twentieth-century concerns about migration and France's "threshold of tolerance" illuminate a deeper history of welfare, a legacy shaped by the social sciences and rooted in theories about social hygiene. As historians of the nineteenth century have shown, disciplinary developments in sociology, demography, and other fields were concerned with overseeing the population with the aim to facilitate national progress. Scholars such as Robert Nye have demonstrated the historical relationships between developing institutions of welfare, social science research, and biological understandings of race.[2] Others, including Alice Conklin, have also highlighted how many of the social science disciplines developing in the nineteenth century were firmly rooted in the imperial project.[3]

Late-twentieth-century discourses about colonial migrants should thus be understood in terms of this deeper context. As such they illuminate the historical role that social scientists and research institutions have played in helping to produce knowledge about population control. Importantly, such recent debates also reveal how legacies of scientific racism continued to inform the post–World War II project to build the welfare state: regulating welfare was not always about guaranteeing citizenship rights. Although scholars have argued that, after World War II, talking about race in such terms became untenable, biological thinking—coupled with concerns about cultural mixing—nevertheless continued to frame the late-twentieth-century debate about the "immigrant question" as well as concerns about the welfare of the nation more generally.

The *Rapatrié* Problem

During the summer of 1962, nearly a million people fled Algeria for France. The exodus placed considerable strain on the city of Marseille, the primary port between the metropole and Africa. Each week, the city received tens of thousands of people who were initially collectively referred to as *rapatriés*, or repatriates. In the early part of the year, about 42,000 arrived each month. These numbers spiked dramatically in May 1962, when over 100,000 arrived, and peaked in June when more than 350,000 landed in the city. The new arrivals camped on the docks, in public squares, in shantytowns, and the city seemed "submerged by a wave of refugees."[4] As local officials struggled to deal with this deluge of newcomers, they questioned the distinctions that central state officials were drawing among Algerians, particularly the central state's reclassification of "Muslim Algerians" as foreigners. In doing so, local officials contributed to an evolving system of social security that—for some people—ultimately disconnected social benefits from political rights.

As Algeria was one of the last colonies to become independent, this was not the first time that French settlers and former colonial subjects left newly sovereign states for mainland France. In 1946, Syria and Lebanon, both French protectorates, gained independence; and in 1954, France withdrew from Indochina. Morocco and Tunisia became independent states in 1956, followed by Senegal in 1960 and most of French West Africa by 1962. During this fifteen-year wave, the total number of settlers and postcolonial migrants arriving in France was approximately 500,000 people.[5] In 1962, however, nearly twice as many came to France in just three months.

Previous waves of postcolonial migrants could go to Marseille's Bureau of Social Aid or to private charities for assistance. These institutions handed out blankets and food to new arrivals and helped them find temporary shelter. However, the exodus from Algeria "overwhelmed all public and private welcoming and social services" and severely strained city resources.[6] Marseille had just begun the large-scale construction of public housing in earnest, and city residents were beginning to move in larger numbers into new apartments. However, after

1962, Marseille's population increased by 500,000 people, which reexacerbated the housing crisis.[7] Most recent arrivals struggled to meet their basic needs, like finding housing and food for their families. Families found shelter where they could, squatting in abandoned warehouses or building makeshift shacks in blooming shantytowns in and around the city.[8]

Marseille residents began to lodge complaints about these newcomers. As one resident wrote to the prefect: "There is a very old wooden barracks behind my house, lacking running water and toilets, which the city should have destroyed long ago. . . . Living in this barracks . . . are between 60 and 70 families."[9] Residents also complained about the dramatic increase in theft, banditry, and especially the increase in prices. As one resident recalled, "If there was a holdup, it was a *rapatrié*, if there was a traffic jam, it was because of a *rapatrié*."[10] As a former *rapatrié* remembered: "None of us had a job or an apartment to sell. It's more that the Marseillais profited from us."[11] According to police reports, crime did increase during the summer of 1962 as organized gangs took advantage of the chaos, staging a series of armed bank robberies. According to one prefectural report, "between June 27th and the last week of July, there were nineteen armed robberies perpetrated in Marseille."[12] But this report also assumed a causal link between the exodus and the crime wave, stating that "seventeen [of the recent robberies] concerned recent repatriates from Algeria."[13]

As anxieties about the dramatic population surge mounted, Mayor Gaston Defferre attempted to quell unrest by outlining municipal and central state efforts to address what he called "the rapatrié problem" in a series of editorials in the *Provençal* newspaper. In one article he wrote, "It will require extraordinary measures to confront this exceptional situation that we find ourselves in."[14]

During the chaotic period of the summer months, discussions of the "rapatrié problem" seemed to refer to the entire mass of new arrivals, including both *pieds noirs* and *harkis*.[15] However, as local and national officials began to discuss lasting solutions to the problem, a clear distinction emerged regarding who were actually going to be fully repatriated.

The *rapatriés* who would become Marseillais were increasingly described as *pieds noirs*, or European settlers. In his editorials published in *Le Provençal*, Defferre outlined municipal and state efforts to accommodate these new arrivals through the construction of housing and employment incentives: "We are working with the central state," Defferre wrote, "to secure the land and means necessary to build housing" and to "welcome the . . . *rapatriés* who will become Marseillais."[16]

Welcoming or integrating the European *rapatriés* into the metropole was not just a goal for the Marseille municipality but "a problem of national scope and character."[17] In particular, government officials were concerned about the arrival of a large population of former settlers who had vehemently opposed Algerian independence. The Organisation de l'armée secrète, or OAS—a group of *pieds noirs* and soldiers—had committed terrorist acts in both Algeria and metropolitan France to protest what they saw as the French government's betrayal and failure to defend their interests in the colony. After the Evian Accords and the end of the war, French officials attempted to negotiate an agreement that would permit *pieds noirs* to remain in Algeria. However, as violence against French settlers escalated, many *pieds noirs* fled the former colony. Therefore, the "installation of the *rapatriés*" was more than just the immediate effort to house these new arrivals; it was the necessity to integrate them as French citizens.[18] Or, as Defferre explained in a *Provençal* article, it was "our duty" to welcome the *rapatriés* just as it was "their duty to become Marseillais."[19]

In order to begin integrating the *rapatriés* into the metropole, the government charged the Ministry of Rapatriés with overseeing the new programs at both local and national levels.[20] These programs were designed to offer short-term relief as well as longer-term social welfare benefits. In addition to securing employment, the ministry also worked with local housing offices to find permanent housing for the *rapatriés*. A 1962 memo from the Minister of Rapatriés to all departmental prefects outlined the "special housing program destined for the *rapatriés* including the construction of 35,000 public housing units by the end of May 1963."[21] The ministry also encouraged existing public housing societies to allocate 10 to 30 percent of housing openings to *rapatriés*. HLM societies "who acted especially in this effort for national solidarity"[22] would be awarded special financial incentives. Despite these directives to construct almost 40,000 new housing units in less than one year, the ministry cautioned local governments against using cheap, prefabricated materials "despite the efficacy and rapidity of these measures."[23] Even in the use of building materials the Ministry of Rapatriés emphasized permanence: integrating the European *rapatriés* into the national fabric was to ensure their long-term status as French citizens.

While the Ministry of Rapatriés oversaw the assimilation of "European repatriates," a branch of the Ministry of the Interior, the Office of Muslim Affairs, was charged with all issues having to do with "Muslim refugees." In particular, the office was concerned with the new legal designation of Muslim Algerians. In a classified memo to all departmental prefects, the Office of Muslim Affairs defined the new status of "Algerians as foreigners."[24] Since 1947, all Algerians—both French-European and Muslim—had had French citizenship. But with Algerian independence all "European *rapatriés*" from Algeria retained their French citizenship, whereas those labeled "Muslim refugees" were reclassified as foreigners. As Todd Shepard has shown, the end of the Algerian War of Independence marked a turning point for legal definitions of Frenchness as Algerian-Muslims were stripped of their (limited) political rights.[25]

In addition to underscoring this new legal status, the memo also outlined the "new directive concerning aid to Algerian migrants," describing how "the accession of Algeria to independence, having fundamentally modified the legal status of Algerians in France, conducts us naturally to rethink the problem of aid to these migrants and to precisely lay out the new orientation of the action of public powers in this domain."[26] The Office of Muslim Affairs was referring, primarily, to the social welfare programs initiated during the Algerian War of Independence. Under the auspices of the Constantine Plan from 1958–1962, the French government had established a substantial welfare regime aimed at, as Amelia Lyons puts it, "winning the hearts and minds" of Algerian families through improving living standards.[27]

If Algerians had been stripped of their political rights—losing their status as French citizens—were they still entitled access to the social welfare programs of the Constantine Plan? In the year following the exodus, state and local officials debated what to do about the large population of Algerians in the metropole, weighing whether the end of their political rights in France also meant the end of their social benefits. These discussions ultimately raised broader questions about changing notions of membership in the nation.

In late 1963, the Service des affaires musulmans at the Ministry of the Interior briefly concluded that Algerians' loss of French political rights also meant the end of their access to welfare benefits. This position was detailed in a memo sent to all departmental prefects stating that the new "policy [for Algerians] translates to the reduction if not the suppression of all aid."[28] This conclusion, however, was met with rapid and vociferous opposition from local officials whose cities were particularly affected by the exodus.

In a series of letters, Marseille Mayor Gaston Defferre, as well as the director of the municipal Bureau of Social Services, vehemently protested against cutting social aid to Algerians.[29] As one memo outlined: "If the accession of Algeria to independence has permitted a different conception of the aid afforded to Algerians, the human problem nonetheless seems to remain the same and cannot be objectively ignored."[30] According to this memo, the exodus had created a humanitarian crisis in Marseille, and the municipal Bureau of Social Aid was digging deep into city coffers to offer services to the newcomers from Algeria. The director of the Marseille Bureau of Social Aid further asserted that "The work of the bureau is not limited to aiding persons of French nationality. . . . The population originating from Algeria, implanted in Marseille, also needs my services, notably the unemployed, the sick, the elderly, and women with children. . . . Considering that the migration of numerous destitute Algerians 'in transit' in our city is enough that they regularly receive aid for goods, meals, and shelter, the Bureau of Social Aid, in such a situation, must respond to considerations both social and humane."[31]

Importantly, the director also criticized Algerians' new status as foreigners, asserting that if they were indeed refugees in France, then the "Algerian consulate [should] take the necessary measures to assure the means of subsistence and shelter to the Algerians recently arrived in France. . . . Except it also seems improbable that the Algerian Consulate can assure financial support to its nationals—in general, foreign consulates do not maintain social services."[32] The director pointed to the ambiguities of trying to impose a refugee status—that is, the legal framework of international asylum—onto a population previously part of the French Empire. Marseille city officials protested that even though Algerians' *legal* status as foreigners was supposedly clear, their *actual* status in France was not.

After considering the concerns expressed by Marseille officials, central state authorities ultimately agreed with them, admitting that "the status of Algerians in France is less than completely defined."[33] As one central state official acknowledged in a memo: "The problem of reordering the auxiliary Muslim refugees in France continues to be fraught [especially concerning] families and the problem of housing."[34] In a report on "Algerian migration and French administration" Michel Massenet, a longtime civil servant, expert on migration policy, and the then central state director of Muslim affairs, stated that "some have concluded . . . that social action in favor of migration must be abandoned" because "Algerians will be—in effect—considered citizens of an independent state and their rights defined according to the rules applicable to foreigners."[35] Massenet reasoned, however, that "this rationale . . . leaves aside an essential problem": that of the large number of Algerians and other migrants in France. This reality, Massenet continued, meant that "the French collective still has some responsibility."[36] Rather than cut all funding previously allocated to French Muslims from Algeria, Massenet recommended "adapting these social programs to follow new circumstances born out of the independence [of Algeria]."[37]

Welfare without Citizenship?

By 1963, central state authorities had decided how to solve the Algerian welfare problem. Instead of ending programs offering aid to Algerians, Massenet proposed the "extension [of these services] to other migrants."[38] In the 1960s, the French government entered into a number of labor agreements with former colonies and Southern European countries including Algeria, Morocco, Senegal, Portugal, and Greece, and workers from these countries began to migrate to France in increasing numbers.[39] According to one official at the Ministry of the Interior: "Migrants come to our country to earn a living and make up an important element of our national economy."[40] Following this logic, migrants therefore deserved access to some basic services during their stay in France. While decolonization was meant to grant former French colonies political autonomy, an important goal following the end of empire was to maintain economic ties with newly independent states. As one official at the Ministry of the Interior stated, "there is much reciprocity in these economic links."[41] As part of this restructuring of older colonial relationships, Algerians—who had been the target of specific social education and welfare programs under the Constantine Plan—became "migrant workers" and were part of a group that included other former colonial subjects as well as workers from Southern European countries.[42] The extension of social programs to all migrants thus served to obscure the imperial legacies within these welfare services. Based on the recommendations made by social scientists and migration experts, these social services also effectively offered welfare benefits without full political membership.

Massenet and other central state authorities began to outline the specific contours of this expansion of social programs, drawing heavily on the institutions and practices established during the Third and Fourth Republics and further developed under the Fifth Republic's Constantine Plan. According to Massenet, "Certain national associations . . . would continue to be funded pending an adaptation of their methods of action and their objectives."[43] In other words, those institutions that could effectively "modify their statutes" by expanding their focus from Algerians to all foreign workers would retain funding.[44] For those that could not adapt, Massenet "envisage[d] a diminishment of their number."[45] Institutions were thus incentivized to modify their programs or risk losing funding.

Two of the organizations specifically chosen to expand their mandates were the Fonds d'action social and SONACOTRAL. In 1963, SONACOTRAL also changed its name from the National Housing Construction Society for Algerian Workers to the National Housing Construction Society for Workers, or SONACOTRA. In addition to these organizations, many local-level institutions, such as ATOM in Marseille, also expanded their focus. In short, many of the same institutions that had overseen social welfare and integration programs for Algerians during the war continued to do so for all "foreign migrants" after 1963.

Although Massenet identified the Fonds d'action social and SONACOTRA as the main administrators of migrant social aid programs, he also recognized that they could not operate in a vacuum, detached from other state institutions. As part of the reorganization of migrant welfare programs, he also helped establish a complex institutional network whereby multiple state ministries—including the Ministry of Urbanism, the Ministry of Labor, and the Ministry of Public Health and the Population—all worked with SONACOTRA and the FAS. According to Massenet, "the principal argument in favor of an inter-ministerial statute has to do with the fact that precisely the problems concerning the social aid of migrants necessitates cooperation between a large number of administrations."[46] His efforts to establish strong ties with France's other major welfare institutions exemplifies how migrant social services could not be so easily separated from the rest of France's comprehensive welfare state.

One of the major goals of these new programs was to create a system of housing for migrant workers. Officials remained concerned about the large number of migrants living in bidonvilles around France. Although state officials had been engaged in slum clearance in earnest since the 1950s, the exodus of 1962 as well as increased labor and postcolonial migration had caused many shantytowns around France to mushroom. For example, the Nanterre bidonville outside Paris was estimated to contain about fourteen thousand people. In Marseille, despite efforts to clear out slums such as Peysonnel, shantytowns continued to sprout around the city. Moreover, camps such as Grande Bastide and Grand Arenas, originally created to house squatters and other "undesirables" after World War II, still suffered from overcrowding and gross mismanagement.

From 1963 to 1973, SONACOTRA helped build approximately 403 dormitories for single male migrant workers around France.[47] These dormitories, or *foyers* as they were called, were often constructed close to industrial areas but far from city centers and access to stores and other necessities. *Foyers* were meant both to provide workers with a roof overhead and to segregate them from the larger population.[48] Although the SONACOTRA *foyers* were open to all migrant males, including those from "Portugal, Turkey, and Greece," state officials were particularly concerned about housing a specific subgroup of migrants whom they believed were forming "an expanding sub-proletariat in the margins of our cities."[49] Officials emphasized that these new migrant welfare programs should be directed "principally" at those from "francophone Africa."[50] In one memo, Massenet explicitly identified "black Africans" in addition to "North Africans" as part of this supposedly troublesome category of migrants.[51] His position was echoed in numerous other government documents, which claimed that "European migrants . . . constitute a labor force . . . in which social integration is easier and more rapid" than it was for workers from North and sub-Saharan Africa.[52] According to the memos and reports from government authorities at both the local and national levels, "foreign workers" from francophone Africa were the particular targets of social welfare programs, even though those programs were supposed to administer to all migrant laborers. State officials discussed the necessity of "putting into place a social apparatus adapted precisely to [black and North Africans'] needs," including an emphasis on "housing, education, employment, and health care."[53] In other words, government officials believed that "foreign laborers" from francophone Africa required special regulation. Controlling the welfare of these migrants was less about guaranteeing their social right to a certain quality of life and more about safeguarding the well-being and safety of the French populace as a whole.

In addition to building *foyers* for single male migrants, SONACOTRA, the FAS, and the other institutions charged with facilitating migrant welfare programs also developed plans to construct housing for "foreign workers and their families." In Marseille, a local branch of SONACOTRA called the Housing and Management Agency for the Mediterranean Region (Logement et gestion immobiliére pour la région méditerranéenne), or LOGIREM, was directed to oversee much of the construction of housing for migrant families, many of whom were assumed to be living in bidonvilles. LOGIREM was one of five special affiliates of SONACOTRA, and each affiliate covered a particular region in France, with branches in Paris (LOGIREP), Metz (LOGI-EST), Lyon (LOGIREL), and Anger (LOGI-OUEST).[54] These institutions were not new creations; most, such as LOGIREM, had been active under the Constantine Plan. After the 1963 reforms, LOGIREM simply redefined its mandate and expanded its focus from Algerians to all "foreign workers and their families."

LOGIREM, along with its affiliates in other regions, proposed plans to construct *les cités de transit*, or transit housing for foreign families.[55] In 1966, the city of Marseille, in partnership with LOGIREM and SONACOTRA, began constructing one such *cité* called La Bricade. The site chosen for the *cité* was in the 15th *arrondissement* of Marseille, in the northern outskirts of the city, about five miles from downtown. According to Mayor Gaston Defferre, the site was chosen "based on the fact that this property is situated at the far limit of all inhabited areas."[56] Defferre further elaborated that "this land is very isolated, moreover, it is unutilizable for normal construction because a section of it is situated in a heavy industrial zone, the other section is located on a rocky embankment improper for construction."[57] Like the reduced-norm housing developments of the late 1950s, La Bricade was also constructed out of cheap "prefabricated materials corresponding to minimum norms."[58] It ultimately housed five hundred families, many of them relocated from bidonvilles around Marseille.

Cités de transit such as La Bricade were intended to serve several purposes. They were primarily meant to rehouse families living in slums and bidonvilles during their "stay" in France. Government officials described these *cités* as temporary homes for families in transit. The very modest facilities, the rudimentary amenities, and even the very names of these developments served to underscore the perception that these families were an impermanent presence in France. Moreover, the geographic location of these developments emphasized the distance between these families and their French counterparts, as many were built well away from other residential areas. Municipal correspondence about La Bricade, for example, took pains to highlight how the site chosen for it was unfit for regular French citizens and therefore perfectly suited to house these "foreign workers and their families."

These *cités* also served another purpose: they were an intermediary step between slum and "normal" HLM-type housing. According to government officials, some foreign families, especially the Portuguese, could often move directly from bidonvilles to HLM apartments. Others—particularly migrants from francophone Africa—needed to be first resocialized in a *cité de transit*. As with the reduced-norm housing projects of the late 1950s, officials similarly identified former colonial subjects as being most in need of civilization in *les cités de transit*. Paradoxically, at the same time that state authorities asserted the need to adapt certain kinds of migrant families to "French ways of life," they also described these *cités de transit* to be temporary housing facilities for supposedly transient families.

In the early 1970s, the central state commissioned several local organizations to study recent migration to France, and the recommendations made by experts working for these institutions reveal the role social scientists have played in framing migration debates. In Marseille, the national FAS funded CLARB or the Comité de liaison pour l'aide et la résorption des bidonvilles (The Liaison Committee for the Aid and Absorption of Bidonvilles) to focus on the particular issues of migrant families. CLARB was a locally based organization directed by several sociologists who specialized in the study of slum clearance and migration. In a report titled, "The Promotion and Housing of Socially Handicapped Families," Sylvie Jarry put the recent wave of migration to Marseille into historical context by explaining that "the Marseille region has traditionally been a destination for diverse migratory waves for nearly a century."[59] She drew parallels between the experience of earlier and more recent migrants to Marseille: "Each of these waves has confronted the problem of adaption and acculturation to French society."[60] However, Jarry distinguished "Latin" immigrants from Southern Europe, who "have not had as much social, cultural, economic, and political difficulty," from "today's immigrants from Afrique Noire and North Africa."[61] She explained that the problems with Latin immigrants "have been relatively minimal . . . because these populations have a certain number of common traits with the French."[62] She went on to say that, while "the majority of Latin immigrants, after a generation or so, have integrated into the French population without too many difficulties, today a large number of immigrant families—originating from . . . Africa . . . find it difficult to integrate into France."[63]

Jarry further discussed what she called the "psycho-sociological consequences" of being a recent migrant from North or sub-Saharan Africa. According to her, most "Maghrebis and Africans . . . remained closely attached to the traditional values of their ethnicity: paternal authority, limited social freedom for women, communal life, and subsistence economies."[64] Once they were transplanted to France, she continued, "they brutally pass[ed] from the rural world to the urban world, from a Muslim civilization to a Judeo-Christian civilization, from an economy of subsistence to an economy of consumerism, from rural employment to industrial employment."[65] According to Jarry, this shift "provoke[d] a series of radical changes of habits, in their behavior, in their manner of thinking, in their manner of being. . . . The immigrant is like a sailor lost in an unknown sea, without map or compass. This inability to express himself renders him as vulnerable as a child."[66] Reports such as Jarry's characterized migrants—particularly those from North and sub-Saharan Africa—as directionless, even vulnerable.

Although the CLARB committee was supposedly discussing problems they believed were relative to recent migrants, the rhetoric invoked in their studies reflected older ideas about migration. More specifically, Jarry's report echoes early- and mid-twentieth-century studies of immigration, including the work of prominent social scientists such as demographer Georges Mauco. In the 1930s, for example, Mauco wrote extensively about the "assimilability" of foreigners in France. He, like many other social scientific experts of that moment, believed that nationalities were also distinct races. Mauco argued that only migrants from certain, preferred European "races" could successfully integrate into French society, while other "races"—namely Africans, Asians, and Jews—could not.[67] Although Jarry did not describe migrants in such racialized terms in her 1976 report, she did link their supposedly cultural differences to their countries of origin. Namely, she argued that Portuguese and other European migrants were more easily absorbed into France than, say, Africans, because they were closer in temperament and cultural values to the French.

Jarry's report also reflects the historical relationship between the social sciences and imperialism. For example, her description of former colonial subjects as "childlike" and in need of special direction illustrates how social scientists have shaped and perpetuated ideas about the civilizing mission. Jarry ultimately concluded that migrants from former French colonies were fundamentally different from the rest of the French populace, and thus that they needed to become *more* French in order to better assimilate into the nation.

According to the recommendations of Jarry and CLARB, *cités de transit* helped facilitate the evolution of postcolonial migrant families. These "foreigners" especially needed assistance and paternal guidance in negotiating the transition to modern French society. They required special social and cultural education to become more civilized. To this end, several local organizations, including ATOM, administered a number of domestic training programs for families living in *cités de transit* such as La Bricade. Like many other colonial institutions, ATOM had previously been dedicated to the social education of Algerian families, but now directed attention to migrant families more broadly. Nonetheless, many of the programs ATOM offered to migrant families strongly resembled those it had offered to Algerian families under the Constantine Plan. For example, it focused especially on training wives and mothers by offering literacy courses and classes in French cooking. It often worked in tandem with LOGIREM to establish cultural and training centers in *cités de transit* around Marseille. ATOM's work exemplified the efforts of many of the other local organizations in major French cities that most often collaborated with the regional branches of the various LOGI institutions.[68] According to the minutes of a regional meeting on the "promotion of migrants," the overarching goal of organizations such as ATOM was to encourage the "evolution" of "unadapted populations."[69] More specifically, their aim was to manage the "quality" of former colonial subjects to make them more palatable and assimilatable to the larger French populace.

The institutionalization and regulation of *cités de transit* reveal several key tensions in officials' understanding of the term "transit." Families were "in transit" because they were in between slum and normal living—between a seemingly indigenous unevolved past and a civilized future—but also because they were ultimately supposed to return to their presumed countries of origin. Based on the studies of social scientists, officials understood migrant families to be both in France temporarily and in need of special education to become more adapted to French ways of life. Such perceptions thus reflect an additional understanding of the term "transit," one that emphasized the potential social and cultural mobility of families from former colonies. Drawing on old imperial tropes, institutions such as LOGIREM, ATOM, and CLARB articulated their special mission to make migrants into proper modern subjects suited to late-twentieth-century living.[70] Their reports contributed to the idea that certain kinds of migrants needed special regulation, and that providing for their welfare was an effort to cultivate migrants' development of French, and therefore more civilized, qualities.

The Threshold of Tolerance: Science, Race, and Welfare

By the 1970s and at the start of a prolonged period of recession, local and national authorities were not only concerned with managing the so-called quality of the migrant population, they were also anxious about limiting its quantity. Since the end of World War II France had pursued a relatively open-door migration policy, but by the mid-1970s many government officials and migration experts concluded that France had reached its threshold of tolerance, or *seuil de tolérance*, and could not absorb any more newcomers without threatening national decline. This idea—that France's foreign population could not exceed a certain measurable number—was partly informed by the postwar population studies of prominent social scientists. It was explored and tested by demographers and sociologists as early as the late 1940s and appropriated by politicians and policymakers in the 1970s. Recently, scholars have explored the threshold of tolerance in terms of the economic downturn of the 1970s and anxieties about immigration.[71] But the assumptions that influenced ideas about France's ostensible tipping point should be placed in a much deeper context by examining how the social sciences have been put into the service of the nation and how statistical enquiry within these disciplines has been harnessed in the effort to oversee the welfare of the polity.

From the 1940s through the early 1970s, migration to France was largely unregulated, as the government left employers to manage the "cheap . . . labor force."[72] In theory, migrant laborers needed a work permit to enter France, and most entered on some kind of visa usually provided by employers. However, after these permits expired, workers typically stayed, often encouraged to do so by employers who wanted to avoid the hassle of training new workers. This approach led to a large increase in the numbers of clandestine or undocumented workers in France. Although local authorities and central state institutions such as the National Institute of Statistical and Economical Study (INSEE) tried to keep count of migrants and foreign workers, in reality they had only a limited idea of the numbers of people coming and going.[73]

It was particularly difficult to keep track of the migration of families. The INSEE relied on data from local reporting to compile the national census, but, as Amelia Lyons has explained, many of the local reports upon which the INSEE relied "reflected inaccurate knowledge about the current state of the French empire."[74] For example, though some regional officials recognized Algerians as foreign nationals, others lumped North and West Africans together; others simply counted the head of the household but not the family, so that a family of four might be counted as one Algerian male worker.[75] Moreover, families found myriad ways to circumvent the system. For example, many families entered France on temporary tourist visas and simply stayed on.

During *les trente glorieuses* this laissez-faire attitude to migration was widely believed to serve the interests of the booming economy. But by the 1970s, the immigrant question was increasingly framed in national debates as problems of number—there were too many foreigners in France—and integration—foreigners threatened to undermine French ways of life. In 1974, President Valéry Giscard d'Estaing approved a ban on future immigration to France. The logic behind the ban was that France needed to curtail migration in order to assimilate the existing foreign population and to prevent further national decline.

The 1974 immigration ban was born out of the widely held assumption that France had reached its threshold of tolerance and could not accommodate any more foreigners. One of the key supporters of the ban was Michel Massenet, who had worked closely with municipal authorities during the 1962 exodus and had overseen the development of migrant welfare services in the 1960s. For him, "the threshold of tolerance was considered to be between 10 and 30 percent—if the proportion of foreigners reached or surpassed that level, trouble was inevitable."[76] In other words, for Massenet, no group—that is, no nation—could tolerate a foreign population that exceeded a certain percentage of the total population. Massenet's characterization of France's immigrant problem echoed the sentiments of many other politicians and government officials. For example, in 1973, Mayor Gaston Defferre published a special editorial in his newspaper, *Le Provençal*, describing "the immigrant problem" in terms of "the high accumulation of foreigners" in France.[77]

After 1974, immigration policies proceeded along three paths: preventing future immigration, encouraging migrants to leave France, and further developing some of the migrant welfare services of the 1960s to better "integrate" foreigners. While some new policies enacted under the ban focused on "assimilating immigrants," others encouraged migrants to go home, reinforcing the idea that they were only a temporary presence in France. For example, in 1977 the state introduced the *aide à retour* program, which offered financial incentives to families if they returned to their country of origin.[78] These attempts to restrict migration to France largely failed. For example, few Algerians, for whom the *aide à retour* program was intended, took up the offer. Instead, a small number of Portuguese and Spanish families profited from the program, especially as the end of the Salazar dictatorship in Portugal and the death of Franco in Spain made returning home easier.

The immigration ban also failed to stop migration due to a loophole that allowed for family regroupment. After the 1974 ban, the population of recent migrants actually sharply increased, as single migrants, who had previously sent remittances home, now sent for their families to join them in France. Moreover, by the late 1970s, migration from France's remaining overseas departments and territories increased as families from Les départements et territoires d'outre-mer (DOM-TOM) sought better opportunities in the metropole. Although people from the DOM-TOM might have appeared—to some—like foreign immigrants, they were actually French citizens and could travel relatively freely in and out of the metropole.

In application, therefore, the ban was largely ineffective. It did not actually stop immigration. It was nonetheless heralded as a necessary stopgap, an important way to aid France's ailing economy and to fix struggling welfare institutions. The importance of the ban, then, has less to do with its ineffective ability to curtail migration and more to do with its reflection of French attitudes about the nation's "tipping point." The ban is significant because it shows how the threshold of tolerance came to be seen as a commonsensical fact.

Massenet and other officials' understanding of the threshold of tolerance was informed by the studies of several prominent social scientists, including the work of Alain Girard. A sociologist and demographer, Girard was a respected academic who spent much of his career at the Institut national d'études démographiques (INED). He conducted research on a number of topics, including public opinion surveys on family life and living standards. Girard was also noted for his work on immigration, and he conducted periodic surveys of French attitudes toward immigrants from the late 1940s through the 1980s.

In one influential study published in 1974, Girard, along with coauthors Yves Charbit and Marie-Laurency Lamy, surveyed people in Lyon, Paris, and Marseille, asking them a variety of questions about immigrants and immigration to France. One of the survey's first questions asked residents about their perceptions of foreign density in their neighborhoods: "In France there is around 1 foreigner for every 13 French people. In the neighborhood where you live, do you have the impression that the proportion of foreigners is less, the same, or higher than the average in France?"[79] According to their responses, 44 percent of residents from the Paris sample believed there were more foreigners in their neighborhoods than in the rest of France; 46 percent of Lyonnais and 43 percent of Marseille all perceived their neighborhoods to have more foreigners than the national average.[80] Girard and his researchers also asked residents to distinguish between the various nationalities representing the population of foreigners in France. They asked: "What is your opinion on each of the following nationalities, good, somewhat good, somewhat bad, or bad?"[81] Averaging the results from the three cities, Girard et al. concluded that most residents (57 percent) had a favorable opinion of Italians and Spanish, followed by Portuguese (42 percent). Residents were ambivalent about Yugoslavians and Turks, with a sizable number declining to respond to this question. At the bottom of the list were "Africains noirs" followed by "nord Africains," who had only 20 percent favorability among residents surveyed.[82] In one of the final questions, Girard and his researchers asked respondents to distinguish further between the various nationalities representing France's foreign population, asking "which foreigners among the following nationalities can adapt themselves to French [society] and which cannot?" An overwhelming 82 percent of residents believed that Italians could integrate with little trouble into French society, followed by Spanish (78 percent) and Portuguese (58 percent). Only 33 percent believed that *africains noirs* could adapt, and only 30 percent believed *nord africains* could. The majority believed that adaptation was not just difficult for black and North Africans; it was actually nearly impossible.[83] Finally, when asked "why [do foreigners] remain foreigners?" the majority of residents responded that "irreducible differences (race, language, mores, religion)" were the main reasons that foreigners had difficulty integrating, followed by their "refusal to integrate." Only 3 percent responded that other factors, including living conditions, "bidonvilles," "isolated housing," or the "nature of work," contributed to the problem.[84]

In this study and others, Girard surveyed public opinion of recent immigration to France. It is important to note that he was particularly interested in assessing French *perceptions* of migration and *attitudes* toward foreigners. For example, in one 1971 study, Girard asked a sample of French residents a series of specific questions relating to housing, work, and schools. "In your opinion," one question asked, "in a locality with around 5,000 inhabitants" what would be "the number of foreigners you would say is too many?"[85] According to the results, residents responded that a foreign population of about 15 percent of the total population would be too high. In a series of questions regarding schools Girard asked: "Out of a class of 30 students, starting at what number of foreign students do you believe the class will be disrupted or held back?" Twenty-three percent of those surveyed responded that a class would be negatively affected starting with only five foreign students, while 26 percent believed the class would be affected once that number hit ten. Girard followed up with the question "if you have a child in a class of 30 students where there are foreigners, starting at what number of foreign students would you place your child in a different school?" Twelve percent said they would remove their child from the school if the number of foreign students reached five, while 26 percent said they would remove their child if the number of foreigners reached ten.[86] Although Girard was interested to assess residents' attitudes toward immigration, it is important to note that his questions in this study were somewhat leading. By asking respondents to name a number at which point the foreign population would be too high, Girard presupposed that there *was* an actual number that could be determined. Respondents' various answers thus served to reify this presupposition.

Despite these potential pitfalls in Girard's and his researchers' survey design, ultimately, they were interested in residents' *subjective* perceptions about recent migrants. In contrast, high-level bureaucrats, politicians, and other policymakers often interpreted this research as part of a growing body of *objective* knowledge about the immigrant problem. In other words, ideas about the threshold of tolerance developed out of the work of social scientists, but became, as Gary Freeman argues, "one of the working assumptions of French policy makers and a large sector of the general public."[87] Michel Massenet, for example, believed that ideas about France's tipping point did not simply reflect French attitudes toward immigration. He believed that that *le seuil de tolérance* was an actual, as he put it, "law of social interaction."[88] According to him, the threshold of tolerance was neither a perception nor even a theory, "it [was] an empirical fact."[89] For Massenet and others, the threshold of tolerance was a tested and proven phenomenon and therefore a natural law of human interaction. He believed "that certain phenomena unfold almost automatically, no matter which Frenchmen compose the host population, no matter which foreigners make up the newcomers."[90] Conflict was inevitable if a foreign population proved too large—and too culturally or racially different—for a host population to absorb.

By the mid-1970s, immigration was increasingly described as a social problem that threatened to lead to national decline, and this perception was fueled by the notion that, as Freeman explains, "culturally and racially diverse groups could not exist peacefully side by side."[91] Implicit in this understanding was the assumption that racial conflict was inevitable, and that ideas about the immutability of cultural and racial differences were themselves not expressions of racism, but merely manifestations of this "natural" law understood as the threshold of tolerance.

Although many credited Alain Girard's research with helping to inform public policy about France's tipping point, Girard himself was deeply troubled about the widespread use of *le seuil* concept.[92] In a 1984 book, *L'homme et le nombre des hommes*, Girard cautioned that "the threshold of tolerance" should not be invoked in the interest of serving "ideologies," and that "it [could] not be established a priori in numeric terms."[93] He specified that the idea was only relevant as an "instrument" to be applied and "tested in each case, without the possibility of extrapolation."[94] In other words, Girard did not necessarily discount the possible invocation of a threshold of tolerance, but cautioned that the idea should *not* be considered an objective, a priori fact.

Girard was not alone in his concerns. Beginning in the mid-1970s, a number of social scientists grew uneasy about the potentially negative implications of studying or even invoking the idea that France had a threshold of tolerance. In 1975, sociologists from the Centre national de la recherche scientifique (CNRS), demographers from INED, and representatives from various state and private organizations including the Marseille-based CLARB and ATOM, convened a conference at the University of Provence titled "The Threshold of Tolerance: Operational Concept or Ideological Notion?"[95] During the conference, several researchers expressed concerns about the "frequent usage" of the phrase in the press and by politicians. They too were concerned that the *seuil* tended to "appear as a scientific law."[96] In one paper, Carmel Camilleri, a professor at Université-Paris V, wrote that "accepting the notion of a threshold of tolerance is to admit there is a point at which racism can be considered legitimate."[97] René Duchac, professor at the University of Provence, questioned if even "speaking of a threshold is to postulate that it exists?"[98] Ultimately, most researchers who participated in the conference concluded that the "threshold of tolerance must be stripped of any pseudo-scientific notions" and that any reference to a threshold must "depend on concrete situations."[99]

To this end the researchers sought to situate recent studies of the threshold of tolerance within the large body of research on immigration since World War II. In his contribution to the conference, René Duchac, for example, looked to some of the earliest postwar studies of migration, drawing attention in particular to Alain Girard and Joseph Stoezel's 1953 two-volume study, *Français et immigrés*. Duchac pointed out that Girard and his fellow demographer, Stoezel, had been conducting statistical surveys of public opinions of foreigners for decades, well before the 1970s preoccupation with the so-called immigrant problem.[100] He also sought to underscore Girard's work on the *subjective* attitudes of French residents toward foreigners. For example, in Girard's surveys from the 1970s, "North Africans" and "black Africans" were singled out as problem migrants, but in the years following World War II, Girard and Stoezel found that Germans ranked at the very bottom of the list of those foreigners French respondents "would wish to welcome." In the 1940s, 72 percent of respondents stated that they did not think Germans were capable of becoming French.[101]

By considering Girard's decades-long program of research on immigration, Duchac hoped to draw an important distinction between the academic study of the *seuil* and what he saw as the ubiquitous and undisciplined use of the concept in public discourse. He concluded, for example, that Girard's research methods were impeccable and his "procedure [for conducting] these studies [was] perfectly legitimate."[102] According to Duchac, Girard carefully identified a research question, tested this very particular question on an appropriate sample of the population, and drew careful conclusions based on the evidence gathered. Duchac's larger point was that the *seuil* should not be accepted as an "an acquired fact." Like Girard, Duchac concluded that the threshold of tolerance should be tested only in particular and controlled cases.[103]

What researchers at this 1975 conference did not potentially consider, however, was how ideas about the threshold of tolerance were fundamentally informed by the relationship and discursive interactions between academic research, government policy, and public opinion. In other words, Girard's and other studies about French perceptions of immigration helped to produce a body of knowledge that informed policymakers' efforts to manage migration. Many of the researchers who participated in the 1975 conference were affiliated with major research centers such as the CNRS and INED, and some had been trained by sociologists and demographers, including Alain Girard himself. In many ways, the *very faith* academics like Girard and Duchac placed in the rigor of their research methods helped to legitimate and elevate the *seuil* from something to be tested in unique and particular contexts to an "operational concept" and a commonsensical fact.

Girard, Duchac, and other researchers nonetheless questioned the viability of the notion of the threshold of tolerance. They were especially concerned about the potential for the *seuil* concept to legitimate potentially racist immigration policies. However, the vocabulary they invoked to describe and analyze their findings, and the way they interpreted their data, not only reveal their confidence in the ability of their methods to render an accurate snapshot of the French population, but also shows the pervasiveness and power of biological thinking to inform their conclusions. For example, in *L'homme et le nombre des hommes*, Girard wrote: "It is natural for a group to conserve that which makes it particular, and to oppose . . . foreign elements. Biology, by its most recent progresses, teaches us that each individual is unique and holds in reserve a defense system against the penetration of foreign elements: the phenomenon of rejection after the transplant of a perfectly healthy organ provides a vibrant illustration. It works the same way for a social body as for an individual body."[104]

In other words, Girard explained how "it is normal, and it is healthy" for a social body—just like a human immune system—to protect itself from foreign contagion.[105] He continued, writing, "a human group is jealous of its culture, like an animal group is of its territory. Whether this is good or bad is a false question. It's a fact without doubt."[106] While Girard was very hesitant to describe the threshold of tolerance as a sociological law, he nonetheless concluded that the desire to safeguard one's culture, one's way of life, was not only human, it was a natural expression of animal behavior.

• • •

Patrick Weil and others have explored how, immediately after World War II, prominent social scientists including Alfred Sauvy and Georges Mauco met to frame a new immigration policy for the post–Vichy Fourth Republic.[107] Some of these experts, such as Georges Mauco, had made a name for themselves as immigration specialists before World War II and had worked for the Vichy regime during the war. During immediate postwar discussions about immigration several, including Mauco, favored establishing policies that resembled the older, interwar system that prioritized maintaining the purity of the nation by limiting certain "undesirable" groups from migrating to France in large numbers. Others argued that the new postwar policies should be devoid of any references to racial or social superiority and should not be based upon such a quota system.

According to Weil, Mauco's proposed system lost out: a color-blind, more republican immigration policy was ultimately adopted from 1940 until the 1970s, when new measures, exemplified by the 1974 immigration ban, signaled a return to more racially tinged policies. By contrast, this chapter shows how ideas about racial hierarchies did not disappear during *les trente glorieuses* but were very much present in discussions between local and national authorities and social scientists. Moreover, the shift to a more racially explicit set of immigration policies after 1974 does not signal a move away from, or disavowal of, republican, color-blind principles but rather underscores the paradoxes always inherent in the republican project. As Gary Wilder, Joan Scott, and others have argued, republicanism has never been wholly and immutably universal but also, fundamentally, differential.[108]

In addition to the immediate postwar debates about immigration policy, the work of several major postwar institutions further illustrates how elements of this older tradition—premised on protecting and managing the population—persisted into the late twentieth century.[109] Created in 1945, the INED was one such institution mandated to effect "a politics of population management clarified by science."[110] The first head of the institute, Alfred Sauvy, asserted that the INED was charged with "promoting the familial and demographic politics of France . . . [in order to] protect the family and the qualitative and quantitative amelioration of the French population."[111] Like many postwar institutions, the INED had its roots in Vichy, specifically, the Fondation française pour l'étude des problèmes humaines (FFEPH). Established in 1941 and led by eugenicist and Nobel Prize–winner Alexis Carrel, the FFEPH was mandated to "stud[y] the most appropriate measures to safeguard, improve and develop the French population."[112] By conducting surveys and statistical analyses, the FFEPH sought "pragmatic solutions" to "human problems," specifically by "improv[ing] the physiological, mental, and social conditions of the population."[113] While the INED abandoned the overtly eugenicist aims of the FFEPH, many of the researchers who worked for the foundation, including Joseph Stoezel, continued to do important work for the INED after the war.

Researchers at both the FFEPH and the INED aimed to put the social sciences to the service of the nation. Specifically, they cultivated a real faith in statistical enquiry or, as Joshua Cole has described it, belief in the "power of large numbers" not only to give a picture of the population but also to improve it.[114] Alain Girard, himself an INED researcher, described how the disciplines of "sociology and demography . . . in their theoretical and applied forms, were born in part out of the relationship between the desire to better know and understand human phenomena and the sentiment that exists about the possibility of acting upon society, to change if not to radically transform it."[115] This faith in scientific enquiry is not merely a product of the nineteenth and twentieth centuries but is also rooted in older legacies, including the scientific revolution and the Enlightenment preoccupation with identifying social "laws." Nineteen seventies discussions about France's threshold of tolerance and the complicated ways in which social scientists and policymakers helped to legitimate the concept should be considered within this deeper context. The 1974 immigration ban and the *seuil* concept reflect the historical role that research institutions have played both in cataloguing the polity and in proposing methods for improving its welfare.

• • •

In the 1960s, migrant families, workers, and political refugees from former colonies began to settle permanently in France in increasing numbers at a moment when their presence was imagined to be temporary. Although there were key continuities in social welfare policies and institutions from the 1950s through the "end" of empire, such programs were reconfigured to accommodate all immigrants, thus obscuring the historical and imperial relationships between the metropole and postcolonial migrants. As families settled in bidonvilles around France, many were eventually relocated to *cités de transit*. For state authorities, these housing developments served dual purposes: they were supposed to house foreign families who were in France temporarily, and they were also supposed to "civilize" them by teaching them to be more French during their stay in France. *Les cités de transit* exemplified a rethinking of certain social-security institutions by serving to detach systems of welfare from understandings of social citizenship. These migrant welfare services, as well as postwar studies of French attitudes toward migration, reveal how concerns about regulating the welfare of the population not only reflect late-twentieth-century notions about social rights but also illuminate deeper legacies rooted in ideas about social and racial hygiene.

Concerns about France's threshold of tolerance continue to shape discussions about the immigrant question in France. Since the late 1970s, anxieties about foreigners have often focused on the neighborhoods where they live. For example, most *cités de transit* were constructed on the outskirts of French cities and, along with HLM and *logement million* developments, helped to form the large public housing complexes known as *les grands ensembles*. By the late 1970s, many of these *cités* had fallen into gross disrepair, and public discourse increasingly associated anxieties about national decline with the perceived crisis in "immigrant neighborhoods." The next two chapters examine these concerns as well as emerging ideas about the politics of urban renewal in those areas known as *les banlieues*.

NEIGHBORHOODS IN CRISIS

In the 1970s, the final *grands ensembles* were constructed on the edges of most major French cities, and their completion coincided with the deepening economic recession. In Saint Marcel, a neighborhood on the outskirts of Marseille, a long-term resident reflected on life in the area since the completion of these large housing developments: "This used to be a tranquil place, there were never any problems, but now it's over and everyone complains about insecurity, [b]urglaries, and depravity. . . . The *cités* are the problem [and] problems are recent here. They came with the arrival of certain people. It's embarrassing to say that because it seems to give credence to racists, but it's not at all like that."[1]

Even though this resident associated local tensions with the recent arrival of newcomers to the neighborhood, Saint Marcel has been an historical site of migration. The neighborhood is due east of downtown Marseille in the 11th *arrondissement* and in the early nineteenth century was mostly farmland. By the late nineteenth century, the area had become rapidly industrialized and attracted a large number of Italian migrants who settled there to work in factories. By the early twentieth century, the population of Saint Marcel had doubled to about five thousand people when Greeks and Armenians also settled in the neighborhood. Until the 1960s, most residents of the village lived in single- or two-story stand-alone stone houses with red-tile roofs. But between 1965 and 1974, two thousand public housing apartments were built in the neighborhood. Most of these housing units formed great high-rise buildings, with the two largest buildings towering over the village at twenty stories apiece. Although the original plans for these *grands ensembles* had included the construction of a shopping center with

This photograph, taken from the roof of Le Corbusier's Unité d'habitation, showcases the contrast between red-roofed, single family homes and large, *grands ensembles* that seem to tower over the older residences.
Photo by author.

access to groceries and other essential goods, rising property prices, compounded by the deepening recession, compelled commercial developers to back out. Without the tax revenue generated by local commerce, there remained few resources with which to finance the maintenance of these *cités*, and the buildings fell into gross disrepair.[2]

The Saint Marcel *grands ensembles* housed many Marseille residents relocated from the city center as well as *pieds noirs* and *harkis* who fled Algeria in 1962. By the mid-to-late 1970s, a growing population of families from France's remaining overseas departments and territories (the DOM-TOM), particularly from the Comoros, also began to settle in the *cité*. During this time a significant number of the nearby factories shut down and unemployment levels in the neighborhood rose dramatically.[3] Some long-term Saint Marcel residents thought about the economic downturn and new arrivals in terms of the longer history of industrialization and migration to the neighborhood.[4] But many others believed that the more recent arrivals were uniquely different from previous ones and created particularly serious social problems.[5]

Saint Marcel residents' anxieties about their neighborhood also resembled growing national fears about the *banlieues* or the outskirts and suburbs of French cities. A June 1973 *Le Nouvel Observateur* article, "The *Banlieues* of Fear," described the peripheries of Paris, Marseille, and Toulouse as grim, barren, and dangerous territories: "Iron bars on the windows, frightened passers-by, deserted streets; it's the hell of the *banlieues*. 30,000 muggings a year—not counting car theft, burglaries, hold-ups, [and] rapes."[6] As the recession deepened, public discourse increasingly associated *les grands ensembles* primarily located in *banlieues* around France with crime, chronic unemployment, and immigrants.[7] Politicians, social scientists, and even residents themselves described these areas as neighborhoods in crisis. Although many of these concerns echoed historical anxieties about cities and the urban poor, talk about these grave problems in the margins of French cities nonetheless characterized the crisis as something new. For many, these neighborhoods were in trouble because of neglect and unemployment. For some, these local problems were also symptomatic of a larger crisis—that of the meaning and future of social citizenship.

Since the late 1960s, rumblings in certain sectors of the French economy had signaled impending trouble, but the OPEC oil crisis of 1973—which triggered a global period of decline—was seen as the turning point in France and the end of *les trente glorieuses*. As the economy stagnated, the promise of full (male) employment that had been one of the cornerstones of the post–World War II welfare state seemed far less attainable. Importantly, as Timothy Smith argues, the recession did not mean that the entire populace was faced with the specter of riskier job prospects.[8] Those with secure pensions and positions were, for the most part, protected by strong labor agreements and continued to benefit from the French welfare state. It was others, notably postcolonial migrants, women, and young people, who were especially affected by the downturn.[9] Since the 1970s, expensive pensions and high wages have outpaced economic growth, which has contributed to very low levels of job creation. This in turn has negatively affected the possibility for a robust and sustained economic recovery. But these larger and complex structural problems, although the subject of some discussion among the French public, have also often been overshadowed by anxieties about the *banlieues* and "immigrant neighborhoods" as being *the* major sources of France's welfare woes.

Although a sizable percentage of France's GDP is spent on pensions and other expenses, beginning in the 1970s, government funding was set aside to address growing concerns about France's "immigrant problem" with the aim of fixing the nation's "crisis neighborhoods." From the late 1970s through the 1980s, several central state ministries partnered with social-scientific research centers and municipal governments to initiate a number of neighborhood renewal programs, notably several projects in Marseille. Their goal was to rehabilitate the decayed urban tissue of rundown neighborhoods as well as the residents who lived in these areas. These revitalization programs were developed by a new generation of urban planners and other experts who wanted to break with earlier town planning approaches they criticized for being too centralized and too prescriptive. This cohort of New Left researchers believed that any successful attempt at urban renewal necessitated the active participation of residents.[10] An important aim of encouraging resident involvement in neighborhood rehabilitation was that, through such activity, residents would learn to create a local public sphere. Such a forum would encourage residents to voice their concerns and opinions about neighborhood renovation, but it would also create a particular kind of space—a civic site—for educating residents about the tenets and duties of French citizenship.

Ultimately, resident involvement in urban revitalization projects raised important questions about who—precisely—was participating in this local public sphere. During urban planning meetings many residents, including former colonial subjects, argued that neighborhood rehabilitation necessitated solving social problems by managing the ethnicity of the local population. In doing so, residents helped to cultivate local perceptions of difference, often by conflating notions of race and class. Despite ongoing national debates about whether difference should be recognized in the French public sphere, these urban renewal programs both implicitly and explicitly acknowledged that identifying the ethnicity of residents was an essential criterion in the campaign to rehabilitate neighborhoods in crisis.

More Power to the People? Resident Participation and Local Public Spheres

In the mid-to-late 1970s, a group of experts and government officials from around the Marseille region convened a series of meetings to consider the housing question and what they called the "social problem of migrants."[11] Many of these experts believed that these particular concerns were emblematic of the broader problems of economic decline and rising unemployment levels. They discussed what they saw as "the very specific nature of the problems posed by these socially handicapped populations and the necessity of finding solutions."[12] According to one local official, a major issue was that the "inhabitants [of these neighborhoods] are not very well known." The official suggested that the solution was not "only renovation" of deteriorating *grands ensembles*, "but a complete revamping" of how they approached the housing problem.[13]

Included in these regional meetings were several specialists representing a new generation of sociologists and urban planners. For these experts, the "migrant housing problem" was symptomatic of a larger issue and formed part of a growing critique of the post–World War II modernization project and state efforts to manage everyday life. As early as the mid-1950s, some researchers, notably sociologist Paul Henri Chombart de Lauwe, began to pay attention to the experiences and lives of ordinary French families living in both old and newly constructed housing.[14] Chombart de Lauwe wanted to introduce a more personalized perspective to what he saw as the impersonal project of large-scale housing construction. By the 1960s, rumblings about a new, mysterious illness called *sarcellite*—which supposedly affected housewives living in France's *grands ensembles*—further reflected growing anxieties that the isolating physical space of public housing might have profound psychological effects on its inhabitants.[15] Such concerns were part of an emerging discourse about the potentially deleterious effects of the modern built environment on ordinary people.[16] Despite the seemingly well-placed intentions of postwar urban planners, many questioned whether the vast, concrete, high-rise apartment complexes clustered on the far outskirts of French cities really improved quality of life.

Such criticisms received renewed attention in the early to mid-1970s as a new school of urbanists declared a decisive break with their predecessors. Although Part I of this book shows how postwar modernization was never top-down but necessarily the product of sustained negotiation between residents and local and central state officials, this post-1968 generation of experts criticized older state institutions, such as the Ministry of Reconstruction and Urbanism (MRU), for imposing what they saw as a centralized, technocratic model for modern living. They claimed that the vast postwar modernization project had done little to account for the actual needs and perspectives of ordinary people. Many in this cohort believed that the best way to counter the alienating effects of the modern built environment was to facilitate better resident participation in the management of their own domestic and neighborhood spaces. Their critique of older planning models was part of a broader shift in housing policy reflected in the renaming of the Ministry of Construction (formerly the MRU) as the Ministry of Public Works and Housing (Ministère de l'équipement et du logement, or MEL). In the 1970s, the MEL began to exit the business of mass-housing construction and focus more on smaller projects such as building single-family homes as well as rehabilitating *grands ensembles* in decline.[17] This shift in French urban planning was also part of a larger international trend influenced by emerging work on social movements and urban geography. For researchers such as sociologist Manuel Castells and geographer David Harvey, urban space and everyday life were important realms of engagement, and attention to these sites permitted researchers to pose new questions about where politics actually happened.[18] Many from this post-1968 generation of academics began to emphasize the necessity of encouraging residents to participate in the construction of urban space.

In France, this New Left cohort of urbanists was influential in the creation of several research centers such as the Marseille-based Centre d'études, de recherches et de formation institutionnelles sud est, or CERFISE.[19] Formed in 1975 by Michel Anselme and Michel Péraldi, CERFISE was the southern spin-off branch of Le centre d'études, de recherches et de formation institutionnelles (CERFI), a Paris research collective of progressive academics from diverse disciplines including urban planning, sociology, and psychology. In Marseille, CERFISE specialized in developing methods and practices that encouraged resident participation in urban rehabilitation programs. CERFISE's studies helped inform the national urban renewal policies and programs implemented later in the 1980s and 1990s.

In 1976, the city of Marseille commissioned CERFISE to study the problem of rundown housing in the *quartiers nord*. In partnership with the city, CERFISE chose to focus on Petit Séminaire, a notoriously run-down *cité* in the 13th *arrondissement*. Petit Séminaire was constructed between 1958 and 1960 and was part of the Opération Million project.[20] A sizable number of *rapatriés* from Algeria had moved into the complex after 1962 and joined an existing population of residents who had been rehoused in this *grand ensemble* following redevelopment projects in downtown Marseille. According to Anselme, the residents of Petit Séminaire formed "a very heterogeneous population" that also included a significant number of Roma.[21] When CERFISE researchers began their study in 1976, there were a total of 240 units in Petit Séminaire, but 70 of these were either vacant or occupied by non-rent-paying vagrants or squatters. There was also no housing management office located on the grounds, which made it difficult for residents to report issues such as broken pipes or other common problems. According to Anselme, his team "went regularly to Petit Séminaire, several times a week, and had meetings with the inhabitants. . . . It was necessary to meet with all the residents, everyone had the chance to speak if they wanted."[22]

CERFISE researchers did not see Petit Séminaire residents as social problems to be worked on but active participants in the project to revitalize their *cité*. They believed that encouraging residents to take part in these weekly meetings was an essential first step in creating a public sphere in Petit Séminaire. According to Anselme, "The emergence of a public sphere (*espace*) in the *cité* became the ritualization of resident meetings."[23] For Anselme, this local public sphere was an overtly political space, a democratic locale, where all residents could voice their opinions and their grievances. It was both an organic and a constructed site, a "setting" that brought residents, social workers, and representatives from the housing management office into dialogue.

For CERFISE researchers, the emergence of a public sphere was also an important step in facilitating good citizenship practices. Resident participation was
important because it was an invitation to enter into civic life and perform the
duties associated with membership in the polity. Implicit in CERFISE's theory was
an understanding of color-blind French republicanism and faith in the idea that
citizens could engage with each other as abstract, undifferentiated individuals
united in the common project to guarantee their own rights as well as to promote the public good.

CERFISE ultimately recommended that Petit Séminaire undergo a comprehensive renovation, and that this project would not be successful unless residents
were involved in all stages of the rehabilitation project. As Anselme recalled in a
1980s article: "We imagined . . . a vast construction site where inhabitants would
have the possibility to participate . . . to invest themselves in one way or another
in this movement to transform their *cité* . . . we felt it possible to requalify the
space of housing, to transform the image of the *cité* to that of the inhabitants, and
to reintegrate the inhabitants into the urban community, to dynamize this co-
habitation of the city."[24] CERFISE's emphasis on the importance of resident
participation in urban planning exemplified a growing consensus among social
scientists and government authorities. As one official at the central MEL wrote in
a circular entitled *Habitat and Social Life*: "It is necessary to furnish a standard of
living (*cadre de vie*) appropriate to the wishes of the population."[25]

In the early 1980s, the MEL developed a comprehensive program to address
the problem of neighborhoods in crisis. In 1982, the Habitat and Social Life commission launched a new initiative they called the "Social Development of Neighborhoods" (Le développement social des quartiers, or DSQ). According to the
commission, "the Ministry of Urbanism and Housing has reoriented its agenda
toward urban innovation, the struggle against social segregation, and the rehabilitation of degraded neighborhoods.[26] The various goals of the DSQ program
were to "struggle against processes of exclusion in urban space, to insert populations in difficulty, [to] promote social, economic, and cultural programs, [to]
ameliorate living conditions in the city, [and to prevent] delinquency."[27] One key
goal for the DSQ programs was to help "insert" so-called problem populations
into the social life of a local public sphere.

To qualify for DSQ funds, neighborhoods had to be officially labeled as areas
"in difficulty" (*quartiers difficiles*) or "sensitive neighborhoods" (*quartiers sensibles*).
In order to receive this designation, a neighborhood was first submitted to a "social and urban diagnostic" that tested "the weakness of the social tissue" and included an analysis of its "economic, urban, and cultural resources [as well as its]
local demographics."[28] In the first phase of the program, from 1981 to 1983, the
commission selected 22 neighborhoods nationwide to be the first recipients of

special DSQ funds. Between 1984 and 1988 the number receiving such funding increased to 148. These neighborhoods were selected because of "the gravity of the problems posed, the accumulation of handicaps, [and] the isolation of the neighborhood from the rest of the metropolitan area."[29] The DSQ initiatives attempted to address a comprehensive set of "problems" including unemployment, poverty, and lack of infrastructure, through "a spatial definition of a perimeter of action."[30] Like the rehabilitation proposal for Petit Séminaire in Marseille, many local DSQ renovation projects encouraged residents to participate in the revitalization of their neighborhoods.

Putting the Theory of Resident Participation into Practice

In 1982, a *cité* called Grand Saint Barthélémy, located in Marseille's 14th *arrondissement*, was labeled a DSQ-funded site.[31] First opened in 1960, this complex was among the first *grands ensembles* completed in Marseille. Saint Barthélémy initially housed families displaced from downtown, including survivors of the 1960 Saint Lazare building collapse.[32] After 1962, *pieds noirs* and a few *harkis* also began to move into the *cité*, along with a growing number of families from the French Antilles and other parts of the DOM-TOM. Local debates about the Saint Barthélémy renovation project illuminate the unexpected ways that theories about resident participation were put into practice and reveal conflicting ideas about the real purpose of neighborhood rehabilitation. For some involved in the renovation project, rehabilitation meant managing the "ethnic density" of the *cité*'s residents. For others, rehabilitation meant ensuring that all of Saint Barthélémy's diverse residents had equal access to the social right to quality housing.

When Saint Barthélémy was marked as a DSQ site in 1982, authorities from the MEL found a vibrant network of local associations already at work there. Saint Barthélémy residents had been forming and participating in cultural, sporting, and housing organizations almost since it was first constructed.[33] In many ways, Saint Barthélémy seemed like an ideal neighborhood in which to test the theory of resident participation in urban renewal.

For example, an early leader in the *cité*, Françoise Ega, helped form a number of local groups. She was an important advocate for resident rights in the 1960s until her early death in 1976. Born in Martinique in 1920, Ega came to France during World War II. Once in France, she met and married her husband, Frantz Ega, who served in the war and also fought in Indochina in the early 1950s.[34] They settled in Saint Barthélémy in the early 1960s, and Françoise Ega worked as a

Saint Barthélémy is located near the center of Marseille's 14th *arrondissement*.

Source: https://commons.wikimedia.org/wiki/File:Marseille_Arrdt_14.svg#/media/File:Marseille_Arrdt_14.svg.
Author: Superbenjamin - Own work. Licensed under CC BY-SA 3.0 via Wikimedia Commons.

housekeeper for several families around Marseille.[35] Once in Saint Barthélémy, she helped to form the Amicale générale des travailleurs antillais et guyanais for Martinicans and other Antilleans living in the neighborhood. The Amicale organized soccer matches, dances, and potlucks, and also invited non-Antillean residents of the *cité* to participate in these festivities. In addition to her activities with the Amicale, Ega also worked with a fellow resident, Severrain Montarello, to open the first neighborhood center, the Espace Culturel Busserine.[36]

For most residents living in Saint Barthélémy in the 1960s, transportation was a major issue, as there was no main bus line linking the *cité* to downtown Marseille. The lack of public transportation made getting to work, accessing government offices, and shopping for goods very difficult for the many residents who had no automobiles, which were still luxury items in the 1960s. Françoise Ega helped spearhead a campaign to bring public transportation to the *cité*. She organized a neighborhood delegation to meet with Mayor Gaston Defferre, who ultimately agreed with their petition and approved the installation of a bus route providing regular access to downtown Marseille.[37]

Ega's activism showcases how, well before Saint Barthélémy was targeted for DSQ-funded renovations, many residents were active in campaigns to improve their neighborhood. In another campaign, this time led by Jacques Marty, president of one of Saint Barthélémy's renters' associations, residents tackled one of the *cité*'s major problems: chronically broken elevators. According to Marty, "the elevators were always out of order, and the *cité* was very poorly maintained."[38] Many of Saint Barthélémy's buildings were over ten stories high. Perpetually schlepping groceries, children, or even furniture up and down ten flights of stairs was more than just a mere nuisance. Moreover, many of the *cité*'s residents were elderly and could not manage the exertion of climbing mountains of stairs. In the mid-1970s, the resident association decided to file a formal legal complaint against the management company, LOGIREM. In order to raise funds to pay the legal fees, the association organized several *bals des ascenseurs*, or elevator dances.[39] As Marty recalled, the legal case regarding the broken elevators "lasted two or three years," but was ultimately resolved when LOGIREM finally agreed to make some repairs.[40] Despite these small victories, however, it was clear by the late 1970s that Saint Barthélémy still required a major renovation.

In 1982, the National Association of Housing Management Offices, in partnership with regional planning officials, created a comprehensive "neighborhood development plan" for the *cité*.[41] The DSQ plan focused on renovating individual apartments—especially old bathrooms and kitchens—and repairing hot-water and heating systems. The plan also targeted common areas, including repairing dilapidated facades, refitting ground-floor lobbies, cleaning up stairwells and open spaces, and applying fresh coats of paint throughout the *cité*. According to the master plan, once a housing unit was renovated, residents already living in Saint Barthélémy could apply to relocate to the newly refurbished apartment. In some cases, residents living outside the neighborhood could also petition to move into the *cité*.

In addition to this detailed outline of the DSQ-funded renovations, the plan also discussed how an emphasis on resident participation in the project would help ensure their access to the right to housing. According to the development plan: "The active intervention of inhabitants in the management process and in the transformation of the neighborhood is an important factor in their 'emancipation.'"[42] Most important, including residents in the rehabilitation process was supposed to support "the most socially fragile families . . . who are most often refused the full right to housing."[43]

The principal way in which residents were formally invited to participate in the project was in the creation of a special *collectif*, or committee, of local authorities and residents who met to discuss various issues related to the rehabilitation process. The *collectif* was comprised of representatives from three Saint Barthélémy *associations de locataires* (or resident renters' associations), employees from the three housing companies that managed buildings in the *cité*, two social workers, a representative from the municipal housing office, and two neutral observers from CERFISE who were there primarily to document the activities of the committee.[44]

The job of the *collectif* was to discuss progress made with the renovations as well as to examine the applications of residents who wanted to move into newly finished apartments. The inclusion of residents in a committee of this type was a notable shift from past practices. Historically, residents had had a very difficult time trying to engage directly with housing management offices. In contrast, the Saint Barthélémy *collectif* permitted residents to meet regularly with housing management representatives, to voice their concerns, and to contribute suggestions about the ongoing project. The committee thus introduced a new layer of accountability into the local management of public housing.

Initially the *collectif* had a purely advisory role. During the first few years of the renovation project, the committee could not make policy and mainly provided feedback on decisions made by local housing officials and urban planners. But in 1984, representatives from the residents' organizations began to demand more authority. During a series of meetings, "Mesdames Tarrin, Gabor, Minot, Castro, and Naggi"[45]—all leaders in Saint Barthélémy's renters' associations—"declared that the *collectif* [should] have real decision-making authority."[46] These residents wanted to play a more decisive role in the rehabilitation of their neighborhood. City and state officials—in keeping with the new emphasis on resident participation—agreed and decided to grant the *collectif* more authority. In 1984, the committee transitioned from playing a purely advisory role to having significant decision-making power. In particular, the *collectif* was charged with evaluating resident applications and deciding which families deserved to move into renovated apartments.[47]

With the *collectif*'s increased power came more questions about the scope and scale of resident participation and the essential purpose of neighborhood revitalization. During a February 1984 meeting, one committee member who was a social worker in the *cité* expressed concern about the *collectif*'s lack of transparency and asserted that other "social groups not represented by the *associations de locataires* should also be invited to attend.[48] More specifically, this *collectif* member was concerned that, out of the many organizations in Saint Barthélémy, only select members of the renters' associations were invited to participate in the committee. According to this social worker, leaders of Saint Barthélémy's renters' associations represented only a narrow cross-section of the *cité*'s total population; most were among the first to have moved to Saint Barthélémy in the 1960s. Many of this first generation of Saint Barthélémy residents represented Marseille's diverse populations and included Italian, Armenian, and Spanish families as well as several from the French Antilles. Nevertheless, the social worker expressed concern that many of these residents perceived their households to be distinctly different from the more recent generations of newcomers to the *cité*, many of whom hailed from North and West Africa as well as from French territories in the Indian Ocean. A report generated by CERFISE echoed this social worker's concerns, observing that "residents who participate[d] in the Associations de locataires have also been living in the *cité* for a long time, some since the beginning," and that they did not identify with their neighbors who had arrived more recently.[49] Both the social worker and CERFISE researchers challenged the *collectif* to discuss issues of transparency, especially the question of which residents were permitted to participate in the rehabilitation project.

In the debate that followed, representatives from the renters' associations stressed their categorical opposition to including other residents and other resident groups in *collectif* meetings, stating they "were very reticent to open the *collectif* to associations that [were] not mandated to represent residents."[50] They asserted that the goal of the *cité*'s many cultural and sporting associations was to facilitate a vibrant social community, not to articulate resident interests regarding the rehabilitation project. They argued that including other Saint Barthélémy associations in the renovation meetings would only serve to muddle the focus of the committee. In an even more curious move, resident members of the *collectif* further justified their opposition to including other residents by asserting that such a step "would render [*collectif*] decisions quasi-public," which they did not believe was "an objective of the *collectif*."[51] What did these resident members of the *collectif* mean by stating that too much transparency could actually be a problem? And why did they assert that transparency was not a central goal of this committee that was supposed to facilitate participation and dialogue among neighborhood actors?

One of the major tasks of the *collectif* was to decide which families already living in Saint Barthélémy merited moving into newly renovated apartments in the *cité*. For many members of the *collectif*, the question of whether other resident groups should be invited to participate in committee decisions was part of this larger issue. During the three years when the *collectif* met, this question of housing allocation dominated most of its time and colored many of the other issues that it considered.

The process of allotting housing generated vociferous and often hostile debate. Some committee members wanted a clear set of "relevant criteria regarding the rules of housing allocation."[52] They wanted to do more to "inform candidates about the decisions of the *collectif*, and about the motivations behind their decisions," especially when a family's application to move into a renovated apartment was denied.[53] In short, they wanted more transparency. Others felt that the *collectif* should remain closed to the larger public, that discussions of resident applications should remain confidential, and that residents need not know all the reasons behind why their bid was denied. Those committee members in favor of less transparency reasoned that "while certain motivations [behind a denied application], such as insufficient financial resources, not paying rent, or even troubles with neighbors, are relatively receivable by the candidates, it's not the same as those [denied applications] that have to do with the equilibrium of the *cités*, the equilibrium between cultural or ethnic communities. If these motivations were explicit, there is a very real risk that the social climate of the neighborhood would deteriorate even more."[54] In other words, some *collectif* members argued that if a family was told that their application had been denied because they had a history of not paying rent, they would probably accept the decision. However, if a family learned that their application to move into a renovated apartment was denied because they were the wrong ethnicity, this *would* be a problem.

At the root of the debate about rehabilitating Saint Barthélémy was the question of whether the race or ethnicity of residents should be a factor in the housing reattribution process. Some, including the social workers and CERFISE observers, strongly believed that managing the ethnicity of residents should not be a priority for the *collectif*. For them, the *collectif*'s ultimate goal was to help Saint Barthélémy families move into renovated apartments. They reasoned that if the *collectif* did decide to utilize ethnic criteria in their decision-making process, this should be—at the very least—acknowledged publicly. Others, particularly most of the *collectif* members who were also Saint Barthélémy residents, believed that the principal goal of the committee was to do something called the "social *reéquilibration* [recalibration or rebalancing]" of the neighborhood, and to do so required managing the ethnic makeup of the *cité* and keeping this process private. They believed that altering the ethnic density of Saint Barthélémy residents was essential to facilitating a successful renovation of the neighborhood.

The phrase "social *reéquilibration*" began to appear in Marseille municipal documents in the early 1980s, but it refers to a concern that began to develop among local and national authorities in the mid-1970s. At that time, as regional officials began to meet to discuss the "immigrant problem," they concluded that one of the central reasons for the issue of run-down housing had to do with the density of migrants living in certain *cités*.[55] According to a 1976 report, "seven Marseille neighborhoods have a foreign population higher than 20%. Two of those are downtown, and the others are more peripheral and are principally situated in the north of the city."[56] During a 1977 meeting of the commission charged with the "social problem of migrants," members discussed the need to "keep the percentage of [migrant] families in *cités* at around 5%."[57] They concluded that adhering strictly to this percentage was the only way to ensure the "social promotion" of migrants. They also proposed that the twenty-seven of Marseille's fifty-four HLM developments that did not already allow "immigrant residents" should begin doing so. Moreover, they proposed "blocking the allocation of housing to migrants in *cités* that already have a high density."[58]

Local authorities' concern about the so-called high density of foreigners in *cités* resembles, in many ways, national anxieties about the threshold of tolerance.[59] In the 1980s, as officials considered ways to rehabilitate neighborhoods in crisis, they believed that a successful DSQ renewal plan must also reconfigure neighborhood demographics. They believed that social *reéquilibration* was an important part of urban renewal. Moreover, they understood social *reéquilibration* to mean limiting the number of those families whom officials called "extra-European" from living in sensitive neighborhoods. Neighborhood rehabilitation, then, meant excluding certain residents as much as it was supposed to facilitate their "insertion" into the local civic corps.

Representatives from the Saint Barthélémy renters' associations who participated in the *collectif* similarly believed that achieving the social recalibration of Saint Barthélémy—rather than inclusive resident participation—should be their primary goal. In a February 1984 meeting, D. Martin, president of one of the *associations de locataires*, expressed concern that the *collectif* "[had] not yet done enough in terms of the ethnic *reéquilibration* of Saint Barthélémy."[60] In a July meeting several months later, Monsieur Dupont, a representative from the municipal housing bureau, echoed this concern, stating that the "procedure followed by the *collectif* has not been of such a nature as to permit a social *reéquilibration* of the neighborhood." In particular, Dupont noted that "the entry of European families has not been encouraged, [and] moreover, the internal allocation of new homes has most often been for extra-European families."[61] In other words, Martin wanted to do more to encourage "European" families to move into renovated apartments in Saint Barthélémy. He also wanted to minimize the number of "extra-European" families who already lived there from being able to relocate to renovated apartments. In response to these comments, S. Gabor of the Association Locataires St-Barthélémy III, stated that "the Amicales de Locataires agree entirely with this proposed direction."[62]

According to archival records of meeting minutes, the committee continued to debate the ultimate purpose of neighborhood rehabilitation for much of 1984. Several members, for example, were vehemently *opposed* to the idea of social *reéquilibration* and were also against considering the ethnicity of housing applicants. During a July 1984 meeting, for example, some protested vociferously against including an ethnic criterion in *collectif* deliberations, stating that "most of the housing demands come from extra-European households." They reasoned that "the application of a selective housing allocation rule would risk increasing the number of vacant housing units in a neighborhood where there is a strong demand for housing." Finally, as the debate continued, several of the social workers "made it known that they could not adhere to an access-to-housing policy founded in such ethnic discrimination."[63]

Despite these protests, by late 1984 the race and ethnicity of housing applicants *were* firmly part of the criteria the committee used when evaluating housing applications. For example, during an October meeting, the committee considered whether a newly renovated apartment should be given to the Diouf family from West Africa, who had lived in Saint Barthélémy for some years and had applied for a new apartment, or to a *"français de souche"* family, who had just moved to the neighborhood in May 1984 and "ha[d] not [even] made any explicit requests to move to the refurbished apartment." Despite heated opposition from the social workers, the *collectif* voted to give the European family "first priority, and the Diouf family second priority."[64]

Tensions came to a head in the spring of 1985 when the two social workers formally resigned from the committee, stating that "the activities of the *collectif* [were] in contradiction to the principles of [their] profession."[65] In a letter to the committee members, they specified their reasons for quitting, stating that "originally, the objectives of the *collectif* were to establish a coherent attribution and relocation policy that spoke to the real needs of the neighborhood."[66] They believed that the primary goal should have been to facilitate the access of *all* families living in Saint Barthélémy to the "right to housing." They concluded their letter by emphasizing that "one of the major reasons for our desire to resign is the utilization of the criterion 'extra-European family' for rejecting housing demands."[67]

The social workers also opposed the way in which the committee conflated perceptions of race and class. They criticized what they called "the amalgamation of 'extra-European families' with 'socially unfit families.' "[68] In other words, they objected to the assumption that non-European families were necessarily also perceived to be uncivilized. They did not believe that the two categories were mutually inclusive. They further opposed "the utilization of ethnic criteria in the attribution of housing," especially when such criteria were not made public and were disguised by internal references to the *social* rather than the *ethnic* equilibrium of the *cité*.[69]

The social workers' critique was supported in a report by CERFISE researchers who had been sitting in on meetings as nonparticipant observers. A 1985 report noted that, ultimately, "the allocation [of housing has taken a] central place in the process of rehabilitation, that is, *positioning the social* reéquilibration *of the neighborhood as a prerequisite and condition of rehabilitation.*"[70] Similarly to the concerns of the social workers, CERFISE researchers criticized how the initial goal to facilitate resident participation in the *cité* had been "subordinated . . . to [the] social *reéquilibration* of the neighborhood."[71] They concluded that the potential success of the rehabilitation project was compromised by the lack of any real comprehensive participation: "We insist on the fact that if these Associations de Locataires represent part of the population, they don't express in any way the will of the entirety of residents . . . in effect . . . this [kind of] participation excludes a large portion of residents."[72] The *collectif* permitted certain residents to have a larger voice in the management of their neighborhood, but housing institutions and local officials only came into contact with "the privileged interlocutors" of the *cité*.[73] The report concluded that "the project of rehabilitation . . . is thus . . . a reestablishment, or in other words, *the reconquering of a social position.*"[74]

Both CERFISE researchers and the social worker members of the *collectif* were critical of how they saw categories of class and race conflated. More specifically, discussions about the need to "recalibrate" Saint Barthélémy focused primarily on encouraging *français de souche*—namely white—families to relocate to the neighborhood. In a 1985 report, two CERFISE researchers observed that long-term Saint Barthélémy residents believed "that the physical and social degradation of [their] *cité* [was] a result of the massive departure of the middle classes and their replacement by a precarious population (*maghrébin* and *comorien* in particular)."[75] As such, CERFISE researchers condemned the ways in which whiteness was associated with the middle classes, while nonwhiteness was correlated with poverty, criminality, and social degradation. Ultimately, they criticized how this conflation of race and class was institutionalized in Saint Barthélémy's untransparent process of housing attribution.

The Saint Barthélémy DSQ project raised questions about varied understandings of public spheres. For CERFISE researchers, creating a local public sphere meant facilitating a democratic forum where all could participate. Yet for some *collectif* members, participation meant creating another kind of interactive space where the ultimate goal was to achieve "social *reéquilibration.*" The ways in which these *collectif* members interpreted participation underscores how public spheres can be constructed as much through excluding some as including others.[76] The rehabilitation controversy in Saint Barthélémy also complicates recent debates about color-blind republicanism in France, especially discussions about the place of difference in the French public sphere. Ultimately, the Saint Barthélémy revitalization project illuminates how categories of race can be implicitly mobilized to designate membership in a social space.

"This *Cité* Is a *Harki Cité!*"

In addition to the Saint Barthélémy DSQ project, several other *grands ensembles* around Marseille were targeted for renovation in the 1980s. One such revitalization project in a *cité* known as Tilleuls also casts light on the complicated relationship between perceptions of difference and the local politics of participation. Furthermore, debates about social *reéquilibration* in this *cité* show how former colonial subjects helped produce understandings of race and ethnicity and how these notions were shaped by the imperial past.

Tilleuls is in the 15th *arrondissement* of Marseille and was constructed as a *cité d'urgence* in 1964 primarily to house *harkis* who had been living in nearby bidonvilles since they had come to France during the 1962 exodus.[77] In the early 1980s, the neighborhood resident association, the Amicale des locataires de la cité des Tilleuls, submitted a revitalization plan to SONACOTRA, which managed the complex. The renters' association wanted to renovate Tilleuls common spaces as well as fix the plumbing and wiring system throughout the *cité*. To do so, the association proposed to utilize new funds made available by a 1977 housing policy reform.

As part of the shift toward encouraging resident participation in urban rehabilitation, in the late 1970s the national Habitat and Social Life Commission advised the MEL to adopt a more "personalized" approach to the housing question.[78] Based on these recommendations, the MEL decided to make some changes to the ways that funds were allocated for housing repairs. From the end of World War II to 1977, the housing ministry had followed a policy known as *aide à pierre*, meaning that government funding for housing was tied to building materials. In other words, if a building was condemned or needed repair, funding went to the city or to the housing management company to purchase materials for renovation. During postwar reconstruction, this policy was intended to more easily channel money and resources to construction companies and financiers tasked with the job of housing the people. But by the late 1970s, the *aide à pierre* policy had become outdated. As a new cohort of urban planners emphasized the need for greater resident involvement in neighborhood revitalization, they criticized the old policy for excluding residents from having a say in how housing resources were utilized. In 1977, the MEL introduced a new policy known as *aide personalisée au logement* (APL), which was alternatively known as *aide à la personne*. Whereas funding had previously been tied to building materials, under the new policy housing money would follow the resident. According to the policy, if a building was condemned or needed renovating, residents could use the APL either to finance repairs or move to a new home. The *aide à la personne* functioned as a kind of voucher and was designed to offer residents the possibility of making choices about their housing needs. Around France, many utilized the *aide à la personne* funds to move out of their aging *grands ensembles* apartments. Some moved to apartments closer to city centers. Others used the funds to finance the purchase of single-family homes. Still others utilized the funding to make repairs to their existing apartments.

In Tilleuls, some families agreed to pool their APL funds in order to renovate parts of the *cité* while others used their vouchers to move out of the complex altogether.[79] According to the minutes of a 1985 meeting between city officials, representatives from SONACOTRA, and the *cité*'s renters' association, "69 families" out of 86 total families living in Tilleuls agreed "to use the *aide personnalisée au logement* . . . to do important work to improve these housing units."[80]

At first glance, it seemed as if the participation experiment had worked exceedingly well in Tilleuls. The *cité*'s renters' association did indeed succeed in convincing enough families to combine their funds to finance a renovation project. But a closer look at other neighborhood debates reveals a much more intricate picture of participation in Tilleuls and shows how resident involvement as well as ideas about social *reéquilibration* were informed by complex notions of identity.

Most of Tilleuls's residents were known as *harkis* who had fought with the French or were employed as colonial functionaries during the Algerian War of Independence.[81] French officials may have considered them to be a distinct category comprised of a well-defined group of people, but many who came to be labeled *harkis* were actually from diverse regions of Algeria and identified with various ethnic groups. Rather than examining Tilleuls's *harki* population as a homogeneous community, considering the multiple ways these residents understood themselves offers a more nuanced understanding of their sense of belonging. For example, a 1984 report on neighbor relations in Tilleuls reveals how residents' relationship to their *cité* and to each other was also shaped by perceptions of ethnic and regional differences informed largely by their experiences of the colonial past in Algeria. According to the report, "It's really between the Maghrebis of different origins where there is the most conflict." It detailed how a group of Tilleuls residents had recently organized to protest the poor state of the plumbing in the *cité*. They circulated a petition, and "a family originally from Kenchela refused to sign it because there were too many Kabyle names on it."[82] The report further explained tensions between "the Kabyles and the Chaouis."[83] Although all were considered to be Berber, the Kabyles were from northern Algeria, whereas the Chaouis were from the eastern part of the country. As one SONACOTRA official wrote, "incidents between [*harkis*] are frequent, in part because they come from diverse regions" of Algeria.[84] In her monograph *Imperial Identities*, Patricia Lorcin has shown how ethnic and political categories were constructed and mobilized in colonial Algeria.[85] The diverse ways in which Tilleuls residents understood their own ethnic and regional differences show how "imperial identities" also informed postcolonial notions of belonging in the metropole.

Although there were tensions among Tilleuls's *harki* population, many residents did, at times, identify as *harki*, often in distinction from other non-*harki* residents. SONACOTRA—which managed Tilleuls—employed a caretaker-handyman to perform odd jobs and repairs around the *cité*. Historically, SONACOTRA had hired someone from among the original *harki* residents of Tilleuls to do this job. According to a 1984 report, a number of residents complained that one such caretaker—who was "the son of a *harki*"—was neglecting his duties. SONACOTRA decided to fire him, but instead of hiring another *harki*, as was the custom, the management company selected a Tunisian man. According to the report, "when the residents found out that the new handyman was a Tunisian immigrant, there was a vociferous outcry against his appointment." The *harki* residents of the *cité* believed that this "recruitment was a provocation, and they actively protested that the post continue to be reserved for one of them."[86] In this particular situation, a *harki* identity took on particular coherence for those residents who believed that they should remain "the dominant group" in Tilleuls.[87] As one resident asserted, "this *cité* is a *harki cité*!"[88]

The *harki* identity took on coherence for Tilleuls residents in other ways as well. By the late 1970s and early 1980s, new families began to move into the *cité* as some of the original families utilized *aide à la personne* funds to relocate. According to a demographic study, "five Algerian, fourteen Comoran, and two Senegalese" families counted among the new residents moving to Tilleuls.[89] Some of these newcomers identified their *harki* neighbors in terms of political and social divisions rooted in their colonial experiences. For example, one SONACOTRA official wrote that tensions between residents also related to the fact that "certain of them were former soldiers in the Indochina campaign, and others were engaged in the events in Algeria."[90] According to this official, former *harkis* who had fought with the French were now living alongside former FLN supporters in Tilleuls. Many of the *cité*'s newer residents viewed their *harki* neighbors as traitors to the cause of Algerian independence and believed them to have collaborated with the French. Such tensions demonstrate how the legacy of imperialism was at work in the everyday lives of Marseille residents, shaping their perceptions of ethnic but also political identity.

As new families continued to move to Tilleuls, many of the original *harki* residents increasingly believed their *cité* was rapidly falling into decline. Although there continued to be sporadic tensions among Tilleuls' *harki* residents, many also associated the "social degradation" of their neighborhood with the arrival of families from other ethnic and racial groups. According to one *harki* resident, "things began to go bad when housing was given to Algerian and Tunisian families."[91]

Another resident voiced a similar sentiment: "How can they put Algerians, Tunisians, and even blacks in here with us today?"[92] In addition to protesting against the arrival of other North African families, some of Tilleuls's original residents "did not like the 'darkening' of their *cité* because of the presence of the Comorans [which they] believed create[d] a general social devaluing of living standards."[93]

Like longtime Saint Barthélémy residents, Tilleuls residents amalgamated perceived social problems with notions of race and ethnicity. According to one Tilleuls resident, problems began when immigrants "came from bidonvilles in the northern neighborhoods. [And those families] are responsible for the degradation of the *cité*."[94] But as one SONACOTRA official pointed out, the original *harki* families—like many others living in post–World War II Marseille—"forg[o]t that even they themselves had lived in bidonvilles before being rehoused in Tilleuls."[95]

Like some of Saint Barthélémy's residents, many in Tilleuls also believed that their neighborhood would benefit from a social *reéquilibration*. Moreover, they understood that the social recalibration of their *cité* depended on having more *français de souche* or "European" families move to the *cité*. As one resident asserted: "They told us that if a *harki* family moves out, they would put a *français de souche* in their place. We were okay with that. But instead, they put immigrants here. . . . And we aren't okay with that!"[96] Local officials similarly suggested that any attempt at a comprehensive renovation of Tilleuls should also be accompanied by an active effort to encourage more "European" families to move into the neighborhood. As an official from the Bureau de l'action sociale française d'origine nord-africaine wrote to the head of Family Housing at SONACOTRA: "it is necessary now . . . that [any] vacant apartments left behind should be given to *français de souche*."[97] Such exchanges between Tilleuls residents and state officials show how ordinary Marseille participated in and contributed to the debate about social *reéquilibration*. These discussions also underscore how diverse residents—including former colonial subjects—helped to produce categories of race and ethnicity.

· · ·

In the 1970s and 1980s, an emerging discourse about France's crisis neighborhoods was shaped by concerns about the economy, the "immigrant question," and a developing critique of postwar town planning. As a new generation of urban planners and social scientists reconsidered ways to manage the built environment, they emphasized the importance of resident participation in the production of neighborhood space. A major goal of nascent urban rehabilitation initiatives—including the DSQ programs of the 1980s—was to encourage the formation of a vibrant public sphere in France's *grands ensembles*. This emphasis on resident involvement was informed both by ideas about French republicanism and by emerging theories about social movements and urban sociology.

But debates about rehabilitation revealed a complicated relationship between the politics of local participation and urban renewal. Many involved in these projects, including residents, believed that neighborhood rehabilitation meant limiting certain kinds of families from living in their *cités*. By conflating perceptions of race and class, residents, urban planners, and housing officials helped to generate urban renewal policies that tended to implicitly discuss racial problems by explicitly addressing social problems. Discussions of the social *reéquilibration* of neighborhoods also show how the colonial past shaped everyday debates about urban renewal, particularly how perceptions of difference informed ideas about resident identity.

Finally, the debate about rehabilitation also reflected a larger national concern about the meaning and future of social citizenship. For some, social citizenship could be realized only through the creation of a local public sphere in which all residents could participate. Following this logic, participation in a local public sphere more fully enabled citizens to engage as undifferentiated, abstract members of the polity. For others, urban decay was a local symptom of the larger "crisis" of the welfare state. For them, the economic downturn and the "immigrant question" were intimately related and revealed both the French state's difficulty to deliver on the post–World War II promise of universal social security and the inability of "immigrants" to grasp the meaning of and the responsibilities associated with social citizenship. While this chapter explored urban renewal and the politics of participation, the next examines how efforts to rehabilitate crisis neighborhoods in the 1980s and 1990s also focused on managing the bodies of so-called *banlieue* youth.

BANLIEUE YOUTH AND THE BODY POLITIC

On the night of February 21, 1995, a seventeen-year-old French-Comoran boy named Ibrahim Ali Abdallah was shot and killed near La Savine, a *cité* in one of Marseille's northern neighborhoods in the 15th *arrondissement*. Ibrahim and his friends, Soulé Ibrahima and Ahamada Saïd, were part of a hip-hop group called B. Vice and had been practicing in a local state-run youth center earlier that evening. Their rehearsal had wrapped up around 10:00 p.m., later than planned, and the boys began to hurry to the bus stop, afraid they would miss the last bus home.[1] It was also Ramadan, and the boys were eager to rejoin their families.

On their way, they passed a number of campaign posters plastered on a wall bordering the street, including several National Front (FN) posters featuring the caption: "France and the French first!" Elections were just a few months away, and Jean-Marie Le Pen was running for president for the third time, while a lawyer named Jean-Pierre Bauman was the FN candidate for the 15th and 16th *arrondissements* of Marseille.[2] Earlier that night, three FN supporters, Robert Lagier, Mario d'Abrosio, and Pierre Giglio, had posted these campaign materials in strategic spots around the neighborhood. After finishing their task, the three men began to patrol the area in their car. They had night-vision goggles and were armed with pistols. One of them, Robert Lagier, was a master marksman with sniper training and a member of a national police shooting club.[3]

The men were parked at the Aygallades intersection near the bus stop when they saw the three boys rushing toward them. As the boys neared the bus stop and the car holding the three FN members, Lagier exited the vehicle and fired. The first bullet whizzed past Soulé Ibrahima's ear. The teenagers, realizing that someone was shooting at them, turned and began running back toward the youth center. Lagier took aim again, aided by his night-vision goggles, and pulled the trigger two more times. Ibrahim was hit in the back and collapsed on the street. He "died several minutes after the paramedics arrived."[4] Meanwhile, the three FN members fled the scene in their car. Later, they claimed that the boys had attacked them first and had thrown rocks at their vehicle. But Soulé and Ahamada told a different story, testifying that the men had opened fire on *them*, unprovoked, and that "they never gave Ibrahim a chance."[5]

In the media frenzy that followed Ibrahim's death, the press focused considerably on the rise of the National Front, particularly how this radical rightist party had been making steady electoral gains since the 1980s. But, curiously, it also focused intensely on Ibrahim's character. Was he a young, upstanding future citizen of the republic—a serious student and role model—as his parents and friends described him? Or was Ibrahim a juvenile delinquent—as the National Front claimed—an immigrant, a thug, and a symbol of all that threatened "True France?"[6] As part of its investigation into Ibrahim's background, the press also closely examined his recreational interests. His heavy involvement in after school programming drew attention to state-sponsored centers and associations, particularly those that promoted hip-hop culture in *banlieues* around France. Many of these programs had grown out of the urban revitalization initiatives of the 1980s and were part of the movement to encourage residents to participate in neighborhood renewal. The press questioned whether such programs were actually working and if Ibrahim's death signaled that investment in *banlieue* youth had ultimately failed to get these young people off the streets.

Many of these youth programs and facilities—including the center where Ibrahim had spent much of his time—were shaped in important ways by the socialist-led reforms of the early 1980s as well as by the political activism of the so-called Beur generation. In 1981, the socialists came to power as a generation of youth—many of whom had been born in France to migrant parents or had come to France at a young age—began to agitate for greater inclusion in the polity. Some of them advocated a specifically French brand of multiculturalism, while others rallied around an antiracist and anti–National Front message. Part of the socialists' sweeping agenda for change was to target this generation by initiating a series of urban renewal programs, first funded as part of the Développment social des quartiers (DSQ) initiatives of the 1980s and later the Politique de la ville policies of the 1990s. As part of these programs, state and local authorities increased funding to local youth centers with the idea that encouraging *banlieue* youth to participate in extracurricular activities was one way to introduce them to the duties of French citizenship. Building on the growing consensus among social reformers and urban planners about the need to partner with residents to regenerate their neighborhoods, these centers often hired young adults from within *cités* to work as key intermediaries between the state and neighborhood youths. These local agents, known as *animateurs*, worked closely with young people to develop new programming that reflected teenagers' interests, including activities that recognized a burgeoning enthusiasm for hip-hop culture. But, above all, *animateurs* worked hard to promote a code of good social conduct for *banlieue* youth.

State authorities and *animateurs* had very gendered understandings of "*banlieue* youth" as both an idea and a category of analysis. Their efforts to rehabilitate crisis neighborhoods and the young residents of these *cités* show how recreational and after-school programming has attempted to manage *banlieue* boys and girls in particular ways. Such efforts also reflect a broader contemporary French discourse about the bodies and practices of so-called immigrant youth and their place in the nation. Twenty-first-century studies have focused considerably on this issue by exploring the ongoing debate about head scarves, particularly how "immigrant girls" and their choices regarding the hijab are often considered an indication of how French they—and their families—aim to be.[7] Few scholars, however, have examined the interrelated themes of gender and citizenship as they pertain to "immigrant boys." This chapter aims to round out the discussion, first by exploring how young activists participated in debates about the right to difference in the 1980s, and then by examining how state actors and local intermediaries have contributed to differential and gendered discourses about *banlieue* youth in the 1990s. In addition to focusing on the practices of girls, extracurricular activities in neighborhood youth centers have also sought to contain and discipline male bodies and to cultivate particularly masculine citizenship practices.

The New Dangerous Classes?

By the late 1970s, the "immigrant question" not only referred to general concerns about the threshold of tolerance but also to growing anxieties about the young so-called foreign population, many of whom were characterized in public discourse as "juvenile delinquents."[8] Unlike with the immigrant workers of the 1960s, it was not assumed that these young people would eventually return to their countries of origin. Most in fact were born in France: they were not actually immigrants at all. But like the foreign laborers who had dominated headlines in the previous decade, "immigrant youth" were similarly characterized in gendered terms as dangerously masculine. The French press, for example, associated male immigrant youth with lawlessness. An article in the *Nouvel Obsevateur* described a spate of crimes committed by "foreign" teenage boys in one of Marseille's *quartiers nord*: "Detectives in Marseille arrested a gang of youth who had committed over a dozen muggings and several rapes. The head of the gang, Mohamed Khouani, was 18 years old, and he had five accomplices including three minors, aged between 14 and 17 years old. They circulated in stolen vehicles, slashing the tires of isolated cars. If the owner returned, they stole his wallet; when it was a woman, they raped her."[9] In addition to the press, government authorities also associated delinquency with young immigrants. For example, a series of reports by the city of Marseille described how "juvenile delinquency among foreigners is markedly higher than among French nationals and has increased much more sharply in the last few years."[10] Such studies attempted to distinguish between supposedly French and immigrant forms of delinquency. "Who are these young foreign juvenile delinquents?" one report asked. "How is the nature of their delinquency distinct?"[11] According to this report, delinquency was "the barometer of social inadaptation" and the "causes [were] multiple and complex" and included "poor education, lack of parental authority, [and] violence encountered in the media and at the movies."[12] The report concluded that "delinquency begins much earlier for immigrants, at seven to ten years old [than it does for French delinquents]." From ten to fourteen years of age, "immigrant delinquency takes the form of mini-gangs. Aggressions are more structured and usually take the form of shoplifting or stealing mopeds."[13]

Concerns about immigrant juvenile delinquency were often linked to "zones with a high density of foreigners."[14] State officials were increasingly concerned about the potential for the "ghettoization" of French neighborhoods: "the acceleration of the segregation of [immigrant] families . . . and rejection by the host population contribute to the rapid development of adolescent delinquency. Delinquency is directly related to the situation of the ghetto."[15] In Marseille, city council members alarmed by the specter of an American form of urban racial conflict referred to certain northern neighborhoods as the "Chicagos" of the port city.[16]

Despite this attention to the problem of juvenile delinquency, it was not a new concern. Historically, it was understood to be a working-class problem. In his work on the late nineteenth century, Jacques Donzelot explored how anxieties about delinquent children were often tied to "deviant" and "pathological" working-class characteristics including "indigence, sloth, and promiscuity."[17] According to Sarah Fishman, late-nineteenth-century social reformers believed that "bad traits created by the environment in one individual could be passed down to the next generation, eventually resulting in a degenerate population."[18] Late-nineteenth and early-twentieth-century experts began to treat delinquency as a social—not a criminal—problem, and one that should be tackled by a cluster of experts including social workers, judges, and teachers. Over time, the central aim was less to punish so-called juvenile delinquents than to rehabilitate them.[19]

Late-nineteenth and early-twentieth-century ideas about delinquency often described the problem in socioeconomic terms. However, late-twentieth-century discourses tended, as Susan Terrio explains, to "focus on delinquency as a cultural lack that threaten[ed] public safety and French values."[20] In other words, while earlier discourses about deviancy naturalized the link between degeneracy and the working classes, late-twentieth-century debates tended to naturalize the links between "immigrant" populations, race, and criminality. Despite these differences, at root, French understandings of juvenile delinquency tended to emphasize the possibility that deviant youth had the potential to become good citizens, and that the state therefore had a responsibility to attempt to mold them into dutiful members of the republic.

In the 1980s, several sociology research centers began to interrogate the so-called specificities of immigrant juvenile delinquency.[21] The Centre d'analyse et d'intervention sociologique (CADIS), and particularly the work of François Dubet, played a pivotal role in shaping how juvenile delinquency was analyzed. His work on French *banlieue* youth also informed government urban redevelopment programs in the 1980s and 1990s.[22] Dubet was a student of sociologist Alain Touraine, who founded CADIS in 1970 and had developed a new "sociological method of intervention."[23] Touraine's ideas about social movements emphasized the role of sociologists in putting "a theory of social action to work."[24] Touraine and his researchers incorporated this method in their studies of labor, antinuclear, and student movements. Dubet also drew on this theory of social action in his study of French *banlieues*. Identifying a common experience was central to this method of sociological intervention, and Dubet set about pinpointing the environmental and experiential factors that he determined best encapsulated the *banlieue* and its effect on young people. Based on his examination of everyday life in these urban areas—of unemployment, poverty, recidivism, and conflict with police—he labeled the experience of living in the *banlieue, la galère*.[25] The term *la galère*, refers to galley slaves and the Old Regime practice of sending condemned criminals to row naval ships. It also invokes connotations of purgatory.[26]

According to Dubet, the experience of *la galère* was particular to young people living in the *banlieue*: "*la galère* is the form of the marginality of youth linked to the end of the industrial world that can neither create stable systems of identification nor assure the integration of newcomers."[27] Although *la galère* affected all young people living in the *banlieue*, for Dubet, the experience was particularly acute for young "immigrants:"[28] "*La galère* is not an experience specific to immigrant youth, but they live it in a particularly acute way . . . overall, immigrant youth are . . . more than the others, excluded and unemployed."[29]

Dubet argued that *banlieue* youth formed what he called "the new dangerous classes," invoking Louis Chevalier's classic study of nineteenth-century Paris.[30]

Chevalier's dangerous classes were produced in the shift from an agricultural to an industrial society. They were the transient and uprooted mass of the new laboring classes, drawn to industrializing cities in search of employment and eventually settling on the city outskirts in areas that came to be known as the *banlieue rouge*.[31] For Dubet, these dangerous classes were being replaced by a new group: young immigrants. *La galère* was a symptom of a world in transition, a shift from an industrial past to a postindustrial present: "*la galère* appears as the *banlieues rouges* breakdown, when modes of social regulation unravel and economic exclusion is exacerbated by unemployment."[32] In the *banlieue rouge*, the working classes identified with a certain experience of work and mobilized to defend their interests. By contrast, Dubet characterized the late-twentieth-century *banlieue* in terms of the common experience of unemployment.[33] *La galère* emerged "in the hole and void left by the destruction of older forms of class consciousness and by the absence of new movements."[34] The *banlieue rouge* was becoming the "*banlieue* of fear," a territory characterized by acts of violence committed by immigrant juvenile delinquents. For Dubet, "today, *la galère* is an action of the dangerous classes . . . [it is] violence and the feeling of living in a jungle . . . [it] is the plaguing and emotional feeling of being enraged."[35] Accordingly, *la galère* was also a symptom of the larger crisis of the welfare state, as young people—including "*banlieue* youth"—struggled to navigate a labor economy that increasingly seemed to limit access to the full complement of social citizenship.

The Beur Generation and the Right to Difference

In the summer of 1981, in a *cité* known as Minguettes in the suburban outskirts of Lyon, clashes between local youth and police were referred to as the "Minguettes rodeos." Extensive media coverage of the conflict showed teenagers running amok, torching cars, smashing bottles, and breaking windows. These television images seemed to give credence to Dubet's theories about the new juvenile delinquency and *la galère*. The insurrection also recalled troubles in other western European countries, notably in Great Britain, which had recently been the site of urban rebellion in the South London neighborhood of Brixton in April 1981. In both France and Britain, such unrest fed general fears about the so-called immigrant problem.

However, after the "hot summer" of 1981—as it was called—young people from different neighborhoods around France began to organize.[36] In 1981, youth from a number of *cités*, including Minguettes, coordinated a series of concerts called "Rock against the Police" that were held in Paris, Lyon, and Marseille.[37] These concerts took their cue from a series of similar events organized by

British youth activists. Like those in Great Britain, these concerts were aimed at protesting police brutality, but also, as one French activist remembered, they were an effort to "help other issues emerge in a more visible way, particularly the social dynamic of the *cités*."[38] In the 1980s, youth-organized concerts, hunger strikes, marches, and other protests marked an important moment of activism when young people of color—including youth from France's *banlieues*—argued for greater inclusion in the polity. Many claimed that, as individual members of the republic, they also had the right to express their cultural and ethnic diversity. Their activities informed developing policies that emphasized the importance of local participation, which ultimately influenced urban renewal programs targeting youth living in *banlieues*.

In 1983, members of a Lyon-based youth organization, SOS Avenir Minguettes, proposed a demonstration on a grand scale, a march for equality and against racism—"inspired by Martin Luther King and Gandhi"—that would begin in Marseille and end in Paris.[39] A poster circulated in Marseille advertising the march called for "equality in the right to a life, equality in the right to respect, equality in the right to happiness."[40] On October 15, 1983, members of SOS Avenir Minguettes joined a number of other groups and protestors in La Cayolle, a *cité de transit* in Marseille. This cluster of run-down reduced-norm housing units symbolized the degraded everyday experiences and housing conditions of many families in France.[41] Before leaving Marseille, the group of some one hundred and fifty marchers passed through other *cités*, notably Saint Barthélémy and La Paternelle. Many of them chanted, "We are the children of the *quartiers nord*."[42] As the marchers made their way to Paris, they traveled through other key cities, including Dreux, the recent site of the election of the National Front.[43] When the marchers reached Paris on December 3, 1983, the participants had grown from the few dozen marchers who had left Marseille to approximately a hundred thousand people who joined in the final day of the demonstration.

The 1983 march helped draw national attention to the issues that many youth living in *banlieues* around France were facing. The intense media coverage of the event also gave, as Saïd Bouamama explained: "youth from the *cités*, particularly those of foreign origin . . . a [new] social visibility."[44] More specifically, the press began to focus on what was being called the "second generation." In a 1980 *Le Monde* article, Tahar Ben Jelloun described: "What we call the second generation. . . . This generation wasn't foreseen. It was born by chance and forgotten. It is there . . . with a vague, vacillating, and mitigating identity. It is also without a future, because it is without work and without bearings. Its past is hazy, gray, and hollow . . . a double rejection: after family, it's France who has rejected it."[45] This "unforeseen" generation was often difficult to describe: some were born in France—either in the metropole or in the overseas departments and territories

(DOM-TOM); others had come to France at a young age. This generation was also difficult to count, as many were French, while others were not technically French citizens.[46]

According to Saïd Bouamama, the media cast these young activists in a positive light: "the thugs, rioters, and delinquents" that had dominated headlines during the Minguettes Rodeos "were transformed into 'nice Beurs.'"[47] "Beur" is a slang term coined by youth whose parents came from former colonies in North Africa. It is an inversion of the derogatory French word "Arabe." Many of the activists who participated in the march understood "Beur" to refer exclusively to children of parents from Tunisia, Algeria, and Morocco. But for other youth activists, the term Beur referred not only to "Maghreb migrants, but also [more generally] to migrant children from Africa [and] Portugal . . . the term expressed the emergence of a multicultural urban identity."[48] In other words, for many, "Beur" referred to young people of North African descent, but for some, it could also signify the collective of all young people who shared the common experience of living in French *cités*. As Marilaure Mahé, a former youth activist from Marseille recalled, the 1983 March for Equality and against Racism became one of the "founding myths" for the generation of Beur youth who came of age in the 1980s and began to foment their political and cultural identities.[49]

This wave of youth activism occurred during a moment of sweeping reform as the socialists took power in 1981. When François Mitterrand was elected president, his party also gained an absolute majority in the parliamentary elections. This was the first Left-led government in the Fifth Republic, and the socialists' victory was all the more notable because elsewhere, in the United States and Great Britain, for example, the 1980 election of President Ronald Reagan and the 1979 appointment of Margaret Thatcher as prime minister, signaled a decisive shift to the right.

Led by Mitterrand, the socialists initiated a number of reforms, including devoting more attention and funding to "immigrant issues." For many recent migrants and their children, the 1981 election seemed like a real moment of possibility for them to obtain greater political rights. A series of immediate reforms reinforced this perception. In 1981, a 1901 law restricting immigrant associations was overturned, allowing the right for non-French nationals to form organizations. Some restrictive measures in the 1974 ban on immigration were mitigated, allowing for easier familial regroupment, which helped to reunite separated families. Strict deportation laws were also eased, which ceased the deportation of young people who had illegally entered France before the age of ten but had lived most of their lives in France.[50] During the "wave of May 1981, a double idea dominated these youth and recent [m]igrants; on the one hand, there was the certitude that a step had been taken towards equal rights. . . . On the other hand, there was widespread hope of an ambitious social policy capable of curbing the degradation of living conditions."[51] Many thus interpreted the election and the initial reforms as concrete steps towards real social and political change.

SOS Racisme was the largest youth organization to emerge out of the 1983 March for Equality and benefited immensely from the newly elected socialist government. It was first led by Harlem Désir, who was born in Paris to a Martinican father and a Jewish mother.[52] Désir had close ties with the Left, and SOS Racisme received most of its financial and political support from the socialist party.[53] The Minister of Culture, Jack Lang, as well as other socialist notables including Georgina Dufoix and Laurent Fabius, were especially supportive of the nascent organization and were included as "godfathers" (les parrains) or key advisers in its ranks. SOS Racisme promoted a general message of antiracism, and slogans like "Hands off my buddy" (Touche pas à mon pôte) and "I like whom I want" became ubiquitous antiracist messages.[54]

For the socialists, SOS Racisme was intended as a response to the rise of the radical Right. Racist attacks and murders of youth of color had been on the rise since the 1970s, and xenophobic, anti-immigrant, and ultranationalist organizations had been growing since the early 1970s.[55] In 1972, Jean Marie Le Pen formed the National Front (FN). Initially considered a fringe group, the party began to gain membership in the mid-to-late 1970s. Some members were pieds noirs and had been active in the Organisation de l'armée secrète during the Algerian War of Independence. Other new FN supporters were industrial and blue-collar workers who had historically formed the backbone of the Left, particularly the French communist party (PCF). Around France, and especially in areas hardest hit by economic depression and unemployment, the FN had been making steady gains and drawing support from both the traditional Left and the Right.[56] In the 1980s, the National Front began to move into mainstream politics, exploding into the national spotlight during the 1983 municipal campaigns.[57] The rise of the radical Right became a central rallying point for SOS Racisme. The FN offered SOS Racisme a definitive position from which to frame its message of antiracism. The socialists hoped to appeal not only to banlieue youth but also the next generation of young French voters, bringing them into the fold of the Left. With this goal in mind, SOS Racisme articulated a broad message promoting universal principles of equality and a moral imperative against racism.[58]

For some activists and members of the socialist government, SOS Racisme was supposed to harness the energy of the Beur generation as well as frame the terms of the movement.[59] However, other youth activists felt that this growing national organization had few ties to local neighborhoods. Many of those involved in the 1983 March for Equality had mobilized explicitly to address discrimination and inequity in everyday life. For them, SOS Racisme's broad message of antiracism did little to deal with the problems of housing and unemployment. As one activist, Kaïssa Titous, remembered: "'Don't touch my buddy!?' This was no longer the fight for equality."[60]

Among a number of other, much smaller organizations that emerged in the 1980s, one, known as Mémoire Fertile, focused on social issues specific to problems in France's *cités*. Between 1986 and 1987, the group organized conferences in four cities: Lille, Marseille, Anger, and Paris. Members of the group centered these conferences on debates about membership in the nation and social rights.[61] One of their key issues was "a new citizenship founded not on nationality, but on residence, rooted in the commune and the neighborhood."[62] For Mémoire Fertile members, this conception of citizenship focused on ordinary people and everyday life, and promoted action from below. Their notion of membership thus encompassed issues that they believed concerned all habitants—notably, housing, employment, education, and racism.[63] For them, this idea of citizenship also legitimated the neighborhood as an important local space for practicing membership.[64] As Saïd Bouamama described: "It is in the street, in society, where we construct action."[65] For Mémoire Fertile, citizenship was not something acquired but practiced.

According to Mémoire Fertile activists, what they called the new citizenship was also explicitly about multiculturalism. They envisioned a kind of belonging that included diverse cultures and peoples who all worked to "find a mode of effective participation."[66] Members of the group "insisted on the existence of a multicultural France [and a] rupture with the myth of a homogeneous nation."[67] The organization argued that the recognition of multiple cultures and communities should no longer be viewed as an obstacle to the political unity of the nation. They rejected the French assimilationist "melting pot."[68] For Mémoire Fertile, multiculturalism was inseparable from *égalité*. Equality was not framed as a moral imperative, but as a necessity and a requirement for living in a diverse society. Its members were not just proponents of a right to culture, they also defined equality as the recognition of cultural difference in the pursuit of social and political parity. For Mémoire Fertile, the right to difference without social, economic, or political equality would only reify injustice.

Although Mémoire Fertile utilized the term "multiculturalism," they were not proponents of communitarianism. They rejected what they saw as the potential balkanization of the public sphere into distinct minority communities. In this sense, their perspective echoed the positions of strict supporters of republicanism, especially those who rejected a so-called Anglo-Saxon model of multiculturalism. Mémoire Fertile instead promoted the idea of a "pluralistic space" in which diverse residents and citizens of France could participate—as individuals, not members of ethnic groups—in the republican institutions of belonging.[69] For

Mémoire Fertile, multicultural citizenship was at once concrete, participative, and plural.[70]

SOS Racisme and its socialist supporters also envisioned a uniquely French brand of multiculturalism. But while Mémoire Fertile advocated a multicultural citizenship grounded in neighborhood participation, SOS Racisme supported a new kind of visibility for difference in the public sphere, by encouraging recognition and celebration of French diversity. SOS Racisme was especially good at utilizing the media to promote its message. For example, the organization's debut event was a concert at the Place de la Concorde in Paris, funded by the Ministry of Culture, that was broadcast live and covered by all the major television networks. In front of a crowd of three hundred thousand people, Harlem Désir appealed to "French of all cultures. . . . To French Jews and French Muslims. . . . To immigrants of first and second generations."[71] The speech was meticulously staged, and as Désir spoke the camera panned from a close-up of his face to a panoramic view of the crowd. After several shots of young audience members, many of them displaying "Hands off my buddy!" banners, the camera refocused on the Eiffel Tower looming proudly in the distance.[72] Finally, it cut quickly to the Minister of Culture, Jack Lang, who looking approvingly at Désir and at the crowd as if affirming these diverse faces of France.

Events such as this SOS Racisme concert were a state-sanctioned celebration of French diversity. Such events helped to attest that a brand of French multiculturalism was possible. Members of Mémoire Fertile, however, were critical of this kind of expression of diversity, or what they called the "folklorization of cultures."[73] They believed that the recognition of cultural difference also had to be incorporated into existing systems of social security. Multiculturalism, for Mémoire Fertile, could not simply be limited to the "celebration of cultures" but was needed to facilitate real social and political equity.[74] Groups such as Mémoire Fertile did not perceive their idea of multiculturalism to be incompatible with French republicanism; they saw it as essential to guaranteeing real fraternity and solidarity among France's diverse residents.

During the early 1980s, as new organizations such as SOS Racisme and Mémoire Fertile presented various messages about citizenship and diversity in France, the increasingly powerful National Front party also articulated its vision of the right to difference. According to the FN, "all cultures were noble" and therefore had to protect their "originality."[75] For the National Front, however, multiculturalism destroyed this "specificity."[76] Instead, FN members asserted that the real right to difference was the preservation of the integrity of French culture. For them, foreign groups should remain foreign. Otherwise, "French culture was in danger of disappearing because of immigration."[77] Immigrants and any appeal in favor of the "mixing" of cultures fundamentally threatened what FN members believed should remain essentially French. The National Front touted "a dogma of the impossibility of peaceful coexistence of different cultures."[78] It thus espoused a new kind of racism premised less on biological inferiority than on the conservation of cultural integrity.[79]

In addition to this message about the right to difference, the National Front also built upon the idea that France had reached its carrying capacity for foreigners. The group drew on the so-called threshold argument, or the notion that immigration needed to be curbed or stopped altogether in order to prevent violent clashes between cultures. With this message, the National Front won huge victories in the municipal elections of 1983. The issues of immigration, crime, and concerns about the ongoing recession dominated the elections in many French cities, including Dreux, parts of Marseille, Roubaix, and the 18th *arrondissement* of Paris.[80] After these wins, the National Front continued to make large gains. In the 1986 national elections, the socialists did not retain enough seats to maintain power and were forced to form a coalition government with the center right Rally for the Republic/Union for French Democracy (RDR/UDF) parties from 1986 to 1989. By the late 1980s, the FN had emerged as a legitimate and increasingly mainstream national political party. With the National Front's electoral successes, the socialist party message began to gradually shift away from the language of multiculturalism. While the FN espoused a politics of the right to difference through the exclusion of immigrants, many socialists returned to a historically leftist approach of encouraging the inclusion of immigrants through a politics of assimilation.[81]

Groups such as the popular SOS Racisme and less well-known Mémoire Fertile on the Left, and the National Front on the far Right, all participated in a discursive debate about the right to difference. While SOS Racisme generally supported the right for French citizens—of all origins—to be visible in the public sphere, Mémoire Fertile members believed that real participation could not be achieved without social and political equality in addition to a robust politics of multiculturalism. Conversely, the National Front utilized the rhetoric of difference to make the case that all peoples—but especially *français de souche*—had the right to protect and preserve their own distinct, unique, and essentially different cultures.

All of these positions formed part of a broad discussion about the possibility of recognizing a multicultural France. These many groups not only embraced the language of republicanism but also sought to both insert themselves into and work to change established political discourses. In doing so, groups from opposite ends of the political spectrum raised important questions about the place of difference in the public sphere. Youth activist members of SOS Racisme and Mémoire Fertile also helped to counter negative characterizations of *banlieue* youth by showing that they could engage in civic discourse as potential citizens of the republic.

Animation and *Animateurs*: The Apprenticeship of Citizenship

Youth activists helped to showcase the political agency of the so-called second or Beur generation. After the 1983 March for Equality and against Racism, many participants in this seminal event returned to their neighborhoods energized to effect real change. Although state officials continued to be concerned about *banlieue* youth and delinquency, increasingly they also began to see these young people as potential partners who shared a common goal to improve French *cités*. As officials approved programs aimed at rehabilitating neighborhoods in crisis, they also searched for ways to encourage what they called the social insertion of *banlieue* youth into the body politic.

In the early 1980s, several state institutions, including the Fonds d'action social (FAS), the Ministry of Youth and Sports, and the Ministry of Culture, began to focus particularly on these young people, especially those living in DSQ-funded sites. An emerging agenda concentrating on the "social promotion" of *banlieue* youth drew on a number of studies commissioned by the Ministry of Youth and Sports and the Ministry of Justice.[82] One such report discussed the need for "general action in the prevention of juvenile delinquency," including the "increase [of] recreational activities for youth in order to prevent social in-adaptation."[83] Another report stated that "a large number of the problems encountered by youth are due to the absence or inadequate number of recreational centers . . . these difficulties are inextricably linked to . . . factors of in-adaptation . . . [including] the lack of sociocultural and sports centers."[84] In other words, the Ministry of Youth and Sports linked the lack of cultural and recreational programming in run-down *cités* to the problem of juvenile delinquency.

Although these studies referred, somewhat generally, to all youth from *cités*, these reports were part of a state-sponsored body of literature that explicitly discussed juvenile delinquency in gendered terms, as a particularly male problem. For example, many studies emphasized how juvenile delinquency was generally more of an issue for boys, including one report that asserted "delinquency is much less serious in girls than boys," and that for every twelve male juvenile delinquents, there was only one girl delinquent.[85] It went on to discuss how certain neighborhood spaces helped to facilitate criminality in young men, particularly how the "tendency to hang out on the street or in public places" led to the formation of "gangs."[86] In addition to the usual problems such as petty theft and vandalism, state reports concluded that these gangs were directly related "to the growing number of *viols collectifs*," or gang rapes, nationwide.[87] According to the studies of several state institutions, the criminality of young men was of utmost concern. These reports suggested that efforts to discipline the bodies and behaviors of young immigrant men could be achieved through the expansion of sports and recreational programs.

According to a ministry publication on the "Insertion of Youth": "Sports are part of the struggle against the marginalization of populations subjected to the effects of the social and economic crisis."[88] More specifically, "the practice of sports permits youth in difficulty to become conscious of the importance of the body in the quest for a place in society."[89] The Ministry of Youth and Sports focused on the physical bodies of *banlieue* youth and on the potential for recreational activities to mold them into the body politic: "Sportive practices . . . also favor the acquisition of a code of good social conduct; in brief, they are factors of insertion, and better still, integration."[90] According to the ministry, integration was the "assembling of different parties to a system and assuring their compatibility as well as the good functioning of the complete system."[91] Recreational activity centers thus encouraged integration, and "the objective of integration is to enter youth into contemporary French society."[92] Building youth centers and increasing recreational programming would encourage *banlieue* youth to become better citizens.[93]

Although these reports mentioned that youth centers should offer a broad range of activities, including tennis, gymnastics, and dance, studies tended to underscore the benefits of so-called classic sports including "soccer . . . [and] boxing," all traditionally male games.[94] Such findings were supported by statements made in interviews by a number of young men from "sensitive neighborhoods" around France. According to one twenty-one-year-old man quoted in a Ministry of Youth and Sports publication, "Sports permit me to be in shape, to be well." Before he started going to his local youth center, he recalled: "I was tired . . . because of a lack of training. Our bodies weren't used to it. . . . Now we train regularly to be in top form."[95] Ministry reports showcased how sports helped discipline male bodies and encouraged boys to become good, fit men.

Based on the recommendations of many of these studies, in the early 1980s the Ministry of Youth and Sports, the Ministry of Culture, and the FAS received increased funding to establish and run youth activity centers—often called Les Maisons des jeunes et cultures (MJCs)—in run-down neighborhoods around France.[96] In Marseille, some MJCs were first established in the late 1970s but were incorporated into the DSQ, and later the Politique de la ville, programs in the 1980s and 1990s. According to the director of the Corderie MJC in Marseille's 7th *arrondissement*: "the MJC is close to the realities on the ground, the grand social problems. . . . [We] service a large number of residents with programming that favors social progress."[97]

Local MJCs affirmed the importance of working with and responding to the needs of the local community. For example, according to an annual report from the Corderie MJC, "[We] count 600 regular participants and permit a large number of Marseillais, from different origins and communities, to participate in a cultural life."[98] MJCs developed programming that "responded to the needs [of the] neighborhood."[99] Such centers also began to increasingly hire youths from the community and "prioritize[d] youth and their access to culture."[100] Youth activity centers affirmed "popular and associational programs . . . as the indispensable bases of real social progress."[101] As one youth leader from the Marseille Corderie MJC articulated, "we are more than a recreational center, this is a space for the apprenticeship of citizenship."[102]

The effort to construct youth centers was an important part of urban rehabilitation projects. These initiatives also reflected the French tradition of *animation*, or the local-level organization of educational and recreational activities.[103] *Animation* has no precise English translation, but the Larousse dictionary defines it as the "methods and means implemented for encouraging the participation of members of a collectivity in the life of a group."[104] According to Larousse , an *animateur* or *animatrice* is a "person charged with organizing and directing the activities of a community."[105] *Animation* is rooted in the history of popular education, particularly the efforts of social Catholic organizations and syndicates to promote the advancement of the working classes in the late nineteenth and early twentieth centuries.[106] In the interwar period, during the Popular Front, the relationship between education and sports was institutionalized with the formation of a new position, the Undersecretary of State for Sports. Léo Lagrange, the first to hold this post, was an important figure in the state-funded popular education movement. He believed that sports encouraged French working-class youth and, by extension, the working classes in general, to better themselves and to cultivate joy for labor and for civic participation. By the 1960s, *animation* emerged as a distinct professional field as *animateurs* began to play educational roles in cultural centers, senior centers, and high schools.

By the 1980s, state officials, including Jack Lang, viewed *animation* as one important way to reach *banlieue* youth in French *cités*.[107] As state funding to local youth centers and other programs increased, the number of *animateurs* hired to work in this developing sector also grew. By 1990, there were around 170,000 permanent employees in *animation*, most of whom worked in neighborhood youth centers. In addition to these salaried workers were about 140,000 part-time workers.[108] Many who formed part of this emerging workforce of *animateurs* had participated in or were influenced by the activism of the beur generation.

As the number of *animateurs* grew, *animation* also became more professionalized. According to Jean-Claude Gillet, *animation* is the space where "educational and strategic pedagogy" meet local participants.[109] *Animation* is "praxis [and] looks to reconcile theory and practice in a dialectical and circular process."[110] *Animateurs* aim to "orient everyday life" and to facilitate participation. The goal of *animateurs* is to encourage the "possibility that each individual, if desired, exercises a power . . . and a capacity to transform things . . . which is the cornerstone of the democratic vision."[111] Thus, participation was central to *animation* and served as both a "remedy for social pathologies" and as a "mode of social control."[112]

From Boys to Breadwinners

Motivated young people from troubled *cités* were viewed as uniquely qualified to act as intermediaries between the state and other young residents. As *animateurs*, these local youth leaders were not only charged with working to keep kids off the streets but also with modeling good citizenship practices. More specifically, one aspect of their responsibilities was to prepare youth living in "sensitive neighborhoods" for the job market. Although local *animateurs* worked with "*banlieue* youth" as a whole, some were especially concerned with making young men employable. Good *citoyens* (or male citizens) were also supposed to be productive breadwinners.

In many cases, young people had already been very active in their communities and it was relatively easy for state officials to identify good candidates for the job of local *animateur*. Such was the case in Marseille's Tilleuls Cité, where a number of neighborhood youths began to petition local authorities for change well before the state-initiated rehabilitation efforts of the 1980s and 1990s. In 1977, twenty-six teenage boys sent a petition to the local branch of the SONACOTRA office. Their *cité* lacked adequate facilities to accommodate its many young residents, and the young men requested funding to construct a soccer field near the housing complex.[113] Most of the boys who signed the petition were under nineteen years of age, except for two young men, Abdelkader Ounnous and Saïd Regaoui, who were in their early twenties. Over the next several years, the two emerged as central figures in the *cité*, initiating projects and working with local authorities to improve infrastructure and facilitate social programming for Tilleuls youth.[114] For example, in 1977, Regaoui met with SONACOTRA and ATOM employees to discuss creating a *centre socio-culturel et sportif*.[115] He and Ounnous subsequently helped to establish the Tilleuls social center, and by the 1980s they had become employees of the state. Their responsibilities were varied and included scheduling after-school programs such as sports and tutoring activities. They were also called on to act as intermediaries between residents and government authorities, occasionally meeting with police if a Tilleuls teenager got into trouble or helping parents communicate in French with local officials.[116]

In various letters and reports, Regaoui and Ounnous described their work in the *cité* as well as articulated their overarching goals as *animateurs*. They believed that their "role . . . must be a social role."[117] Their efforts were not just to "help children with their [school]work," but to "promote the integration of youth through different clubs and youth centers."[118] They stressed that local youth must participate in their community and become "aware of their responsibilities."[119] According to Regaoui and Ounnous, Tilleuls youth had three principal needs: they required better access to social activities, better tutoring for younger children, and job training for older teens and young adults. They believed that *animation* could do more than just keep *cité* youth out of trouble. For them, it facilitated the apprenticeship of citizenship.

Regaoui and Ounnous also understood that *animation* could help young people from the neighborhood make the transition to adulthood by preparing them for the job market. Like much of France in the 1980s, Tilleuls residents suffered from high levels of unemployment, which hovered around 42 percent in the *cité*.[120] According to a 1986 report, Ounnous was "concerned primarily with training those youth who need it, and then trying to help them through the job application process, and helping those already with training to find a job."[121] For Ounnous and Regaoui, employment was central to their understanding of the meaning of social integration.

Although Regaoui and Ounnous often referred to Tilleuls youth in general terms, they were especially interested in helping the young men in the *cité*. In a 1983 report Ounnous noted that he focused "especially" on finding jobs for "young men, ages 19–25."[122] In particular, he "play[ed] the role of mediator [and] facilitator between young men and employers."[123] For example, in 1983, several young men submitted applications to the Société nationale des chemins de fer français (National Society of French Railways [SNCF]), and Ounnous met with the local head of SNCF personnel to discuss their applications.[124]

In a letter sent to nineteen local organizations, Ounnous and Regaoui further articulated their goals for the young men in their community, particularly what they called the ability for Tilleuls men to "blossom" through having a "good trade, a good job, a good home."[125] The two helped promote the idea that good male citizens were also good breadwinners and thus articulated a very masculine notion of citizenship. In doing so, they reflected an earlier conception of social citizenship, a notion rooted in the state-sponsored and paternalistic welfare initiatives of the nineteenth and twentieth centuries. By the late twentieth century, however, this understanding of a male breadwinner model of social citizenship was becoming increasingly untenable. The stagnating French economy and the changing labor market were helping to fundamentally call into question older models of welfare that had been premised on full (male) employment and the limitation of risk.[126] Nonetheless, Regaouis and Ounnous firmly believed that if they helped prepare young men in their *cité* for the job market, the state had a duty to stimulate the economy and to encourage job creation.

Regaoui and Ounnous worked very hard for the young men of Tilleuls. What did they do for the girls? They scheduled after-school programming for all Tilleuls youth, including elementary-school-age boys and girls, but ultimately devoted a great deal of time to the young men of the *cité*. Several factors help to explain their focus. In a 1977 meeting that included Regaoui and Ounnous as well as representatives from SONACOTRA and FAS, the participants decided to distinguish the *animation* of boys from that of girls in Tilleuls. According to the meeting minutes, they decided that "the *animation* of . . . girls" must be handled delicately "because of the particular susceptibility of French Muslim families regarding the condition of women."[127] As discussed at length in the previous chapter, Tilleuls was originally a *cité de transit* for primarily *harki* families. In their discussions about Tilleuls youth, local officials and *animateurs* believed that the cultural and religious background of the residents necessitated treating girls differently. They ultimately decided that ATOM would handle the *animation* of girls in the neighborhood by offering special programs focusing on domestic skills as well as literacy classes.[128] This decision reflected the colonial past and the historical role of institutions such as ATOM and FAS to facilitate the "evolution" of colonized women.[129]

Such efforts to establish a differential and gendered system of social programming not only perpetuated the legacy of imperialism but also the deeper history of *animation* in France. Historically, youth programming, such as the popular *colonies de vacances* of the late nineteenth through mid-twentieth centuries, included boys and girls in gendered forms of participation in camp life. As Laura Lee Downs has shown, these *colonies* were "governed by a clearly gendered organization of space and activities" that served to "prepar[e] the man and woman of the future as citizens who would accede to their gendered places within the nation."[130] In addition to the *colonies*, late-nineteenth-and early-twentieth-century sports and athletic clubs also catered more exclusively to teenage boys and young men than they did to women and girls. As Pierre Arnaud and others have explored, many of these athletic associations were founded after the massive defeat of 1870 and were firmly established during the Third Republic. According to Arnaud, "physical activities and sporting practices were fundamentally shaped by republican ideology," and a French culture of sport was constructed with overtly military aims to "incorporate and mobilize the masses . . . through physical instruction."[131] These various histories—the colonial past as well as the gendered culture of sports and recreation in France—all informed *animation* practices in the late twentieth century. In the 1980s and 1990s, youth centers in *cités* similarly sanctioned the cultivation of particularly masculine citizenship qualities through various kinds of physical training.

Although *animation* in the late twentieth century was intended to shape future citizens in general, youth centers encouraged especially gendered notions of belonging. Boys often played soccer and almost never took sewing classes, while girls rarely engaged in hard contact sports. Of course, not all activities were overtly gendered; *animateurs* and *animatrices* often designed activities such as canoeing or other types of field trips that included both boys and girls together. Nonetheless, the point here is to draw attention to the various ways in which citizens are, as Judith Surkis puts it, sexed, and how bodies are endowed with various kinds of meaning.[132] In this sense, *animation* for "immigrant girls" was an attempt to measure their so-called level of adaptation to French ways of life. Young male immigrant bodies and their levels of physical fitness were perceived to be indicators of the ability of these boys to become productive, disciplined breadwinner citizens.

"L'opération rap": Hip-Hop and *Animation*

Youth centers such as the one in Tilleuls focused on a broad range of recreational and job-training activities. By the mid-1990s, many centers also began to offer programs based on burgeoning youth interests in hip-hop music and culture. Such programming reflected local and state officials' efforts to encourage youth participation in urban rehabilitation. Despite this commitment to recognizing and affirming teenage interests, many officials also perceived hip-hop to be a potentially insidious form of youth culture. Hip-hop exemplified all that was imagined to be dangerous about *banlieue* youth—particularly young men—at the same time that state officials, including *animateurs*, identified hip-hop programming as a potentially useful way to encourage the apprenticeship of citizenship.

First emerging in the United States in the late 1970s, hip-hop originated in New York neighborhoods including Brooklyn and the South Bronx, which had large communities of African Americans and Puerto Ricans as well as migrants from Jamaica, Haiti, and the Dominican Republic.[133] During block parties, DJs began to blend together musical genres such as reggae, soul, and funk, and several built special large sound systems to accommodate their musical experimentation. Pioneering DJs, including Jamaican-born DJ Cool Herc and Grandmaster Flash, began extending the breaks in songs—by letting the vocals drop out so the baseline could dominate—in response to enthusiastic crowds who wanted the music to last longer so they could keep on dancing. Some dancers began creating special moves to fill up these extended breaks in songs. They called themselves B-boys and B-girls, although they are often referred to as break dancers. In order to liven up the audience, masters of ceremonies (MCs) began to help DJs by rhyming impromptu—or free styling—over the music. MCs also began writing and recording full-length songs of spoken word, or rap.

In the early years of hip-hop in the United States, many of these burgeoning artists believed that hip-hop culture was also a means for social critique. Hip-hop activists, particularly former South Bronx gang member Afrika Bambaata, began organizing neighborhood block parties in the name of "knowledge, wisdom, understanding, freedom, justice, and equality." He also helped form an association called the Zulu Nation, and this group promoted hip-hop as a specific and authentic culture expressed through the three artistic modes of music, dance, and graffiti. Branches of the Zulu Nation sprang up throughout New York, spreading to Los Angeles and other U.S. cities in the early 1980s. In 1983, Bambaata toured Europe with members of the Zulu Nation that included DJs, graffiti artists, MCs (or rappers), and B-boys.

Many French hip-hop artists describe Bambaata's Rock Steady Tour as their first important introduction to hip-hop culture. As one former B-boy recalled after meeting Bambaata at a performance in one of Paris's *banlieues*: "The idea of Bambaata was huge—everyone knew it—it's to make positive all the resentment one has against the system. Okay, we are responsible, we can't just sit back. . . . we take ourselves in hand, we develop our own culture, and we make use of it."[134]

In Marseille, a vibrant underground hip-hop culture began to thrive in the late 1980s and early 1990s.[135] Some groups were featured on local radio stations that also played American hip- hop.[136] Others began to gather in prominent parts of the city, such as in front of city hall or the opera house, to dance.[137] Some groups, such as IAM, ultimately achieved national and even international recognition.[138] Others performed mainly in local open-mic events, talent shows, or benefit concerts.[139]

B. Vice, of which Ibrahim Ali Abdallah was a member, was one such locally known group. Formed in 1989 in La Savine, the group was composed of a diverse group of teenage boys from the 15th *arrondissement*. The name "B. Vice" stood for "Bloc venant de l'intérieur comme de l'extérieur" and alluded to the diversity of its members, which the group described as "Comoran, French, Malagasy, and Maghrebi."[140] Some had been born in France to parents who had migrated from former colonies. Others had come to France as children. One member, Mbaé Tahamida Mohamed, known as MT Soly or sometimes just Soly, came to Marseille from the Comoros. The Comoros, an archipelago of islands in the Indian Ocean, was a former colony and part of the French DOM-TOM. In a 1974 referendum, the majority of the population voted for independence, while one of the islands, Mayotte, chose to stay with France. This started a wave of migration, as those Comorans who wanted to remain French chose to leave the Comoros, often by way of Mayotte or Madagascar, before making their way to the metropole.[141] MT Soly and his family migrated to Marseille via Madagascar and joined the growing community of Comorans settling in the city. By 1989, MT Soly had found B. Vice.

The members of B. Vice initially engaged in all elements of hip-hop culture: some danced, others composed lyrics, and a few of them tagged walls around their neighborhood.[142] According to MT Soly, at first B. Vice practiced wherever they could, "in stairwells, parking lots, or in a nearby abandoned post office."[143] Over time, they gave up tagging as those "nocturnal activities were less and less appreciated by [the] public."[144] They developed an aesthetic style that included a "blend of humorous and engaged lyrics, dance and theater."[145]

By the early 1990s, local and central state officials began to take notice of groups such as B. Vice. In 1991, Minister of Culture Jack Lang began to set aside funding for hip-hop.[146] In Marseille, a regional council created a new institution, L'association départemental pour le développement des actions de prévention (The Departmental Association for the Development of Actions of Prevention, or ADDAP). The primary goal of the ADDAP was *la lutte contre l'exclusion*, or the struggle against exclusion, and it focused on programs addressing "peri- and post-educational problems."[147] The ADDAP helped to form a program they called *l'opération rap* and began funding several "young adolescent groups with the goal to develop rap music."[148] The ADDAP continued the practice of looking to young leaders in "sensitive neighborhoods" to act as liaisons between youth and state institutions. State officials thus began to view hip-hop as a means of engaging "in the promotion of citizenship and the struggle against exclusion."[149]

In 1991, several of the original members of B. Vice applied for funding from ADDAP to form an association they called La Sound Musical School. They first learned about these new resources for hip-hop from *animateurs* at their local youth center, La Savine Centre Social.[150] According to MT Soly and Ali Ibrahima, who together helped found La Sound Musical School, they wanted to create a space to teach "interested neighborhood youth about hip-hop culture," including MCing, music sampling, and dance.[151] With help from local and state funds, La Sound Musical School took charge of two small rooms on the ground floor of one of La Savine's HLM buildings in 1993.[152] The association began to offer practice space for local youth who had formed hip-hop groups of their own, and it also began to stage a number of neighborhood concerts.

By the mid-1990s, La Sound Musical School had five permanent employees, and they "were very much invested in the *animation* of their association."[153] These *animateurs* earned diverse certificates, including diplomas in popular education, business, and accounting—"all with the goal to better manage their association and to better *encadrer* their members."[154] The term *encadrer* conveys a number of meanings in French, including to supervise, to lead, but also to frame, to direct. As MT Soly and the other directors of La Sound Musical School worked to guide and manage local youth, they too sought direction and training to better run their center. They became part of the professionalizing field of *animation*.

This 1993 photo of B. Vice performing in Vitrolles, a suburb of Marseille, showcases both the MCing and dancing talents of its members. Downstage, three members of B. Vice are rapping, including Patrick T. on vocals, and Saïd A. as MC, while, upstage, B-boy L. Dine dances. The photo captures each of the performers in motion; the blurred lines of the four figures signify their dynamic movements and energy. To the right of the photo, the audience is also a dynamic participant in the scene. Several audience members are grinning, and one has raised his arm in the air, presumably keeping time with the downbeat of the music. Photo courtesy of MT Soly.

As La Sound Musical School and its *animateurs* continued to receive state funding to develop hip-hop programming, they also increasingly drew on the rhetoric of citizenship and civic participation in articulating their goals for the center. According to the school's directors, the center was a space for "dialogue, for sharing knowledge and culture," but also a place for "debates about violence, family, religion, delinquency, racism, and civic responsibility with the goal to develop the expression of citizenship among the youth."[155] According to MT Soly, hip-hop culture was more than just a means of expression for *banlieue* youth; it was also a means for social inclusion. For example, in one project "on the theme of citizenship" MT Soly worked with a dozen neighborhood youth to help them write and record a CD of ten original hip-hop songs. The name of the project was "Si 't'es citoyen," which can mean both "if you are a citizen" and "if you are a *good* citizen."[156] MT Soly and the other directors of La Sound Musical School also believed that they had a responsibility as "ambassadors from

Marseille's *quartiers nord*," to contrast negative media images of their neighborhoods by calling attention to how many residents of these *cités* "were responsible
citizens."[157]

La Sound Musical School developed a robust schedule of classes for the youth
of La Savine. In addition to original programming that included hip-hop instruction in dance, writing lyrics, and improvisation, they expanded their services to
include classes in new forms of technology such as navigating the Internet and
using video and multimedia equipment.[158] It was one of many local associations
around France that partnered with other youth centers and state officials with the
objective of "animating" youth from the *cités*. La Sound Musical School became
part of the growing network of institutions that encouraged the social and cultural integration of *banlieue* youth through their active participation in neighborhood programs. Hip-hop was increasingly viewed as an important and legitimate part of local efforts. As *animation* continued to grow as a professional field,
animateurs also received training to acquire a number of hip-hop-specific certificates and diplomas.

Hip-hop programming began to flourish in youth centers around France in
the 1990s at about the same time as a national debate about hip-hop began to
gather steam. One nationally known group, Nique ta mère (Fuck Your Mother,
or NTM), was at the center of a veritable hip-hop affair. While many state officials and *animateurs* saw hip-hop in youth centers as a possible way to reach out
to *banlieue* youth, NTM was charged with promoting the very type of delinquent
behavior that state officials were trying to discourage. In 1995, NTM participated
in a Bastille Day concert protesting two recent municipal elections that had voted
National Front members into the office of mayor in Toulon and Orange. During
the concert, NTM encouraged the crowd to yell "Nique la police!" or "Fuck the
police!" at the guards hired to provide security for the event.[159] The group was
ultimately found guilty of the obscure—and rarely prosecuted—charge of orally
abusing public authorities. NTM members received an "unprecedented sentence
of six months in prison," a 50,000 franc fine, and were banned for life from recording hip-hop albums or performing at concerts.[160]

Although the sentence was later reduced and the group was eventually permitted to return to recording, the NTM affair, as it came to be called, illustrated the
very ambivalent position of hip-hop culture in the French public sphere. In the
debate surrounding the affair, hip-hop itself was often characterized as a particularly dangerous, provocative, and insidious form of youth expression that threatened to undermine France's tradition of high culture. Critics were concerned
about the glorification of violence and the rejection of authority in the music. They
also condemned the pervasiveness of misogynistic themes in hip-hop culture as

This 1993 photo of La Sound Musical School's atelier in La Savine shows, in the foreground, a young girl sitting still at an electric piano and sound sampler. She is gazing with interest at the keys before her while MT Soly leans over her right shoulder. MT Soly is instructing the girl and appears to be in the act of speaking. His hands are blurred as the camera captures them in motion, gesturing. The girl's image is in focus, and she is framed by the equipment in the atelier, including a computer monitor and sound system in the background. In the right background sit two young men. They are Hassany, a DJ with B. Vice and a founding member of La Sound Musical School, and Hamidou, a young member of the group 45 Niggaz. Like MT Soly, they too are out of focus, because the camera catches them in motion, talking to each other. Photo courtesy of MT Soly.

exemplified by the name of the group, Nique ta mère, or "Fuck Your Mother." Hip-hop seemed to embody what was so very dangerous about "*banlieue* youth" in general, and young "immigrant" men in particular.

In addition to growing criticism about the broad dangers of hip-hop, a number of sociologists began to examine what they viewed to be specific problems within hip-hop *animation*. Several studies considered the question of gender and hip-hop in youth centers.[161] One such study compared the different spaces where boys and girls practiced hip-hop dance, noting that B-boys often danced in youth centers as well as on street corners and other public spaces, whereas girls often practiced more exclusively within the enclosed space of the MJC. While hip-hop instruction for boys often emphasized improvisation and competition with other male dancers, girls often took classes that focused on learning pre-choreographed steps to be performed in recital-type settings. These studies thus examined how state-sponsored hip-hop programming reproduced gendered ways of being and belonging, particularly by encouraging boys to occupy and help create masculinized public spaces while girls remained in interior and appropriately feminine spaces. Although the goal for many hip-hop *animateurs* was to "get kids off the street" and create a forum for the apprenticeship of citizenship, the programs they helped to develop ultimately worked to contain the bodies of male and female youth in distinctly different ways.

It is within this larger context that local groups such as B. Vice and associations like La Sound Musical School continued their activities. By 1995, some original members of B. Vice, including MT Soly, were working exclusively at La Sound Musical School, while other younger members, including seventeen-year-old Ibrahim Ali Abdallah, continued to write and perform with B. Vice. The local success of both La Sound Musical School and B. Vice reveals the extent to which state efforts to partner with local intermediaries succeeded in creating a vibrant associational life for many youth living in France's *cités*. But Ibrahim's untimely death also raised important questions about race, masculinity, and membership in the nation and exposed the ambivalent place of *banlieue* youth within the body politic. Ibrahim died in 1995, the same year as the NTM affair, and in the media frenzy following his death, the press not only drew on the trope of *la galère* to make sense of his murder, but also focused especially on his character. Did Ibrahim, like the members of NTM, exemplify what was insidious about hip-hop culture and immigrant youth in general? Or was he a victim, an innocent, and an upstanding member of the community?

After Ibrahim's death, newspaper reporters and television crews descended on La Savine and interviewed representatives from the National Front as well as Ibrahim's friends and family. In a number of statements made to the press, far-right politician and National Front spokesman Bruno Mégret asserted that Ibrahim and his friends had been the aggressors. "The Comoran and his friends," Mégret was quoted as saying, "viciously attacked" the three FN members and threw rocks at their car.[162] He went on to state that if the three men "hadn't been armed, they probably would have been killed."[163] He also asserted that the entire incident was "the fault of massive and uncontrolled immigration." Although Mégret's comments were very much an expression of the extremism of the radical Right, they nonetheless also echoed pervasive and commonsensical ideas about "immigrant" male bodies, ideas that circulated widely in the press. To Mégret, the very presence of the three boys on a dark street at night was intrinsically threatening. It was therefore natural to assume that they had been up to no good. By drawing on pervasive tropes associating foreign young men with criminal behavior, Mégret was able to claim that Ibrahim and his two friends were the aggressors, the perpetrators, and therefore Lagier, d'Abrosio, and Giglio were correct in having acted in self-defense.

Mégret also drew on widespread assumptions that associated immigrants with racial difference and national decline. Supposed foreigners were easily identifiable as not French because they looked different, and, as such, their very presence undermined the nation. This general tendency to conflate the category "immigrant" with assumptions about race becomes all the more obvious given that many of the people who were identified as immigrants, or "of immigrant origin," were undeniably French. Moreover, in his statements, Mégret identified Ibrahim as a foreigner, as "the Comoran," and this appellation ignored the very complex colonial relationship of the Comoros to the French metropole. Some Comorans in Marseille were French citizens because they were from the island of Mayotte, which voted to remain part of the DOM-TOM. Other Comorans in Marseille did not—as yet—have French citizenship because they hailed from those islands of the former colony that had chosen independence. Finally, Mégret's comments to the press also attest to how commonsense assumptions about race and gender marked Ibrahim as necessarily criminal. As one of Ibrahim's friends later recalled in an interview, "Ibrahim was murdered because he was black."[164]

While Mégret cast Ibrahim as a perpetrator in his statements to the press, other media reports characterized him as a victim. In one *Provençal* article, a reporter went to La Sound Musical School to interview Ibrahim's friends and described the "mixed emotions on the faces of thirty youths who met in the small local musical association of La Savine . . . in one corner, a young Comoran cries quietly. Another . . . sits on the ground, his head in his hands. A third bites his lips."[165] This article underscored Ibrahim's participation in state-sponsored youth activities and how he was positively influenced by this programming. The article also characterized Ibrahim as a young man who took civic participation seriously, who "regularly gave concerts and participated in rap festivals in Marseille and the region," and who sought to both critique and improve the problem of *mal-vie* or *la galère* in the *cité*.[166] Remembering Ibrahim, one friend said, "[He] was never a guy who bummed around."[167]

Media coverage also eulogized Ibrahim as a productive member of the community and as a son and future citizen of the republic. Following his murder, the family and friends of Ibrahim organized a peaceful march down the Canebière, Marseille's main avenue and, according to the *Le Provençal*, "15,000 people participated in the demonstration."[168] The press also reported that Marseille notables and local leaders marched alongside Ibrahim's family, including then mayor

Robert Vigouroux, who asserted, "My place is here, to demonstrate against a murder, against all racism, and to help all Marseille communities listen to each other."[169] Then president of SOS Racisme, Fode Sylla, even flew from Paris to Marseille to join the march.[170] Some participants carried posters that read "Don't touch my buddy!" others carried banners demanding "Justice for Ibrahim."

In the weeks following Ibrahim's death, the National Front members Lagier, d'Abrosio, and Giglio were arrested. All three pled not guilty to the charges, claiming they had acted in self-defense. During the trial, both Soulé Ibrahima and Ahamada Saïd, Ibrahim's friends who had survived the attack, testified as witnesses for the prosecution, and their accounts contradicted the stories of the FN members. According to the two boys: "They pulled out their guns and opened fire. Without any apparent reason."[171] Forensic evidence from the crime scene corroborated the boys' stories. No rocks were strewn about the street, and there was no indication that any rocks had made contact with the car. Lagier was ultimately sentenced to fifteen years in prison for murdering Ibrahim, while d'Abrosio and Giglio were charged with lighter offenses and only served about a year each in prison.

· · ·

Recent efforts to manage the bodies of *banlieue* youth reveal how state institutions, local authorities, and public discourse more broadly have viewed "foreigners"—particularly young men—to be both likely delinquents and potential citizens. Although discussions about immigrant girls and the head scarf continue to capture the French imagination, debates about the *animation* of young *banlieue* men illustrate how a very masculine conception of social insertion and citizenship has taken shape. *Animation*, including the state-sponsored physical training of the body, was seen as an integral part of the broader effort to rehabilitate run-down neighborhoods. This attention to urban revitalization was not just a product of state initiatives but was also shaped by the activism of the so-called second generation that came of age in the early 1980s, and began to advocate for greater inclusion within the polity. Nineteen eighties debates about the possibility of a specifically French brand of multiculturalism, and discussions about the right to difference, informed urban rehabilitation policies, particularly the emphasis on partnering with *banlieue* youth to effect change. In the 1990s, state institutions, including local youth centers, began increasingly to work with youth in *cités*, offering hip-hop recreational activities as part of the local *animation* agenda.

For both state authorities and local intermediaries—many of whom came from the *banlieue*—the apprenticeship of citizenship was a major goal of such programming. Such efforts to rehabilitate "crisis neighborhoods" and the young residents of these *cités* have contributed to gendered *animation* practices and, by extension, to gendered notions of citizenship. Ibrahim's story draws attention to the pervasive ambivalence about the place of "immigrant young men" in France, particularly anxieties about the ability of these men to become upstanding members of the republic.

Epilogue

In 2000, a group of Marseille residents formed an association they called Un centre ville pour tous (A Downtown for Everyone) and also framed a "Declaration of Resident Rights," in which they stated that housing was a social right and that all Marseille residents deserved a certain quality of life and standard of living.[1] The group was formed in response to city plans to redevelop key areas of downtown Marseille—notably the rue de la République, a major boulevard that divided the Panier and Belsunce neighborhoods and linked the tourist areas around the Vieux Port to new commercial developments near La Joliette to the north. Beginning in the 1990s, the city of Marseille implemented a robust plan to drastically remake the boulevard. In partnership with a number of international firms as well as semiprivate French development companies, the city began to buy out and shutter local businesses as well as raise the rents of the numerous apartments that lined the length of the avenue. Many members of Un centre ville pour tous owned small street-level shops or lived in apartments along the rue de la République. In response to city efforts, local activists advocated for greater resident participation in these neighborhood renewal initiatives and encouraged municipal authorities to collaborate with Marseille citizens to rejuvenate public spaces, refurbish run-down housing, and cultivate a "decent habitat."[2]

For municipal authorities, the ultimate goal of the project was to attract major international retailers to Marseille, including H&M and Starbucks, and to create a new stock of luxury and newly renovated apartments that they hoped would entice young professionals and other white-collar workers to settle downtown. To members of Un centre ville pour tous, however, this plan was nothing more than an effort to gentrify the city center and push Marseille's historically diverse, working class residents to the peripheries of the city. Indeed, many municipal authorities viewed the rehabilitation of the rue de la République as the modern expansion—as well as the conclusion—of the late-nineteenth-century project to Haussmannize Marseille. While city officials saw the urban renewal plan as the much needed effort to galvanize the local economy, some residents criticized city hall for merely trying to whiten the city center. According to members of Un centre ville pour tous, it was Marseille's very diversity, which they described in terms of the various "ethnic origins and historical moments of arrival of Marseillais," which constituted "the social thickness and layers" of the city.[3] The rue de la République rehabilitation effort is part of a much larger, seven billion Euro project called Euroméditerranée that was initiated in 1995 and includes sweeping plans to revitalize numerous neighborhoods and to create a new commercial center with luxury residences and hotels. Marseille's tourist center describes the undertaking as "the largest state economic development and planning project since the construction of the business district of La Défense in Paris."[4] According to their website: "The greatest architects are working to redesign Marseille's profile."[5] Supporters of the plan say that it will not only stimulate the economy, which has been ailing for decades, but it will also help to counter Marseille's notorious reputation for being a tough and dangerous town. Many of the Euroméditerranée-funded projects, including a number of community and performing arts centers around Marseille, have already been completed, and proponents of the initiative emphasize how such public works attract tourists and simultaneously cater to Marseille residents who use such facilities for local theater productions, art installations, and other events. Opponents argue that despite these gestures Euroméditerranée is still explicitly about exclusion, and the master plan ultimately serves to limit certain kinds of Marseillais from fully participating in the social life of the city. Still others assert that this most recent scheme is just the latest in a long series of historical efforts to discipline urban space and police the city's residents.

The controversy surrounding the rehabilitation of the rue de la République, as well as the larger Euroméditerranée project, illuminate a number of historical tensions that have not only impacted Marseille but also defined France in the late twentieth century. Like most major French cities, Marseille became a vast construction site after World War II. Elected officials, including long-term mayor Gaston Defferre, local *techniciens*, central state bureaucrats, social scientists, and—importantly—Marseille residents have engaged in complex negotiations about how to manage the city's built environment. Immediately after the war, such discussions starkly illustrated the monumental task of postwar reconstruction in France and highlighted the need to radically rethink what ordinary people could expect in terms of their basic quality of life. In the three decades that followed, local debates about town planning not only focused on rebuilding but also emphasized how the material reconstruction of urban space also had the potential to improve the everyday lives of Marseille residents. Since the 1970s, however, the struggling French economy, coupled with persistently high unemployment levels and the deterioration of France's public housing stock, served to call into question the idea that the grand postwar urbanism project could permanently transform people's lives for the better.

In the last thirty years, renewed efforts to rehabilitate decayed urban tissue contributed to a reevaluation of the role that residents could play in constructing the places where they live. In Marseille, Un centre ville pour tous is one of many local organizations that are partly funded by the state and engage in a lively debate about neighborhood rehabilitation. Their efforts illustrate how city spaces are also contested sites where diverse actors cultivate various ideas about urban living. Their campaigns also demonstrate how such urban renewal programs still highlight debates about *which* residents are actively participating in the project to improve modern life. Importantly, the activities of members of Un centre ville pour tous underscore how expectations about comfort have informed the ways in which ordinary people understand the meaning of welfare, as well as imagine their relationship to the modern French state.

This book has examined how the history of postwar modernization is also an imperial story and, together, these constitutive processes have profoundly shaped the production of knowledge about social citizenship in France since 1945. It argued that neighborhood-level negotiations fundamentally informed evolving ideas about membership in the nation, and that these local contestations reveal how the institutionalization of social citizenship also created new spaces for exclusion. Commonsense assumptions about racial, social, and spatial differences have structured a differential system of housing in France.

The postwar project to build a robust welfare state was also an attempt to construct a new kind of social space, a site for redefining and strengthening the relationship between citizens and the state. Significantly, structuring the space of the welfare state has contributed to a reconceptualization of republicanism in late-twentieth-century France. Since World War II, French citizens have increasingly described membership in the nation in terms of their rights to a quality of life and to a certain standard of living. Expectations about social citizenship have become an important part of how republicanism is understood as ordinary people, elected officials, and policymakers reenvisioned the social contract to also guarantee the people's welfare. This cultivation of a new notion of republicanism has also necessitated imagining that social rights—in addition to political and civil rights—are universal.

This faith in a republican model of membership grounded in social rights has helped to produce the idea that the French public sphere is a kind of essential and timeless space, the site where abstract undifferentiated citizens can have unfettered access to comprehensive citizenship rights. But by historicizing the process through which the public sphere came to be understood as universal, and by exploring the particular ways in which social spaces have been constructed over time, this book illuminates the unevenness of the postwar effort to construct a robust welfare state. More specifically, it shows how perceptions of race, class, and spatial differences have played an essential role in forging understandings of belonging. This study thus provides an important corrective to the myth of republican citizenship in France, a myth grounded in commonsense assumptions about the universality of rights and the homogeneity of the citizenry.

The merits of engaging in a spatial study of welfare resonate beyond the French case. For nearly two decades, scholars inspired by the so-called spatial turn, have shown how particular attention to the question of space can allow for a more robust examination of issues of race, migration, class, and empire. This book argues that the study of the modern welfare state demands a new treatment, one that seriously considers the physical and imagined places where people dwell and define their sense of the meaning of well-being. Moreover, it proposes that such a situated concept of welfare—whether in modern Europe, the United States, or Latin America—has also been shaped by the imperial project. Such an approach makes it evident that social citizenship is constructed not only within "imagined communities" but also through practices, in this case practices involving contested spaces and enjoyed rights.

Notes

The following abbreviations are used in the notes:

ADBR   Archives Départementales des Bouches-du-Rhône

AMM   Archives Municipales de Marseille

CACF   Centre des Archives Contemporaines, Fontainebleau

INTRODUCTION

1. Letter from Slimane T. to Mayor Gaston Defferre, September 16, 1940, AMM 418 W 1, 1.

2. Letter from Abdallah T. to Mayor Gaston Defferre, September 14, 1960, AMM 418 W 1, 1.

3. Letter from Arnaud R. to Mayor Gaston Defferre, February 7, 1962, AMM 468 W 179, 1.

4. Ibid., 2.

5. For studies of postwar reconstruction, see Danièle Voldman, *La reconstruction des villes françaises de 1940 à 1954: Histoire d'une politique* (Paris: L'Harmattan, 1997); Hubert Bonin, Sylvie Guillaume, and Bernard Lachaise, *Bordeaux et la Gironde pendant la reconstruction, 1945–1954: Actes du colloque de Talence tenu du 16 au 18 Novembre 1995* (Talence: Editions de la Maison des sciences de l'homme d'Aquitaine, 1997); James A. Huston, *Across the Face of France: Liberation and Recovery, 1944–63* (Lafayette, Ind.: Purdue University, 1984); Andrew Shennan, *Rethinking France: Plans for Renewal, 1940–1946* (Oxford: Oxford University Press, 1989); Cecil O. Smith Jr., "The Longest Run: Public Engineers and Planning in France," *The American Historical Review* 95, no. 3 (1990): 657–692.

6. For the history of French public housing construction, see Brian Newsome, *French Urban Planning, 1940–1968: The Construction and Deconstruction of an Authoritarian System* (New York: Peter Lang, 2009); Jean-Marc Stébé, *Le logement social en France: 1789 à nos jours*, 2nd ed. (Paris: Presses universitaires de France, 2002); Didier Cornuel and Bruno Duriez, *Le mirage urbain: Histoire du logement à Roubaix* (Paris: Anthropos, 1983); Sabine Effosse, *L'invention du logement aidé en France: L'immobilier au temps des trente glorieuses* (Paris: Comité pour l'histoire économique et financière de la France, 2003); Jean-Paul Flamand, *Loger le peuple: Essai sur l'histoire du logement social en France* (Paris: Editions La Découverte, 1989).

7. For the classic French study of late-nineteenth-century anxieties about disease, degeneration, and national decline, see Louis Chevalier, *Classes laborieuses et classes dangereuses à Paris pendant la première moitié du XIXe siècle* (Paris: Plon, 1958). Other notable studies of the social question include Robert A. Nye, *Crime, Madness, and Politics in Modern France: The Medical Concept of National Decline* (Princeton, N.J.: Princeton University Press, 1984); George L. Mosse, *Nationalism and Sexuality: Respectability and Abnormal Sexuality in Modern Europe*, 1st ed. (New York: H. Fertig, 1985); Andrew Robert Aisenberg, *Contagion: Disease, Government, and the "Social Question" in Nineteenth-Century France* (Stanford, Calif.: Stanford University Press, 1999); David S. Barnes, *The Making of a Social Disease: Tuberculosis in Nineteenth-Century France* (Berkeley: University of California Press, 1995); Ruth Harris, *Murders and Madness: Medicine, Law, and Society in the*

fin de siècle (Oxford: Oxford University Press, 1989); Daniel Pick, *Faces of Degeneration: A European Disorder, c.1848–c.1918* (Cambridge: Cambridge University Press, 1989).

8. For discussion of social citizenship, see T. H. Marshall, *Citizenship and Social Class, and Other Essays* (Cambridge: Cambridge University Press, 1950).

9. Geoff Eley, *Forging Democracy: The History of the Left in Europe, 1850–2000* (Oxford: Oxford University Press, 2002), 290.

10. For more recent studies of the history of human rights and rights discourses in the twentieth century, see Samuel Moyn, *The Last Utopia: Human Rights in History* (Cambridge, Mass.: Harvard University Press, 2010); Stefan-Ludwig Hoffmann, ed., *Human Rights in the Twentieth Century* (Cambridge: Cambridge University Press, 2011). See also Mark Mazower, *Dark Continent: Europe's Twentieth Century* (New York: Knopf, 1999).

11. For studies exploring how access to housing came to be understood as a fundamental right, see Minayo Nasiali, "Citizens, Squatters and Asocials: The Right to Housing and the Politics of Difference in Post-Liberation France," *The American Historical Review* 119, no. 2 (April 2014): 434–459; Bruno Duriez and Michel Chauvière, eds., *La bataille des squatters et l'invention du droit au logement, 1945–1955* (Villeneuve d'Ascq: Groupement pour la recherche sur les mouvements familiaux, 1992).

12. For discussion of the rise of *les grands ensembles* in France, see Annie Fourcaut, *Un siècle de banlieue parisienne: 1859–1964* (Paris: L'Harmattan, 1988); Annie Fourcaut, Frédéric Dufaux et al., *Le monde des grands ensembles* (Paris: Créaphis, 2004).

13. See Jacques Donzelot, *The Policing of Families* (New York: Pantheon Books, 1979).

14. For studies of the institutionalization of systems of social security in comparative perspective, see Seth Koven and Sonya Michel, "Womanly Duties: Maternalist Politics and the Origins of Welfare States in France, Germany, Great Britain, and the United States, 1880–1920," *The American Historical Review* 95, no. 4 (October 1990): 1076–1108; Peter Baldwin, *The Politics of Social Solidarity: Class Bases of the European Welfare State, 1875–1975* (Cambridge: Cambridge University Press, 1990); Susan Pedersen, *Family, Dependence, and the Origins of the Welfare State: Britain and France, 1914–1945* (Cambridge: Cambridge University Press, 1993); Frances Gouda, *Poverty and Political Culture: The Rhetoric of Social Welfare in the Netherlands and France, 1815–1854* (Lanham, Md.: Rowman and Littlefield, 1995); E. P. Hennock, *The Origin of the Welfare State in England and Germany, 1850–1914* (Cambridge: Cambridge University Press, 2007). For the institutionalization of welfare in France, see Rachel G. Fuchs, *Poor and Pregnant in Paris: Strategies for Survival in the Nineteenth Century* (New Brunswick, N.J.: Rutgers University Press, 1992); Paul V. Dutton, *Origins of the French Welfare State: The Struggle for Social Reform in France, 1914–1947* (Cambridge: Cambridge University Press, 2002); Janet R. Horne, *A Social Laboratory for Modern France: The Musée Social and the Rise of the Welfare State* (Durham, N.C.: Duke University Press, 2002); Timothy B. Smith, *Creating the Welfare State in France, 1880–1940* (Montreal: McGill-Queen's University Press, 2003); Philip Nord, *France's New Deal: From the Thirties to the Postwar Era* (Princeton, N.J.: Princeton University Press, 2010). In Britain, see Jane Lewis, *The Politics of Motherhood: Child and Maternal Welfare in England, 1990–1939* (Montreal: McGill-Queen's University Press, 1980); Richard Wall, *The Upheaval of War: Family, Work and Welfare in Europe, 1914–1918* (Cambridge: Cambridge University Press, 1988); Geoffrey Finlayson, *Citizen, State, and Social Welfare in Britain 1830–1990* (Oxford: Oxford University Press, 1994); Kathleen Jones, *The Making of Social Policy in Britain, 1830–1990* (London: Athlone Press, 1994); Simon Wood, *From the Cradle to the Grave, Social Welfare in Britain, 1890s* (London: Hodder and Stoughton Educational, 2002). In the United States, see Carole Haber and Brian Gratton, *Old Age and the Search for Security: An American Social History* (Bloomington: University of Indiana Press, 1994); Molly Ladd-Taylor, *Mother-Work: Women, Child Welfare, and the State, 1890–1930* (Urbana: University of Illinois Press, 1994); Michael B. Katz, *In*

the Shadow of the Poorhouse: A Social History of Welfare in America (New York: Basic Books, 1996); Elna C. Green, *Before the New Deal: Social Welfare in the South, 1830–1930* (Athens: University of Georgia Press, 1999).

15. For social insurance, family benefits, and gender and class in welfare states, see Baldwin, *The Politics of Social Solidarity*; Geoff Eley and Atina Grossmann, "Maternalism and Citizenship in Weimar Germany: The Gendered Politics of Welfare," *Central European History* 30, no. 1 (1997): 67–75; as well as the other contributors to this special issue: "Women and the Welfare State in the Weimar Republic," *Central European History* 30, no. 1 (1997); and Fuchs, *Poor and Pregnant in Paris*.

16. In *The Social Project*, Kenny Cupers discusses how central state authorities, social scientists, architects, and urban planners formed a network of experts charged with cultivating postwar housing institutions and modes of expertise. In *At Home in Postwar France*, Nicole Rudolph similarly explores postwar housing construction but focuses especially on the interiors of modern mass housing to show how central state authorities managed the domestic spaces of French citizens. Kenny Cupers, *The Social Project: Housing Postwar France* (Minneapolis: University of Minnesota Press, 2014); Nicole Rudolph, *At Home in Postwar France: Modern Mass Housing and the Right to Comfort* (New York: Berghahn, 2015).

17. Cupers and Rudolph show how modernization was less a project defined by a monolithic central state, and more a process that cultivated postwar housing institutions as well as forged new modes of expertise for managing the interiors and exteriors of modern mass housing. Cupers, *The Social Project*, and Rudolph, *At Home in Postwar France*.

18. See Cupers, *The Social Project*; Rudolph, *At Home in Postwar France*.

19. See George Steinmetz, *Regulating the Social: The Welfare State and Local Politics in Imperial Germany* (Princeton, N.J.: Princeton University Press, 1993), 149. See also Smith, *Creating the Welfare State in France, 1880–1940*.

20. Paul Steege, Andrew Stuart Bergerson, Maureen Healy, and Pamela E. Swett, "The History of Everyday Life: A Second Chapter," *Journal of Modern History* 80 (June 2008): 358–378, here 366.

21. See, for example, Voldman, *La reconstruction des villes françaises de 1940 à 1954*; Newsome, *French Urban Planning, 1940–1968*; also Cupers, *The Social Project*; Rudolph, *At Home in Postwar France*.

22. See Lyons, *The Civilizing Mission in the Metropole*. Lyons's work builds on earlier studies of population management in the colonies. As Paul Rabinow, Gwendolyn Wright, and others have shown, there was also an imperial dimension to the social question as colonial functionaries in cities such as Rabat and Algiers developed methods for regulating urban space and colonial subjects in the late nineteenth and early twentieth centuries. Paul Rabinow, *French Modern: Norms and Forms of the Social Environment* (Chicago: University of Chicago Press, 1995); Gwendolyn Wright, *The Politics of Design in French Colonial Urbanism* (Chicago: University of Chicago Press, 1991); Zeynep Celik, *Urban Forms and Colonial Confrontations: Algiers under French Rule* (Berkeley: University of California Press, 1997). For studies of welfare and empire in the British context, see Jordana Bailkin, *The Afterlife of Empire* (Berkeley: University of California Press, 2012).

23. For the pivotal edited volume that showcased the new imperial history, see Frederick Cooper and Ann Laura Stoler, eds., *Tensions of Empire: Colonial Cultures in a Bourgeois World* (Berkeley: University of California Press, 1997). Other notable new imperial histories include: Antoinette M. Burton, *Burdens of History: British Feminists, Indian Women, and Imperial Culture, 1865–1915* (Chapel Hill: University of North Carolina Press, 1994); Julia Clancy-Smith and Frances Gouda, eds., *Domesticating the Empire: Race, Gender and Family Life in French and Dutch Colonialism* (Charlottesville: University Press of Virginia, 1998); Lora Wildenthal, *German Women for Empire, 1884–1945* (Durham, N.C.:

Duke University Press, 2001); Emmanuelle Saada, *Empire's Children: Race, Filiation, and Citizenship in the French Colonies* (Chicago: University of Chicago Press, 2012).

24. For several studies that work within the "colonies as laboratory" paradigm, see Isabel Hull, *Absolute Destruction: Military Culture and the Practices of War in Imperial Germany* (Ithaca, N.Y.: Cornell University Press, 2005); and Lyons, *The Civilizing Mission in the Metropole.*

25. In a number of works Marcel Roncayolo has argued against the conception that Marseille is a marginal city, instead emphasizing its importance as a Mediterranean and colonial metropole. See, for example, Marcel Roncayolo, *L'imaginaire de Marseille: Port, ville, pôle* (Marseille: Chambre de commerce et d'industrie de Marseille, 1990).

26. See Junko Takeda, *Between Crown and Commerce: Marseille and the Early Modern Mediterranean* (Baltimore: Johns Hopkins University Press, 2011).

27. Emile Témime and a number of his students have written extensively on the history of migration in Marseille. See Emile Témime and Pierre Echinard, *Migrance: Histoire des migrations à Marseille* (Aix-en-Provence: Edisud, 1989); Renée Lopez and Emile Témime, *Histoire des migrations à Marseille. 2, L'expansion marseillaise et l'invasion italienne* (Aix-en-Provence: Edisud, 1990); Emile Témime, *Marseille transit: Les passagers de Belsunce* (Paris: Autrement, 1995). See also Mary D. Lewis, *The Boundaries of the Republic: Migrants Rights and the Limits of Universalism in France, 1918–1940* (Stanford, Calif.: Stanford University Press, 2007).

28. Claude McKay, *Banjo* (London: X Press, 2000), 57.

29. For discussion of Marseille's imagined spaces, particularly how Marseille came to be understood in terms of a north-south divide, see André Donzel, *Marseille: L'expérience de la cité* (Paris: Anthropos, 1998); and André Donzel, *Le nouvel esprit de Marseille* (Paris: L'Harmattan, 2014).

30. For scholarship on the history of urban development in Marseille, see André Donzel, ed., *Métropolisation, gouvernance et citoyenneté dans la region urbaine marseillaise* (Paris: Maisonneuve et Larose, 2001); Donzel, *Le nouvel esprit de Marseille*; Michel Peraldi and Michel Samson, *Gouverner Marseille: Enquête sur les mondes politiques marseillais* (Paris: La Découverte, 2005); Marcel Roncayolo, *Les grammaires d'une ville: Essai sur la genèse des structures urbaines à Marseille* (Paris: Ecole des Hautes Etudes en Sciences Sociales, 1996).

31. Not all so-called problem neighborhoods are located in the suburbs of major French towns; for example, Paris's eighteenth *arrondissement* is often described as being a *banlieue*.

32. For discussion of French *banlieues* as contested and constructed spaces, see: John Merriman, *The Margins of City Life: Explorations on the French Urban Frontier, 1815–1851* (New York: Oxford University Press, 1991); Annie Fourcaut, *La banlieue en morceaux: La crise des lotissements défectueux en France dans l'entre-deux-guerres* (Grâne: Créaphis, 2000); Danièle Voldman, ed., *Désirs de toit: Le logement entre désir et contrainte depuis la fin du XIXe siècle* (Grâne: Créaphis éditions, 2010); Yankel Fijalkow and Marcel Roncayolo, *La construction des îlots insalubres: Paris 1850–1945* (Paris: L'Harmattan, 1998).

33. Many Haussmannization projects, particularly in Paris, also pushed families out of cities into the rapidly growing *banlieue*. On the Haussmannization of Paris and the construction of the *banlieue*, see David Harvey, *Paris, Capital of Modernity* (New York: Routledge, 2003).

34. These single-family homes and other dwellings were referred to as *pavillons* and were built on lots known as *lotissements*.

35. On the invention of the *quartiers nords*, see Michel Peraldi, Claire Duport, and Michel Samson, *Sociologie de Marseille* (Paris: La Découverte, 2015).

36. On the social production of space, see Henri Lefebvre, *The Production of Space* (Oxford: Blackwell, 1991).

37. On navigating and thereby appropriating or transforming urban space, see Michel de Certeau, *The Practice of Everyday Life* (Berkeley: University of California Press, 1984). For other discussions of the transformative potential within everyday life and practices, see Guy Debord, *The Society of the Spectacle* (New York: Zone Books, 1994).

38. The study of everyday life has been shaped by a number of historiographic contributions, notably Alf Lüdtke and his work on Alltagsgeschichte in Germany; Alf Lüdtke, ed., *The History of Everyday Life: Reconstructing Historical Experiences and Ways of Life* (Princeton, N.J.: Princeton University Press, 1995). See also Patrick Wright, *On Living in an Old Country: The National Past in Contemporary Britain* (London: Verso, 1985); and Henri Lefebvre, *Critique of Everyday Life*, special ed. (London: Verso, 2008). For more recent discussions of major themes in everyday life studies, see Ben Highmore, *Everyday Life and Cultural Theory: An Introduction* (London: Routledge, 2002); Ben Highmore, *The Everyday Life Reader* (London: Routledge, 2002); Steege et al., "The History of Everyday Life"; and Harry Harootunian, *History's Disquiet: Modernity, Cultural Practice, and the Question of Everyday Life* (New York: Columbia University Press, 2000), 21–22.

39. Steege et al., "The History of Everyday Life," 362.

40. Agnes Heller quoted in Wright, *On Living in an Old Country*, 8.

41. Wright, *On Living in an Old Country*, 15.

42. Paul Gilroy, *"There Ain't No Black in the Union Jack": The Cultural Politics of Race and Nation* (Chicago: University of Chicago Press, 1991), 49.

43. Steege et al., "History of Everyday Life," 361.

44. Wright, *On Living in an Old Country*, 7.

45. Dominique Schnapper, for example, has written extensively on the question of republicanism in France and strongly defends the idea of abstract, undifferentiated citizenship. See, for example, Dominique Schnapper, *Le communauté des citoyens: Sur l'idée moderne de nation* (Paris: Gallimard, 1994).

46. Jeremy Jennings, "Citizenship, Republicanism, and Multiculturalism in Contemporary France," *British Journal of Political Science* 30, no. 4 (2000): 577.

47. For French-language studies on immigration as a social problem, see François Dubet, *La Galère: Jeunes en survie*, Mouvements (Paris: Fayard, 1987); François Dubet and Didier Lapeyronnie, *Les quartiers d'exil*, coll. L'épreuve des faits (Paris: Editions du Seuil, 1992); Milena Doytcheva, *Une discrimination positive à la française: Ethnicité et territoire dans les politiques de la ville*, Alternatives Sociales (Paris: La Découverte, 2007); Alain Finkielkraut, *La défaite de la pensée: Essai*; Sylvie Tissot, *L'état et les quartiers: Genèse d'une catégorie de l'action publique* (Paris: Seuil, 2007); Dominique Schnapper, *Exclusions au cœur de la cité*, Collection "Sociologiques" (Paris: Anthropos, 2001); and Jacques G. Petit and Christine Bard, *Intégration et exclusion sociale: D'hier à aujourd'hui* (Paris: Anthropos, 1999).

48. Although small in number, several recent French-language studies have begun to consider race as a viable category of analysis, notably: Didier Fassin and Eric Fassin, eds., *De la question sociale à la question raciale: Représenter la société française* (Paris: La Découverte, 2006); Pap N'Diaye, "Pour une histoire des populations noires en France: Préalables théoriques," *Le Mouvement social*, no. 213 (2005): 91–108; Sylvain Pattieu, "Souteneurs noirs à Marseille, 1918–1921 Contribution à l'histoire de la minorité noire en France," *Annales histoire, sciences sociales*, no. 6 (novembre–décembre 2009): 1361–1386; Emmanuelle Saada, *Les enfants de la colonie: Les métis de l'empire français entre sujétion et citoyenneté* (Paris: La Découverte, 2007).

49. For discussions of race as a category of analysis in English-language scholarship on France, see Herrick Chapman and Laura Levine Frader, *Race in France: Interdisciplinary Perspectives on the Politics of Difference* (New York: Berghahn Books, 2004); Alec G. Hargreaves, *Immigration, 'Race' and Ethnicity in Contemporary France* (London: Routledge, 1995); Sue Peabody and Tyler Edward Stovall, *The Color of Liberty: Histories of Race in*

France (Durham, N.C.: Duke University Press, 2003); Maxim Silverman, *Race, Discourse, and Power in France* (Aldershot: Avebury, 1991); Tyler Edward Stovall and Georges Van den Abbeele, *French Civilization and Its Discontents: Nationalism, Colonialism, Race* (Lanham, Md.: Lexington Books, 2003); Herman Lebovics, *Bringing the Empire Back Home: France in the Global Age* (Durham, N.C.: Duke University Press, 2004); and Elizabeth Ezra, *The Colonial Unconscious: Race and Culture in Interwar France* (Ithaca, N.Y.: Cornell University Press, 2000). See also Naomi Davidson, *Only Muslim: Embodying Islam in Twentieth-Century France* (Ithaca, N.Y.: Cornell University Press, 2012). For discussions of race as a category of analysis elsewhere in Europe, see Rita C. K. Chin, *After the Nazi Racial State: Difference and Democracy in Germany and Europe* (Ann Arbor: University of Michigan Press, 2009); University of Birmingham Centre for Contemporary Cultural Studies, *The Empire Strikes Back: Race and Racism in 70s Britain* (London: Hutchinson, in association with the Centre for Contemporary Cultural Studies, University of Birmingham, 1982); Rita C. K. Chin, *The Guest Worker Question in Postwar Germany* (Cambridge: Cambridge University Press, 2007); Paul Gilroy, *"There Ain't No Black in the Union Jack"*; Tina Campt, *Other Germans: Black Germans and the Politics of Race, Gender, and Memory in the Third Reich* (Ann Arbor: University of Michigan Press, 2004); and Heide Fehrenbach, *Race after Hitler: Black Occupation Children in Postwar Germany and America* (Princeton, N.J.: Princeton University Press, 2005).

50. For recent discussions of Habermas and the public sphere, see Craig Calhoun, ed., *Habermas and the Public Sphere* (Boston: MIT Press, 1992); Dena Goodman, "Public Sphere and Private Life: Toward a Synthesis of Current Historiographical Approaches to the Old Regime," *History and Theory* 31 (1992): 1–20; Roger Chartier, *The Cultural Origins of the French Revolution* (Durham: University of North Carolina, 1991); Keith Michael Baker, "Public Opinion as Political Invention," in his *Inventing the French Revolution* (Cambridge: Cambridge University Press, 1990); Margaret C. Jacob, "The Mental Landscape of the Public Sphere: A European Perspective," *Eighteenth-Century Studies* 28 (1994): 95–113; and William Reddy, "Postmodernism and the Public Sphere: Implications for an Historical Ethnography," *Cultural Anthropology* 7 (1992): 135–169. See also the special forum in *French Historical Studies*, vol. 17 (1992).

PART I: MODERNIZING THE IMPERIAL CITY

1. An address by Le Corbusier to M. Claudius Petit, Minister of Reconstruction and Town Planning, on the inauguration of the Unité d'Habitation à Marseilles, October 14, 1952. http://www.fondationlecorbusier.fr/corbuweb/morpheus.aspx?sysId=13&IrisObjectId=5234&sysLanguage=en-en&itemPos=58&itemCount=78&sysParentName=home&sysParentId=64.

2. Corbusier has been both celebrated and maligned for his contribution to brutal modernism, and many have associated his housing prototypes with public housing designs in France as well as in other parts of Europe and the United States. But as Kenny Cupers points out, France's *grands ensembles* are in no way exact replicas of the Unité, and he has described a much more complex process through which architects, urbanists, and high-ranking French officials shaped postwar urbanism. See Kenny Cupers, *The Social Project*.

3. The phrase *"la maison du fada"* is a mix of French and Provençal. In Provençal, the word *fada*, means, literally, to be bewitched by fairies.

4. "Corbusier, Should He Be Condemned?" article clipping from *Le Provençal*, n.d., in Le Corbusier dossier, MMA 439 W 64.

5. Ibid.

1. "WE HAVE THE RIGHT TO A HOME!"

1. *Le Monde Ouvrier*, September 16, 1946.

2. Marius Apostolo, "Justice par effraction: Les squatters de Marseille et de provence, 1946–1954," in *La bataille des squatters*, ed. Duriez and Chauvière, 105.

3. Frederick Cooper, *Africa since 1940: The Past of the Present* (Cambridge: Cambridge University Press, 2002), 43.

4. Ibid., 41–42.

5. For studies on the ends of empire and post-1945 efforts to redefine citizenship in Britain and France, see Kathleen Paul, *Whitewashing Britain: Race and Citizenship in the Post-war Era* (Ithaca, N.Y.: Cornell University Press, 1997); Todd Shepard, *The Invention of Decolonization: The Algerian War and the Remaking of France* (Ithaca, N.Y.: Cornell University Press, 2006); Ian R. G. Spencer, *British Immigration Policy since 1939: The Making of Multi-Racial Britain* (New York: Routledge, 1997).

6. Historians have challenged the teleological thinking about rights discourses, specifically the tendency to describe human rights as a natural evolution from the Enlightenment to the 1948 Geneva Convention. For scholarship challenging the essentialization of human rights discourses, see Stefan-Ludwig Hoffmann, "Introduction: Genealogies of Human Rights," in *Human Rights in the Twentieth Century*, ed. Hoffmann; and Moyn, *Last Utopia*.

7. For discussion of race after 1945 and immutable cultural difference, see Martin Barker, *The New Racism: Conservatives and the Ideology of the Tribe* (Frederick, Md.: Alethia Books, 1982).

8. For studies of late-nineteenth and early-twentieth-century urban planning and social reform, see Chevalier, *Classes laborieuses et classes dangereuses à Paris pendant la première moitié du XIXe siècle*; Donzelot, *Policing of Families*; Elsie Canfora-Argandoña and Roger-Henri Guerrand, *La répartition de la population: Les conditions de logement des classes ouvrières à Paris au 19e siècle* (Paris: Centre de sociologie urbaine, 1976); Roger-Henri Guerrand, *Les origines du logement social en France* (Paris: Éditions ouvrières, 1966); Ann-Louise Shapiro, *Housing the Poor of Paris, 1850–1902* (Madison: University of Wisconsin Press, 1985).

9. Rosemary Wakeman, "Reconstruction and the Self-Help Housing Movement: The French Experience," *Housing Studies* 14, no. 3 (1999): 355–366, here 356.

10. Ibid.

11. In Britain, the 1919 Housing Act established the Council Housing system.

12. For discussion of the post–World War I housing crisis and subsequent social movements, see Tyler Edward Stovall, *Paris and the Spirit of 1919: Consumer Struggles, Transnationalism, and Revolution* (Cambridge: Cambridge University Press, 2012).

13. Flamand, *Loger le peuple*, 147.

14. Duriez and Chauvière, *La bataille des squatters*, 12.

15. Flamand, *Loger le peuple*, 147. Nearly one million homes were destroyed or desperately needed renovation in Britain. As one British POW recalled upon returning to his family's flat after the war, "you could not tell where the decay stopped and the bomb damage started." Quoted in Kesia Reeve, "Squatting since 1945," in *Housing and Social Policy: Contemporary Themes and Critical Perspectives*, ed. Peter Somerville and Nigel Sprigings (New York: Routledge, 2005), 200.

16. Wakeman, "Reconstruction and the Self-Help Housing Movement: The French Experience," 357.

17. Duriez and Chauvière, *La bataille des squatters*, 16.

18. Jacques Sbriglio, *Le Corbusier: L'unité d'habitation de Marseille et les autres unités d'habitation à Rezé-Les-Nantes, Berlin, Briey en Forêt et Firminy* (Paris: Fondation Le Corbusier, 2004), 120.

19. Marius Apostolo, "Justice par effraction: Les squatters de Marseille et de provence, 1946–1954," in *La bataille des squatters*, ed. Duriez and Chauvière, 105–106.

20. Their actions paralleled those of many homeless around Europe, particularly families in Great Britain. Many desperate British families began to reside illegally in rural military camps or unoccupied buildings in cities including Birmingham, Bristol, and London. For discussions of the postwar British housing crisis and the squatters' movement, see James Hinton, "Self-Help and Socialism, the Squatters' Movement of 1946," *History Workshop*, no. 25 (Spring 1988): 100–126; Noreen Branson, *History of the Communist Party of Great Britain 1941–1951* (London: Lawrence and Wishart, 1997), 118–128.

21. Apostolo, "Justice par effraction," 106.

22. Some of the local associations that participated in Henri Bernus's meeting included the Fédération Provençale des Sinistrés (Provençal Federation of Disaster Victims) and the Evacués et Réfugiés (Evacuated and Refugees).

23. Apostolo, "Justice par effraction," 108.

24. Ibid., 107.

25. Ibid., 109.

26. *Monde Ouvrier*, August 9–14, 1947.

27. Louis Guéry, "Façons de faire: Chroniques locales des années squats," in Duriez and Chauvière, *La bataille des squatters*, 170–173. In Britain, squatters also chose their squats strategically, including a number of luxury flats in the Duchess of Bedford House in Kensington, London. See Dianna Murray Hill, "Who Are the Squatters?" *Pilot Papers* 1, no. 4 (November 1946): 11–27.

28. *Monde Ouvrier*, August 9–14, 1947.

29. For discussion about the post-liberation moment in Marseille, see Robert Mencherini, *La libération et les entreprises sous gestion ouvrière, Marseille, 1944–1948* (Paris: L'Harmattan, 1994); and Robert Mencherini, *Ici-même: Marseille 1940–1944: De la défaite à la libération* (Marseille: J. Laffitte, 2013).

30. Many members of the provisional government favored the creation of a robust parliamentary system. Others, especially Charles de Gaulle, strongly condemned such a move. Blaming the parliament of the Third Republic for the defeat in 1940 and for Vichy, de Gaulle instead asserted the need for a strong executive branch. When he was ultimately outvoted, he resigned in disgust in 1946 and declared his retirement from public life.

31. In Great Britain, squatters' demands for shelter called into question the very mandate of the newly elected labor government to deliver on its promises of sweeping social change.

32. Letter from Henri Bernus, leader of Comité d'entente de squatters to the Prefect, February 27, 1947, ADBR 12 O 378.

33. For discussion about police raids, forced evictions, and collaboration with the Germans during World War II in Marseille, see Simon Kitson, "The Police and the Deportation of Jews from the Bouches-du-Rhône in August and September 1942," *Modern and Contemporary France* 5, no. 3 (August 1997): 309–319; Simon Kitson, "French Police, German Troops and the Destruction of the Old Districts of Marseille, 1943," in *Policing and War in Europe*, ed. Louis Knafla (Westport, Conn.: Greenwood Press, 2002), 133–144; Diana F. Ryan, *The Holocaust and the Jews of Marseille: The Enforcement of Anti-Semitic Politics in Vichy France* (Champaign: University of Illinois Press, 1996).

34. Letter from Henri Bernus, leader of Comité d'entente de squatters to the Prefect, February 27, 1947, ADBR 12 O 378.

35. Ibid., emphasis in the original.

36. Op-ed by Louis Haffray, *Monde Ouvrier*, April 5–11, 1947.

37. Ibid.

38. For discussion of efforts of peripheral groups to establish a moral authority in order to legitimate claims, see Partha Chatterjee, *The Politics of the Governed: Reflections on Popular Politics in Most of the World* (New York: Columbia University Press, 2004).

39. Mazower, *Dark Continent*, 194.

40. Mark Mazower has shown how the allies "repeatedly declared" the importance of defending "the rights of man . . . [as] one of the major purposes of the war." Mazower, *Dark Continent*, 149. Samuel Moyn has argued how "human rights . . . as a war slogan" was more of a "throwaway line [than] a well considered idea." Moyn, *Last Utopia*, 5.

41. Mark Mazower, *No Enchanted Palace: The End of Empire and the Ideological Origins of the United Nations* (Princeton, N.J.: Princeton University Press, 2008), 65; For additional studies on human rights and empire, see Roland Burke, *The Politics of Decolonization and the Evolution of International Human Rights* (Philadelphia: University of Pennsylvania Press, 2010); Fabian Close, "Source of Embarrassment: Human Rights, State of Emergency and the Wars of Decolonization," in *Human Rights in the Twentieth Century*, ed. Hoffmann, 237–257; Alice L. Conklin, "Colonialism and Human Rights: A Contradiction in Terms? The Case of France and West Africa, 1895–1914," *The American Historical Review* 103, no. 2 (1998): 419–442; and A. W. B. Simpson, *Human Rights and the End of Empire: Britain and the Genesis of the European Convention* (Oxford: Oxford University Press, 2001).

42. Jeannette Beaunez interview, conducted in 1985, in Geneviève Dermenjian, ed., *Femmes, familles et action ouvrière: Pratiques et responsabilités féminines dans les mouvements familiaux populaires 1935–1958* (Villeneuve d'Asq: Groupement pour la recherche sur les mouvements familiaux, 1991), 71.

43. Jean Moretton interview, conducted in 1984, in Duriez and Chauvière, *La bataille des squatters*, 135–136.

44. Memo to Ministry of Interior, Direction des Services Financiers et Contentieux Re: Eviction of Squatters, February 21, 1951, ADBR 12 O 378.

45. Created in 1939, the association was originally called the Ligue Ouvrière Chrétienne (LOC). The LOC was comprised of mostly working-class women and was the counterpoint to the Jeunesse Ouvrière Chretienne (JOC). In 1941, the LOC became the Mouvement Populaire des Familles. See Memo from Commissaire de Police, Direction Général de la Sureté Nationale, Ministry of Interior, to the Chef du Service Départemental des Renseignements Généraux, Marseille. Signature illegible. February 17, 1951, ADBR 12 O 378. See also Bruno Duriez, *Chrétiens et ouvriers en France, 1937–1970* (Paris: Atelier, 2001); and Bruno Duriez, ed., *Les Catholiques dans la République, 1905–2005* (Paris: Les éds. de l'atelier/Les éds. ouvrières, 2005).

46. *Des logement pour le peuple: Une solution propose par le Mouvement populaire des familles* (Paris: Les Editions Ouvrières, 1947), 16.

47. Op-ed by Louis Haffray, *Monde Ouvrier*, April 5–11, 1947. Such claims support recent scholarship demonstrating how many political Catholics—in an attempt to distance themselves from their far right leanings of the 1930s and 1940s—embraced postwar human rights talk as compatible with Christian ideas about the sacredness of the person. Such claims also reflect the emphasis some Catholic activists placed on social rights. For studies of personalism, political Catholicism, and postwar participation in human rights debates, see Samuel Moyn, "Personalism, Community, and the Origins of Human Rights," in *Human Rights in the Twentieth Century*, ed. Hoffmann, 85–106; and John Hellman, *Emmanuel Mounier and the New Catholic Left, 1930–1950* (Toronto: University of Toronto Press, 1981).

48. *Des logement pour le peuple*, 25.

49. This blurring of the universal language of human rights with the rhetoric of duty within a community is echoed in Catholic thought elsewhere. For example, in his 1942

work, *The Rights of Man and Natural Law,* Jacques Maritain wrote: "I have stressed the rights of the civic person . . . of the human individual as citizen." Mazower, *Dark Continent,* 193.

50. *Des logement pour le peuple,* 16.

51. *Monde Ouvrier,* February 25–March 3, 1950; *Monde Ouvrier,* July 22–28, 1950; *Monde Ouvrier,* numéro spécial, December 1950.

52. For example, French communists earned 26.2 percent, or the majority of the vote, in the 1945 election over the nascent MRP and the SFIO. And a somewhat reluctant de Gaulle also included communists in the cabinet of his provisional government. See M. Adereth, *The French Communist Party: A Critical History (1920–1984), from Comintern to the "Colours of France"* (Manchester: Manchester University Press, 1984), 141.

53. Eley, *Forging Democracy,* 289.

54. From two Thorez speeches, one at the tenth party congress in 1945, another to a group of coal miners in northern France. Both quoted in Adereth, *French Communist Party,* 141.

55. On political Catholicism in Europe and participation in the resistance, see Tom Buchanan and Martin Conway, eds., *Political Catholicism in Europe, 1918–1965* (Oxford: Oxford University Press, 1996); Jacques Duquesne, *Les Catholiques sous l'occupation* (Paris: B. Grasset, 1966); Duriez, *Les Catholiques dans la République.*

56. The Jeunesse Ouvrière Chrétienne (JOC), the precursor to the MPF, was strictly anticommunist in the interwar period. For a study of Catholic and communist tensions in the interwar period, see Susan B. Whitney, *Mobilizing Youth: Communists and Catholics in Interwar France* (Durham, N.C.: Duke University Press, 2009). For discussion of the "third way" politics of fascism, see Zeev Sternhell, *Neither Right nor Left: Fascist Ideology in France* (Princeton, N.J.: Princeton University Press, 1996); Hellman, *Emmanuel Mounier.*

57. Several members of the MPF, for example, joined the French resistance after 1943.

58. In Great Britain communists also played a role in the squatters' movement. While communist involvement helped bolster support for the movement in France, in Britain there was more widespread anticommunist sentiment. See Hill, "Who Are the Squatters?"

59. Letter from Prefect of the Bouches-du-Rhône to the Ministry of the Interior, March 14, 1947, ADBR 12 O 378; see also Report to the Ministry of the Interior, circa 1950, signature illegible, ADBR 12 O 378.

60. Note sur le Problème Squatter à Marseille, February 15, 1952, ADBR 12 O 378.

61. Note for the Prefect regarding the Marseille Squatter Problem, September 26, 1951. From A. Carli, ADBR 12 O 378.

62. Report from the Office of the Prefect of the Bouches-du-Rhône, September 26, 1951, ADBR 12 O 378.

63. Letter from the Prefect of the Bouches-du-Rhône to the Ministry of the Interior, March 14, 1947, ADBR 12 O 378.

64. A. Carli, Note for the Prefect Regarding the Marseille Squatter Problem, September 26, 1951, 4, ADBR 12 O 378, 5.

65. Letter from Prefect to Ministry of the Interior, March 14, year illegible, ADBR 12 O 378.

66. Letter from Prefect to Ministry of the Interior, circa 1949, ABDR 12 O 378.

67. Report to the Prefect of the Bouches-du-Rhône regarding the Marseille Squatter Problem, September 26, 1951, ABDR 12 O 378.

68. Wakeman, "Reconstruction and the Self-Help Housing Movement: The French Experience," 360.

69. For discussion of the role of Catholics in shaping French welfare institutions, see Nord, *France's New Deal.*

70. For the history of French public housing construction, see Newsome, *French Urban Planning, 1940–1968*; Jean-Marc Stébé, *Le logement social en France: 1789 à nos jours*, 2nd ed. (Paris: Presses universitaires de France, 2002); Cornuel and Duriez, *Le mirage urbain*; Effosse, *L'invention du logement aidé en France*; Flamand, *Loger le peuple*; Voldman, *La reconstruction des villes françaises de 1940 à 1954*.

71. Flamand, *Loger le peuple*, 135.

72. Raul Dautry, quoted in Flamand, *Loger le peuple*, 203.

73. According to a 1946 census, 63 percent of French homes did not have running water and only 5 percent had indoor toilets. Duriez and Chauvière, *La bataille des squatters*, 16.

74. For example, one central goal for MRU officials was to make modern amenities a standard feature in every home.

75. On modernism and shaping the built environment in the interwar and post–World War II periods on both sides of the Atlantic, see Christopher Klemek, *The Transatlantic Collapse of Urban Renewal Post-war Urbanisms from New York to Berlin* (Chicago: University of Chicago Press, 2011), 11; *Karl D. Qualls, From Ruins to Reconstruction: Urban Identity in Soviet Sevastopol after World War II* (Ithaca, N.Y.: Cornell University Press, 2009); *Gail Radford, Modern Housing for America: Policy Struggles in the New Deal Era* (Chicago: University of Chicago Press, 1996); *Nancy Stieber, Housing Design and Society in Amsterdam: Reconfiguring Urban Order and Identity, 1990–1920* (Chicago: University of Chicago Press, 1998).

76. For recent work on housing in Eastern and Soviet Europe, see Mark B. Smith, *Property of Communists: The Urban Housing Program from Stalin to Khrushchev* (DeKalb: Northern Illinois University Press, 2010); Kimberly Elman Zarecor, *Manufacturing a Socialist Modernity: Housing in Czechoslovakia, 1945–1960* (Pittsburgh: University of Pittsburgh Press, 2011). For studies of urban planning and social control in colonial Africa, see Rabinow, *French Modern*; Wright, *Politics of Design in French Colonial Urbanism*.

77. In addition to France, in Germany reconstruction also emphasized national rebirth. For studies of German reconstruction and coming to terms with the past, see Neil Gregor, *Haunted City: Nuremberg and the Nazi Past* (New Haven, Conn.: Yale University Press, 2008); Brian Ladd, *The Ghosts of Berlin: Confronting German History in the Urban Landscape* (Chicago: University of Chicago Press, 1998); Gavriel D. Rosenfeld and Paul B. Jaskot, eds., *Beyond Berlin: Twelve German Cities Confront the Nazi Past* (Ann Arbor: University of Michigan Press, 2008).

78. Raul Dautry, quoted in Flamand, *Loger le peuple*, 135.

79. Both Philip Nord's *France's New Deal* and Brian Newsome's *French Urban Planning* discuss continuities in welfare and housing institutions from the 1930s to the 1940s. See also Danièle Voldman, *Fernand Pouillon* (Paris: Payot, 2006), and Voldman, *La reconstruction des villes françaises de 1940 à 1954*.

80. Brian Newsome, "The Struggle for a Voice in the City: The Development of Participatory Architectural and Urban Planning in France, 1940–1968" (PhD diss., University of South Carolina, 2002), 62. In West Germany, allied leaders relied on regional and municipal officials and urban planners affiliated with the Third Reich to help articulate postwar plans for the new Germany.

81. In 1946, the provisional government ratified a new constitution, thereby establishing the Fourth Republic. With its strong parliament and a relatively weak executive branch, the French Fourth Republic looked a lot like the Third Republic. Like it, the Fourth Republic also had a staggering number of governments, with at least fourteen different administrations between 1947 and 1956. The head of the ministry often changed as frequently as the governments. For example, de Gaulle-appointed Dautry left the ministry in 1946 when de Gaulle resigned from the government. The MRU was briefly led by the staunch communist François Billoux, until he, along with all the other communist cabinet

members, were purged from the government in 1947. Adereth, *French Communist Party*, 148.

82. Danièle Voldman, "Aménager la region parisienne (février 1950–aout 1960)," *Cahiers de l'Institut d'histoire du temps présent*, no. 17 (1990): 49–54.

83. In Britain, the sluggishness of the postwar economy similarly slowed construction. In 1944, the British parliament passed the Housing (Temporary Accommodation) Act, which allowed for the construction of prefabricated homes intended to shelter families until new housing estates could be completed. Although it took several years before these prefabs were constructed in any significant numbers, by the early 1950s some families did benefit from this program. For studies of post–World War II reconstruction and planning in Britain, see Nicholas Bullock, *Building the Post-War World: Modern Architecture in Britain* (New York: Routledge, 2002); Alison Ravetz, *Council Housing and Culture: The History of a Social Experiment* (London: Routledge, 2001).

84. See Flamand, *Loger le peuple*, 198; and Newsome, "The Struggle for a Voice in the City," 118.

85. Note sur le Problème Squatter à Marseille, February 15, 1952, ADBR 12 O 378.

86. Memo from Feron, Director of Construction in the Ministry of Reconstruction and Urbanism to the Departmental Delegate of the Bouches-du-Rhône in Marseille, December 1, 1951, ADBR 12 O 378; Memo from Director of Territory Management in the Ministry of Reconstruction and Urbanism (signature illegible) to the Prefect of the Bouches-du-Rhône, November 22, 1952, ADBR 12 O 378.

87. Emile Temime, *Le camp du Grand Arénas, Marseille 1944–1966* (Paris: Autrement, 2001), 21.

88. At the onset of the war in Indochina, a large number of Vietnamese laborers were detained in Grand Arenas as potential enemy combatants to the state. Témime, Le camp du Grand Arénas, 34.

89. Témime, *Le camp du Grand Arénas*, 18.

90. For discussion of multiple uses of concentration camps after World War II, see Harold Marcuse, *Legacies of Dachau: The Uses and Abuses of a Concentration Camp, 1933–2001* (Cambridge: Cambridge University Press, 2001).

91. For example, Tara Zahra has recently shown how national claims to children in refugee camps became integral to the project of rebuilding Europe; Tara Zahra, *The Lost Children: Reconstructing Europe's Families after World War II* (Cambridge, Mass.: Harvard University Press, 2011). For more detailed discussion of concentration camps near Marseille, see Robert Mencherini and Yves Jeanmougin, *Mémoire du camp des Milles, 1939–1942* (Marseille: Métamorphoses-ben en l'air, 2013).

92. Interview: MB quoted in Témime, *Le camp du Grand Arénas*, 84.

93. The Grand Arenas barracks were designed by architect Fernand Pouillon and constructed in just several weeks. See Voldman, *Fernand Pouillon*, 85–90.

94. Témime, *Le camp du Grand Arénas*, 110.

95. Interview: CT quoted in Témime, *Le camp du Grand Arénas*, 86.

96. Ibid., 118.

97. Ibid.

98. Interview: JR and JS quoted in Témime, *Le camp du Grand Arénas*, 188.

99. *Monde Ouvrier*, March 3–9, 1951.

100. *Monde Ouvrier*, January 20–26, 1951.

101. *Des logement pour le peuple*, 30.

102. Ibid., 17–20.

103. Note sur le Problème Squatter à Marseille, no date, ADBR 12 O 378.

104. The Castors—a social Catholic group—were dedicated to housing poor French families and between 1950 and 1954 constructed about 8,000 houses in Marseille, Lille,

and Lyon. See also Wakeman, "Reconstruction and the Self-Help Housing Movement: The French Experience."

105. The national MPF, although initially affiliated with social Catholicism, officially broke with the Catholic Church in 1949. In Britain, the squatters' movement had also disbanded by the 1950s as the government relocated squatting families, stepped up efforts to build prefabs, and gradually expanded housing estates. See Hinton, "Self-Help and Socialism, the Squatters' Movement of 1946," 115–116.

106. For discussion of the rise of Christian Democratic parties in Europe, see Eley, *Forging Democracy*; Mazower, *Dark Continent*. For study of reconstruction in the growing Cold War context, specifically increasing hostilities between Christian Democrats and communists, see Patrick Thaddeus Jackson, *Civilizing the Enemy: German Reconstruction and the Invention of the West* (Ann Arbor: University of Michigan Press, 2006), 124–129.

107. Mazower, *Dark Continent*, 289.

108. Though a comprehensive history exploring Cold War tensions between communist dockworkers—who were also against the colonial wars—anticommunist French politicians, and the CIA in Marseille has yet to be written, the following secondary and primary sources begin to shed some light on this period. "Labor: The Most Dangerous Man," *Time Magazine*, March 17, 1952; "France: Death to Carlini!" *Time Magazine*, November 24, 1947; Alfred Pacini and Dominque Pons, *Docker à Marseille* (Paris: Payot/ Rivages, 1996); Rosemarie Scullion, "On the Waterfront: Class Action and Anti-Colonial Engagements in Paul Carpita's *Le Rendez-vous des quais*," *South Central Review* 17, no. 3 (Autumn 2000): 35–49; Alfred W. McCoy, *The Politics of Heroin: CIA Complicity in the Global Drug Trade* (Brooklyn, N.Y.: Lawrence Hill Books, 1991).

109. Letter from H. De Mouzon, head of Municipal Bureau of Hygiene to Departmental Engineer and Dr. Girbal, the municipal council member delegate of hygiene, January 12, 1956, AMM 483 W 223.

110. Departmental Director of Hygiene to the Prefect of the Bouches-du-Rhône, July 28, 1956, AMM 483 W 223.

111. Ibid.

112. Ibid.

113. Prefect of the Bouches-du-Rhône to Marseille Mayor Gaston Defferre, August 6, 1956, AMM 483 W 223.

114. Letter from Head of the TAM and Cleaning Services, Jean Mondet, to Marseille Secretary General, Jean Poggioli, August 1956, AMM 483 W 223.

115. Letter from R. Calloud, Departmental Satellite of Ministry of Reconstruction and Housing to Marseille Secretary General Jean Poggioli, September 17, 1956, AMM 483 W 223.

116. Report to the Prefect of the Bouches-du-Rhône regarding the Marseille Squatter Problem, September 26, 1951, ADBR 12 O 378.

117. Ibid.

118. For a discussion of the asocial category in terms of early 1960s debates about slum clearance, see Minayo Nasiali, "Ordering the Disorderly Slum: 'Standardizing' Quality of Life in Marseille Tenements and Bidonvilles, 1953–1962," *Journal of Urban History* 38, no. 6 (November 2012): 1021–1035.

119. See, for example, Chevalier, *Classes laborieuses et classes dangereuses*; Nye, *Crime, Madness, and Politics in Modern France*.

120. After World War II and the racial politics of the Third Reich, such terminology was supposedly no longer viable. French officials' use of this term, therefore, shows key continuities across the so-called 1945 divide. The utilization of the term "asocial" also underscores how racialized thinking was not imported from the Nazis but was central to French officials' understanding during both the Vichy regime and the Fourth Republic. For studies

on eugenics and biological notions of race, see Götz Aly, Peter Chroust, and Christian Pross, *Cleansing the Fatherland: Nazi Medicine and Racial Hygiene* (Baltimore: Johns Hopkins University Press, 1994); Michael Burleigh, *Death and Deliverance: "Euthanasia" in Germany c. 1900–1945* (Cambridge: Cambridge University Press, 1994); Stefan Kühl, *The Nazi Connection: Eugenics, American Racism, and German National Socialism* (Oxford: Oxford University Press, 1994); Richard Sonn, "Your Body Is Yours: Anarchism, Birth Control, and Eugenics in Interwar France," *Journal of the History of Sexuality* 14, no. 4 (2005): 415–432. For studies on the Vichy regime and France's role in initiating the deportation of Jews, see Robert O. Paxton, *Vichy France: Old Guard and New Order, 1940–1944* (New York: Knopf, 2001).

121. Letter from Engineer and Head of Departmental Services of the Ministry of Reconstruction and Housing to Marseille Secretary General Jean Poggioli, November 21, 1956, AMM 483 W 223.

122. Letter from R. Calloud, Departmental Satellite of Ministry of Reconstruction and Housing to Marseille Secretary General Jean Poggioli, September 17, 1956, AMM 483 W 223.

123. Note sur le Problème squatter à Marseille, no date, ADBR 12 O 378.

124. Ibid.

125. Demographic study of Grand Arenas shows that most residents were originally from colonies within the French Empire, and many were marked as having French "nationality." Report by R. Auzelle, Head of Urban Planning, city of Marseille, May 24, 1956, AMM 483 W 254.

126. Note sur le Problème squatter à Marseille, February 15, 1952, ADBR 12 O 378.

127. Ibid.

128. Témime, *Le camp du Grand Arénas*, 103.

129. Interview: CT quoted in Témime, *Le camp du Grand Arénas*, 86.

130. Letter from Jean Frassinet, Deputy from the Bouches-du-Rhône at the National Assembly to the Minister of Reconstruction, the Prefect of the Bouches-du-Rhône, Marseille Mayor Gaston Defferre, the Cleaning Services, September 15, 1959, AMM 483 W 254.

131. See, for example, Hannah Arendt, *The Origins of Totalitarianism* (New York: Harcourt Brace, 2004).

2. "WE HAVE THE RIGHT TO COMFORT"

1. Gaston Defferre interview in *Enterprise*, AMM 100 II 416.

2. Mayor Gaston Defferre, "The Role of the Mayor," n.d., AMM 483 W 257.

3. See Colette Ysmal, *La carrière politique de Gaston Defferre* (Paris: Fondation nationale des sciences politiques, 1965), 40–41; and Gaston Defferre interview from *Enterprise*, November 5, 1963, AMM 100 II 416.

4. For Marseille Mayor Gaston Deffere's multiple references to Marseille as the "California of Europe" and "Second City of France," see AMM 483 W 118; 483 W 257; and 100 II 416.

5. For discussion of early-twentieth-century urban planning and development projects in Marseille, see Donzel, *Le nouvel esprit de Marseille*.

6. Report from Marseille Mayor Gaston Defferre to the Central State regarding the City of Marseille's economic and social activities; March 23, 1961, AMM 483 W 118. See also Emmanuel Todd, *The Making of Modern France: Ideology, Politics and Culture* (Oxford: Blackwell, 1991).

7. Nonelected central state officials did, of course, play an important part in shaping postwar policies. Many of them did not claim any particular political allegiance and thus weathered the political upheavals of the Fourth and early Fifth Republics. See Cupers, *The Social Project*.

8. For studies of modernization in post–World War II France, see Herrick Chapman, *State Capitalism and Working-Class Radicalism in the French Aircraft Industry* (Berkeley: University of California Press, 1991); Herrick Chapman, "Review: Modernity and National Identity in Postwar France," *French Historical Studies* 22, no. 2 (1999): 291–314. For studies on central state institutions and urban development, see Newsome, *French Urban Planning 1940–1968*; Kenny Cupers, *The Social Project*; Jeane Haffner, *The View from Above: The Science of Social Space* (Cambridge, Mass.: MIT Press, 2014). For a classic study of modernization in a "provincial city," see Rosemary Wakeman, *Modernizing the Provincial City: Toulouse, 1945–1975* (Cambridge, Mass.: Harvard University Press, 1997).

9. For discussion of how welfare states and institutions help produce gendered categories, see Carole Pateman, "The Patriarchal Welfare State," in *Democracy and the Welfare State*, ed. Amy Gutman (Princeton, N.J.: Princeton University Press, 1988), 231–260; Kathleen Canning, *Gender History in Practice: Historical Perspectives on Bodies, Class and Citizenship* (Ithaca, N.Y.: Cornell University Press, 2005). For a discussion of gender and domestic space in the French context, see Nicole Rudolph, "At Home in Postwar France: The Design and Construction of Domestic Space, 1945–1975," PhD diss., New York University, 2005.

10. "Apartment of an Intelligent Couple," *Marseille Magazine*, n.d. on clipping but circa 1953, AMM 439 W 64.

11. Ibid.

12. Ibid.

13. Ibid.

14. But while Rudolph discusses how "comfort" was a concept that the French public learned from their exposure to modern mass housing, this chapter underscores how ordinary people articulated their own ideas about comfort—ideas that both shaped and sometimes contradicted developing discourses about modern living. Rudolph, *At Home in Postwar France*, 8.

15. Introduction, Study of Housing Needs, City of Marseille and Institut national de la statistique et des études économiques, December 20, 1960, ADBR 12 O 1839.

16. Study of Housing Needs, City of Marseille and Institut national de la statistique et des études économiques, December 20, 1960, 13, ADBR 12 O 1839.

17. Ibid., 11.

18. Ibid.

19. Ibid., 13.

20. Special issue of Marseille chamber of commerce periodical, n.d., 61, ADBR BETA 1004.

21. Victoria De Grazia, *Irresistible Empire: America's Advance through Twentieth-Century Europe* (Cambridge, Mass.: Belknap Press of Harvard University Press, 2005), 342.

22. Marseille City Council Meeting Minutes, October 12, 1959, 76, AMM 599 W 179.

23. Ibid., 80.

24. See, for example, Dossier de demandes de logement 1960, AMM 418 W 1; Dossier de demandes de logement 1963, AMM 418 W 2.

25. For detailed discussion of this period of experimentation at the MRU, see Rudolph, *At Home in Postwar France*, esp. chap. 1.

26. For an overview of housing and welfare in Sweden, see Helena Mattsson and Sven-Olov Wallenstein, eds., *Swedish Modernism: Architecture, Consumption and the Welfare State* (London: Black Dog Publishing, 2010).

27. For studies of post–World War II reconstruction and planning in Britain, see Nicholas Bullock, *Building the Post-War World*; Alison Ravetz, *Council Housing and Culture*.

28. Lyons, "Invisible Immigrants: Algerian Families and the French Welfare State, 1947–1974," 151.

29. Whereas previously, multiple architects and urban planning teams often worked on a single large development, under the new ZUP, a single team was responsible for constructing the various apartment buildings in a single *grand ensemble*. Although results were mixed, ZUP projects also attempted to create the infrastructure necessary to supporting large-scale housing developments, as many ZUPs included plans for constructing grocery stores, schools, and other necessities. See Rudolph, *At Home in Postwar France*, 189–190.

30. For a discussion of *les grands ensembles* and social mobility, see Annie Fourcaut, "Les premiers grands ensembles en région parisienne: Ne pas refaire la banlieue?" *French Historical Studies* 27, no. 1 (Winter 2004): 295–218.

31. Demande de Logement, Letter from Marseille resident named Dégand, n.d., circa 1969, AMM 540 W 9.

32. Letter from Nicolas L. to Municipal Housing Office, October 28, 1960, AMM 418 W 1.

33. Letter from Slimane T. to the Municipal Housing Office, letter received on September 9, 1960, AMM 418 W 1.

34. Ibid.

35. Ibid.

36. Ibid.

37. Paul Ginsborg, "The Politics of the Family in Twentieth-Century Europe," *Contemporary European History* 9, no. 3 (November 2000): 438.

38. Merith Niehuss, "French and German Family Policy 1945–60," *Contemporary European History* 4, no. 3 (November 1995): 293–313; here 300.

39. For a recent study of the family and normative understandings of gender, see Camille Robcis, *The Law of Kinship: Anthropology, Psychoanalysis, and the Family in Twentieth-Century France* (Ithaca, N.Y.: Cornell University Press, 2013).

40. Letter from Alexis G. to Municipal Housing Office, July 7, 1960, AMM 418 W 1.

41. Letter from Abdallah T. to Mayor Gaston Defferre, September 14, 1960, 1, AMM 418 W 1.

42. Ibid.

43. Letter from Mohamed B. to Mayor Gaston Defferre, September 20, 1960, redirected to Municipal Housing Office, 1, AMM 418 W 1.

44. Ibid., 2.

45. It is also worth noting that Mademoiselle D. A. was probably illiterate and paid a scribe to write the letter for her, evident from the differences between the handwriting of the letter and her own signature, written in painstaking block letters as "DIB." Letter from Mademoiselle D. A. to Marseille Housing Office, June 21, 1960, 2, AMM 418 W 1.

46. Letter from Abdelkader R. to Mayor Gaston Defferre, October 22, 1960, redirected to the Municipal Housing Office, 1, AMM 418 W 1.

47. Philippe Sanmarco, "Le clientélisme, comment ça marche? Clientélisme et politique en région Provence Alpes Côte d'Azur," in *Démocratie et territoires* (Université d'Aix-Marseille: Centre d'études en sciences sociales appliquées et appuis, recherche, éducation pour la négociation locale sur les environnements, 2003), 1–3.

48. Paul Jankowski, *Communism and Collaboration: Simon Sabiani and Politics in Marseille, 1919–1944* (New Haven, Conn.: Yale University Press, 1989), 14.

49. Jankowski, *Communism and Collaboration*, 16.

50. Ibid., 13.

51. Ibid.

52. For studies of clientelism and popular politics in North American cities, see Peter McCaffery, *When Bosses Ruled Philadelphia: The Emergence of the Republican Machine,*

1867–1933 (University Park: Pennsylvania State University Press, 1993); James J. Connolly, *The Triumph of Ethnic Progessivism: Urban Political Culture in Boston, 1900–1925* (Cambridge, Mass.: Harvard University Press, 1998).

53. For studies of patronage in early modern France, see Robert Harding, *Anatomy of a Power Elite: The Provincial Governors of Early Modern France* (New Haven, Conn.: Yale University Press, 1978); Sharon Kettering, *Patrons, Brokers and Clients in Seventeenth-Century France* (Oxford: Oxford University Press, 1986); Rouland Mousnier, *Les institutions de la France sous la monarchie absolue*, vol. 1: *Société et état* (Paris, 1974), 85–93. For early modern Europe more broadly, see F. W. Kent, Patricia Simons, and J. C. Eade, eds., *Patronage, Art, and Society in Renaissance Italy* (Oxford: Oxford University Press, 1987); Paula Clarke, *The Soderini and the Medici: Power and Patronage in Fifteenth-Century Florentine Society* (New York: Oxford University Press, 1991).

54. The Marseille city council was comprised of 63 members. After the first round of elections in 1953, the socialist party (SFIO) only won 18 percent of the vote, which amounted to 15 council members. The communists, led by François Billoux, had 24 council members, while the center right, conservative parties, and independents (MPR and RPF) contributed a smattering of elected officials to make up the rest of the council. Ysmal, *La carrière politique de Gaston Defferre*, 39–42.

55. Georges Marion, *Gaston Defferre* (Paris: Albin, 1989), 185. For a study of the PCF after 1958, see David Scott Bell and Byron Criddle, *The French Communist Party in the Fifth Republic* (Oxford: Oxford University Press, 1994).

56. For example, Guerini, who lost the mayoral election to incumbent Gaudin in the 2008 Marseille municipal elections, was the head of the OPHLM in the late 1960s.

57. Transcript of Marseille City Council Meeting Minutes, January 20, 1959, AMM 599 W 179. See also Transcript of Marseille City Council Meeting Minutes, July 6, 1959, 20–23, AMM 599 W 179.

58. Pacini and Pons, *Docker à Marseille*, 115.

59. Housing Commission Meetings: August 3, 1953; October 2, 1953; October 16, 1953; September 25, 1953, in AMM 468 W 179.

60. Ibid.

61. Ibid.

62. Transcript from Marseille City Council Meeting, July 6, 1959, 22–23, AMM, 599 W 179.

63. Pacini and Pons, *Docker à Marseille*, 115.

64. Ibid.

65. For further evidence of clientelistic practices between the socialist party and Marseille residents, see dossier: *Comité d'entente des locataires HLM de Montredon*, AMM 468 W 179.

66. See *Les demandes de logement* dossier, AMM 540 W 9.

67. Memo from the Marseille Commissariat de Police to Monsieur le Commissaire Divisionnaire in the Commissaire Central, June 26, 1960, AMM 483 W 149.

68. Ibid.

69. Of the eight families living in one of the collapsed buildings, four families were Italian, two were Spanish, and two were French. See Studies of Saint Lazare families and victims of Collapse, AMM 483 W 149.

70. Memo from Assistance Publique à Marseille to Gaston Defferre, Regarding: Furniture, rue du Caire, January 6, 1961, AMM 483 W 149; Memo from Marseille Secretary-General Jean Poggioli to Marseille Mayor Gaston Defferre, July 2, 1960, AMM 483 W 149.

71. Memo from Albert Villard, Head Architect, to Marseille Secretary-General Jean Poggioli, July 1, 1960, AMM 483 W 149.

72. Ibid.

73. *Le Provençal*, June 28, 1960.

74. *La Marseillaise*, June 28, 1960.

75. Louis Gazaganaire, *La Marseillaise*, July 12, 1960.

76. Memo from Marseille Secretary-General Jean Poggioli to Marseille Mayor Gaston Defferre, July 2, 1960, AMM, 483 W 149, 3.

77. Louis Gazaganaire, *La Marseillaise*, July 12, 1960.

78. Ibid.

79. Louis Gazaganaire, *La Marseillaise*, July 13, 1960.

80. Ibid.

81. Louis Gazaganiare, *La Marseillaise*, July 12, 1960.

82. Ibid.

83. The Saint Lazare disaster situates the efforts of the Marseille PCF within the broader history of communist involvement in local politics. As Tyler Stovall and Annie Fourcaut have shown for the Parisian red belt, and others have demonstrated in other European cities, notably Berlin and Vienna, historical explorations of local politics, everyday life, and municipal communism have offered a much more complicated picture of Europe's communist parties, one that richly supplements studies of the workplace and, especially for the post–World War II period, studies focusing on the problem of Stalinism and the party line. For classic studies of Paris's red belt, see Fourcaut, *Un siècle de banlieue parisienne 1859–1964*; Tyler Stovall, *The Rise of the Paris Red Belt* (Berkeley: University of California, 1990). For scholarship on communism and local politics in other European cities, see Helmut Gruber, *Red Vienna: Experiment in Working-class Culture, 1919–1934* (New York: Oxford University Press, 1991); Pamela E. Swett, *Neighbors and Enemies: The Culture of Radicalism in Berlin, 1929–1933* (Cambridge: Cambridge University Press, 2004); Sara Ann Sewell, "Bolshevizing Communist Women: The Red Women and Girls' League in Weimar Germany," *Central European History* 45, no. 2 (June 2012): 268–305.

84. Cesare Mattina has described Marseille as "a plural city, formed by a multitude of neighborhoods . . . each with their own unique identity." Cesare Mattina, "Des médiateurs locaux: Les presidents des comités d'intéret de quartier autour de la rue de la République," in *Métropolisation, gouvernance et citoyenneté dans la region urbaine marseillaise*, ed. Donzel, 269–291; here 269.

85. I credit one of the anonymous reviewers of the manuscript for first making this point and for encouraging me to situate CIQs within the broader history of associational life in France.

86. Peraldi and Samson, *Gouverner Marseille*, 18.

87. Mattina, "Des médiateurs locaux," 269–291; here 269.

88. As Michel Peraldi and Michel Samson explain: "Very quickly, *notables* [i.e., elected officials and politicians] saw in CIQs a beneficial political machine [that was] easy to harness." Peraldi and Samson, *Gouverner Marseille*, 8.

89. Mattina, "Des médiateurs locaux," in Donzel, *Métropolisation, gouvernance et citoyenneté*, 269–291; here 270. See also Albert Rochu, *Les années Defferre* (Paris: Alain Moreau, 1983), quoted in Mattina, "Des médiateurs locaux," 269–291.

90. For example, both Lyon and Toulon have a formalized network of neighborhood associations called Les comités d'intérêts locaux.

91. See dossier: CIQ Sainte Marthe, in AMM 483 W 10.

92. Memo from J. Couteaud, Engineer and chief of the Marseille *ponts et chaussés* to Marseille Mayor Gaston Defferre, July 4, 1956, AMM 483 W 223.

93. Petition to mayor Gaston Defferre from residents of the La Renaude housing complex, July 1968, AMM 468 W 179.

94. Memo from Arnaud R., president of the Association des locataires du group HLM, Saint-Charles 3eme, to Marseille Mayor Gaston Defferre, February 7, 1962, AMM 468 W 179.

95. Memo from President of the Belle-de-Mai CIQ to Marseille Secretary-General Jean Poggioli, November 21, 1963, AMM 483 W 10.

96. Letter from Jean Maquart to Jean Poggioli, January 6, 1964, 1–3, AMM 483 W 10.

97. Ibid., 3.

98. Letter from Marseille Secretary-General Jean Poggioli to President of the Belle-de-Mai CIQ, January 13, 1946, AMM 483 W 10.

99. Pacini and Pons, *Docker à Marseille*, 22.

100. See Shannon Lee Fogg, *The Politics of Everyday Life in Vichy, France: Foreigners, Undesirables, and Strangers* (Cambridge: Cambridge University Press, 2009).

101. Pacini and Pons, *Docker à Marseille*, 13.

102. As such, their story not only contributes to a more nuanced understanding of the politics of everyday life in postwar Marseille but also adds more broadly to studies of migration and belonging, particularly scholarship treating the importance of local space in shaping notions of identity. In recent years, studies of Berlin's predominately Turkish neighborhood of Kreuzberg, or London's Southeast Asian community along Brick Lane, have contributed an important European perspective to the already robust study of space and identity formation in North American cities. For work on Kreuzberg, see Levent Soysal, "Rap, Hip-hop, Kreuzberg: Scripts of/for Migrant Youth Culture in the World City Berlin," *New German Critique* 92 (Spring–Summer 2004): 62–81. For Southeast Asians in East London, see Claire Alexander, "Making Bengali Brick Lane: Claiming and Contesting Space in East London," *The British Journal of Sociology* 62, no. 2 (June 2011): 201–220. For extensive work on identity and space in American cities, particularly Los Angeles, see George J. Sanchez, *Becoming Mexican American: Ethnicity, Culture and Identity in Chicano Los Angeles, 1900–1945* (New York: Oxford University Press, 1993); Mark Wild, *Street Meeting: Multiethnic Neighborhoods in Early Twentieth-Century Los Angeles* (Berkeley: University of California Press, 2005); Isabela Seong-Leong Quintana, "National Borders, Neighborhood Boundaries: Gender, Space and Border Formation in Chinese and Mexican Los Angeles, 1871–1938," PhD diss., University of Michigan, 2010.

3. ORDERING THE DISORDERLY SLUM

1. *Marseille Magazine*, no. 28 (1954), 22–23, AMM 439 W 25.

2. Letter from Médecin Directeur du Bureau Municipale d'Hygiène to Doctor Girbal, adjoint délègue a l'Hygiène, Re: Dénonciation de taudis Enclos Peysonnel, November 16, 1951, AMM 439 W 25.

3. For studies of the Algerian War of Independence, see Raphaëlle Branche and Charles Robert Ageron, *La guerre d'indépendance des Algériens: 1954–1962* (Paris: Perrin, 2009); Benjamin Stora, *Histoire de la Guerre d'algérie (1954–1962)*, 4th ed. (Paris: La Découverte, 2004).

4. Scholarship on the "social question" and the development of social-scientific methods includes Donzelot, *Policing of Families*; Horne, *Social Laboratory for Modern France*; Aisenberg, *Contagion*.

5. Studies of nineteenth-century anxieties about urban decline and the pathologies of modern life include Chevalier, *Classes laborieuses et classes dangereuses*; Nye, *Crime, Madness, and Politics in Modern France*; Pick, *Faces of Degeneration*; Barnes, *Making of a Social Disease*.

6. Gabrielle Hecht, *The Radiance of France: Nuclear Power and National Identity after World War II* (Cambridge, Mass.: MIT Press, 1998), 28.

7. Rabinow, *French Modern*, 9. For other discussions of the technocrat and technocracy, see Kuisel, *Capitalism and the State in Modern France*; Richard F. Kuisel, *Ernest Mercier: French Technocrat* (Berkeley: University of California Press, 1967).

8. Gabrielle Hecht specifically employs the term *techniciens* in *The Radiance of France*.

9. Rabinow, *French Modern*, 9.

10. The urban planning and public health departments collaborated closely at the municipal and departmental levels, each contributing empirical data on slums and residents. Members from the four departments also sat on two key councils: the council of public health and the council of urban planning. These councils were comprised of local architects, engineers, and medical doctors with particular expertise in issues of urban planning and public health.

11. Jean B. and Marcel Coen, "M. l'Abbé Pierre, connaissez-vous l'enclos Peysonnel, Cour des Miracles de tous les épaves de Marseille," *Marseille Magazine*, no. 28, (1954), 22–23, AMM 439 W 25.

12. Ibid.

13. Ibid.

14. Ibid., 25.

15. On colonial exhibition and putting "natives on display," see Yael Simpson Fletcher, "Capital of the Colonies: Real and Imagined Boundaries between Metropole and Empire in 1920s Marseille," in *Imperial Cities: Landscape, Display and Identity*, ed. Felix Driver and David Gilbert (Manchester: Manchester University Press, 1999), 134–151; Nadja Durbach, "London, Capital of Exotic Exhibitions from 1830 to 1860," in *Human Zoos: Science and Spectacle in the Age of Colonial Empires*, ed. Pascal Blanchard (Liverpool: Liverpool University Press, 2008), 81–88.

16. The Canebière is the main road that runs through downtown Marseille. Jean B. and Marcel Coen, "M. l'Abbé Pierre, connaissez-vous l'enclos Peysonnel, Cour des Miracles de tous les épaves de Marseille," *Marseille Magazine*, no. 28, (1954), 24, AMM 439 W 25.

17. Pamphlet from the Ministère de la reconstruction et du logement, *La lutte contre les taudis et la rénovation de l'habitat défectueux*, 13–18, AMM 439 W 31.

18. Ibid.

19. Ibid.

20. André Hardy, *Rapport de l'habitat défectueux et la politique du logement*, 1951, 1, AMM 439 W 31.

21. Ibid.

22. Ibid.

23. Memo from the Ministère de la reconstruction et de l'urbanisme to Direction de l'aménagement du territoire service des affaires foncières, de l'habitat et du logement, February 10, 1952, 1, AMM 439 W 31. For a more detailed discussion of Robert Auzelle's contribution to postwar French urbanism, as well as the housing studies more specifically, see Kenny Cupers, *Social Project*, 73–74.

24. Memo from the Ministère de la reconstruction et de l'urbanisme to Direction de l'aménagement du territoire service des affaires foncières, de l'habitat et du logement, February 10, 1952, 4, AMM 439 W 31.

25. Letter from Médecin directeur du bureau municipale d'hygiène to Doctor Girbal, *adjoint délègue á l'hygiène*, Regarding the *Dénonciation de taudis Enclos Peysonnel*, November 16, 1951, AMM 439 W 25.

26. Ibid.

27. "Terrains Peysonnel, Enquête Sommaire, Ville de Marseille, Directions des services techniques, Bureau central d'études," September 29, 1954, AMM 439 W 25.

28. Ibid.

29. Ibid.

30. If any resident of the *îlot* desired to receive mail, they all apparently gave their address as 1 rue Peysonnel no matter where they lived in the slum. As was the custom for

many in Marseille at the time, most mail was delivered to a local bar and collected later by its owner.

31. For documentation on quantitative methods for determining sociability and *salubrité* scores, see AMM 439 W 25; 483 W 254; 468 W 179.

32. For instances when local *techniciens* noted "nationality," see multiple household studies from AMM 439 W 25.

33. See multiple household studies from AMM 439 W 25.

34. Studies on the ambiguous position of colonial subjects as "not quite French" include Clifford D. Rosenberg, *Policing Paris: The Origins of Modern Immigration Control between the Wars* (Ithaca, N.Y.: Cornell University Press, 2006); Lewis, *Boundaries of the Republic*.

35. For a discussion of the developing French immigration system, see Rosenberg, *Policing Paris*.

36. Fogg, *Politics of Everyday Life in Vichy, France*.

37. Ibid., 88.

38. For example, individual housing studies for the rue des Honneurs, and the *Abris de Defense Passive* did not note the nationality of residents, AMM 483 W 254.

39. Moreover, in 1956 studies of two slums, Feracci distinguished between the French and the Spanish residents of the *boulevard Corderie* and the Russian, Armenian, and French residents of the Camp de Sainte Anne; AMM 483 W 254.

40. For discussion of local perceptions and assumptions about Marseille's downtown port district, see Mary Dewhurst Lewis, "The Strangeness of Foreigners: Policing Migration and Nation in Interwar Marseille," *French Politics, Culture and Society* 20, no. 3 (Fall 2002): 65–96.

41. Another possibility for why Feracci added the nationality category might have pertained to the allocation of family benefits. He might have wanted to determine whether slum families were eligible for benefits called *les allocations familiales*, allowances that were intended to supplement monthly earnings and help French families. Families often used these benefits to supplement their rent payments. Therefore, noting the nationality of a family could have been an indicator of the amount of monthly income families were entitled to and whether or not they could afford the rent in new public housing. Interestingly, in the studies where Feracci documented the nationality of a family as well as whether they were entitled to *les allocations familiales*, he noted that quite a few non-French families were receiving monthly benefits—for example, in Camp de Sainte Anne, several families Feracci noted as Armenian. In addition to Armenians, in other *îlots insalubres* around Marseille, Italians, Greeks, and several Russians also received *allocations familiales*. It is possible that these families were French even though Feracci noted otherwise. However, in a town where clientelism played a large role in everyday life, it is not surprising that families with some connections could still procure monthly benefits even if they were not French.

42. For studies of Marseille slums and tenements in the 1950s and 1960s, see AMM 483 W 254.

43. Gaston Defferre letter to MRU, December 12, 1960, 1, AMM 455 W 44.

44. Letter from Lacroix, Directeur des Services Techniques de la Ville de Marseille, to Directeur Départemental du Ministère de la Construction, n. d., AMM 455 W 44.

45. Projet de Construction de 240 Logements de Transition, AMM 455 W 45.

46. Clearing Marseille's city center of slums and redeveloping downtown was a key goal for the municipal government. Officials had to decide on new locations for housing displaced residents, and the barren and eclectically developed city outskirts became the most desirable choice.

47. Letter from Mayor Gaston Defferre to Monsieur Leroy, Directeur Général de l'Agence Technique Caisse des Depots and Consignations Re: La Paternelle, June 12, 1959, AMM 455 W 45.

48. Projet de Construction de 240 Logements de Transition, Marseille Municipal Archives, 455 W 45.

49. Ibid.

50. Ibid.

51. Letter from Pouchot, Société marseillaise mixte de construction et d'aménagements communaux to Gaston Defferre, July 16, 1959, AMM 483 W 167.

52. Memo from Société central pour l'équipement de territoire to Prefect, October 26, 1959, MMA, 483 W 167; Memo from Poggioli, Secretary-General to Pouchot, March 18, 1961, AMM 483 W 167.

53. Letter from Pouchot, November 4, 1959, AMM 483 W 167.

54. Poggioli to Commissaire de Police, September 5, 1964, AMM 483 W 167.

55. Letter from Poggioli, April 1960, AMM 483 W 167.

56. The Fonds d'action sociale (FAS) was initially created in 1947 under the name Fonds d'action sanitaire et social. Its main purpose was to provide some financial assistance to workers and families in search of better housing and some services promoting hygiene. In 1956, the Ministry of the Interior created a fund for the construction of housing for Algerian workers in the metropole, or SONACOTRAL. This credit society was supposed to work with HLM offices to create dormitory-style housing for the single-male Algerian workers in the metropole. For more discussion see Lyons, "Invisible Immigrants: Algerian Families and the French Welfare State, 1947–1974"; Amelia Lyons, *Civilizing Mission in the Metropole.*

57. Sophie Josset, *Le FAS: 1958–1998.* Internal Report commissioned by the Fonds d'action sociale, 1998. From the private library of the FASILD, 11.

58. Marc Bernadot, "Une politique du logement: Sonacotra (1956–1992)" (Sorbonne, 1997), 48.

59. Circular no. 65 from the Ministry of the Interior, February 10, 1958, quoted in Josset, *Le FAS*, 13.

60. See Lyons, *Civilizing Mission in the Metropole*, 48.

61. From Gaston Defferre: Financement du Programme des 2,000 logements, n. d., AMM 455 W 44.

62. Gaston Defferre to Pierre Sudreau, MRL, October 24, 1960, AMM 483 W 245; Poggioli, Secretary-General to Prefect, January 9, 1961, AMM 483 W 245; Poggioli to Prefect, December 21, 1961, AMM 483 W 245.

63. Letter from Gaston Defferre to Pierre Sudreau, October 24, 1960, AMM 483 W 245.

64. Gaston Defferre to SONACOTRAL, February 1, 1961, AMM 455 W 44.

65. Poggioli to Prefect, December 21, 1960, AMM 483 W 245.

66. Hauw, David, "Les opérations de relogement en habitat collectif à Casablanca, de la vision des aménageurs aux pratiques des habitants" (PhD diss., Université François Rabelais, Tours, 2004), 35.

67. For recent work on the local experience of the Algerian War of Independence in the metropole, see Raphaëlle Branche, Sylvie Thénault, and Marie-Claude Albert, *La France en guerre, 1954–1962: Expériences métropolitaines de la guerre d'indépendance algérienne* (Paris: Autrement, 2008).

PART II: THE WELFARE CITY IN DECLINE?

1. *Le Provençal*, August 26, 1973.

2. Ibid.

3. Ibid.

4. Ibid.

5. *Le Provençal*, August 26, 1973.

6. Ibid.

7. *Le Provençal*, August 29, 1973.

8. *Le Provençal*, August 27, 1973.

9. *Le Provençal*, August 30, 1973.

10. *Le Meridional*, August 26, 1973.

11. Another group called the French Committee for a Pan European Union published an article calling on the government to "cease activities [committed] by the north African underworld in France." *Le Meridional*, August 27, 1973.

12. *Le Meridional*, August 27, 1973.

13. *La Marseillaise*, August 29, 1973. See also "Two Algerians Succomb to Their Wounds," *La Marseillaise*, August 31, 1972.

14. See crime reports in *Le Provençal*, August 31–September 2, 1973.

15. *Le Provençal*, August 31, 1973.

4. MANAGING THE QUALITY AND QUANTITY OF THE POPULATION

1. See William Schneider, *Quality and Quantity: The Quest for Biological Regeneration in Twentieth-Century France* (Cambridge: Cambridge University Press, 1990).

2. See Robert A. Nye, "The Bio-Medical Origins of Urban Sociology," *Journal of Contemporary History* 20, no. 4 (October 1985): 659–675. See also Cesare Lombroso, Mary Gibson, and Nicole Hahn Rafter, *Criminal Man* (Durham, N.C.: Duke University Press, 2006).

3. For the most recent discussion of social science and imperialism, see Conklin, *In the Museum of Man*.

4. Jordi and Témime, *Marseille et le choc des décolonisations: Les Rapatriements*, 1954–1964, 67.

5. Ibid., 151.

6. Ibid., 71.

7. Memo from director of public health to the prefect, October 8, 1962, ADBR 12 O 1793.

8. For discussion of the 1962 exodus and *rapatriés* in Marseille and France more broadly, see Jean-Jacques Jordi, *1962, l'arrivée des pieds-noirs* (Paris: Ed. Autrement, 1995); Jean-Jacques Jordi, *De l'exode à l'exil: Rapatriés et pied-noirs en France: L'exemple marseillais, 1954–1992* (Paris: L'Harmattan, 1993).

9. Memo regarding complaint of Monsieur P. to the prefect, October 8, 1962, ADBR 12 O 1793.

10. Jordi and Témime, *Marseille et le choc des décolonisations*, 71.

11. Ibid.

12. Ibid., 72.

13. Ibid.

14. Gaston Defferre article, *Le Provençal*, clipping, circa 1962, ADBR 12 O 1792.

15. The term *pieds noirs*—literally "black feet"—referred to the diverse population of settlers in Algeria and included people from France as well as other parts of southern Europe such as Spain and Malta. As Michel Abitbol points out, the term also applied to Algeria's Jewish population. Granted French citizenship in 1870 under the Crémieux decree (although their citizenship was revoked during the Vichy regime), Algerian Jews formed an important part of the exodus of 1962 and, as French citizens, qualified for the many programs aimed at fully repatriating *pieds noirs* and integrating them into the polity. See Michel Abitbol and Alan Astro, "The Integration of North African Jews in France," *Yale French Studies* 85 (1994): 248–261; and Nancy Wood, "Remembering the Jews of Algeria," in *French Civilization and Its Discontents*, ed. Tyler Stovall and Georges van den Abbeele (Lanham, Md.: Lexington Books, 2003), 251–270.

16. Gaston Defferre article, *Le Provençal*, clipping, circa 1962, ABDR 12 O 1792.

17. Ibid.

18. Ibid.

19. Ibid.

20. Minstère des rapatriés, Notice de renseignements sur le prêt du ministère des rapatriés pour l'achat d'un logement, n.d., ADBR 12 O 1791.

21. Memo from G. Pompidou, Le premier minister, to all departmental Prefects, September 1, 1962, ADBR 12 O 1791.

22. Ibid.

23. Ibid.

24. Memo from Jacques Aubert, Service des affaires musulmans, Ministry of the Interior, to all French departmental Prefects, September 17, 1963, AMM 468 W 150, 1.

25. As Todd Shepard argues, this legal distinction excluded Algerians from the new definition of Frenchness based on "common-sense understandings of racial or ethnic difference"; Shepard, *Invention of Decolonization*, 12.

26. Memo from Jacques Aubert, Service des affaires musulmans, Ministry of the Interior, to all departmental Prefects. September 17, 1963, AMM 468 W 150, 1.

27. See Lyons, "Invisible Families."

28. Memo from Jacques Aubert, Service des affaires musulmans, Ministry of the Interior, to all departmental Prefects. September 17, 1963, AMM 468 W 150, 2.

29. See letters in AMM 468 W 150, particularly: Letter from Jean Calvelli, Director of the Cabinet, Marseille Mayor's office to Bouches-du-Rhône Departmental Prefect, January 16, 1964; Letter from Marseille Mayor Gaston Defferre to Bouches-du-Rhône Departmental Prefect regarding continued aid for Algerians, April 22, 1964.

30. Memo to Bouches-du-Rhône Departmental Prefect, Re: Aide aux Nord-Africains, Subvention du département, March 24, 1964, AMM 468 W 150, 2.

31. Ibid., 1–2.

32. Ibid., 2.

33. Memo from Jacques Aubert, Service des affaires musulmans, Ministry of the Interior, to all departmental Prefects. September 17, 1963, AMM 468 W 150, 2.

34. Memo from Ministère des rapatriés: service d'accueil et de reclassement des français d'Indochine et des français Musulmans, to all French departmental prefects, May 28, 1963, ADBR 12 O 1791.

35. La migration algérienne et l'administration française by Michel Massenet, report, no date but circa 1964, CACF 19770391, art. 9, 2.

36. Ibid., 3.

37. Ibid., 4.

38. Ibid., 7.

39. See Silverman, *Deconstructing the Nation*, 43. See also James D. Le Sueur, *The Decolonization Reader* (New York: Routledge, 2003).

40. Memo from Jacques Aubert, Service des affaires musulmans, Ministry of the Interior, to all departmental prefects. September 17, 1963, AMM 468 W 150, 1.

41. Ibid.

42. For discussion of French "amnesia" following the Algerian War of Independence, see Benjamin Stora, *La gangrene et l'oubli: La mémoire de la guerre d'Algérie* (Paris: La Decouverte, 1991).

43. La migration algérienne et l'administration française by Michel Massenet, report, n. d. but circa 1964, CACF 19770391, art. 9, 6.

44. Ibid.

45. Ibid., 5.

46. Ibid., 8.

47. Mireille Ginesy-Galano, *Les immigrés hors la cité: Le système d'encadrement dans les foyers, 1973–1982* (Paris: L'Harmattan/CIEM, 1984), 47–48.

48. The dormitories often had strict rules about visitors, and some even maintained curfews. Even though conditions were often poor—with exceptionally unsanitary conditions and few amenities—residents paid rent, and these fees tended to be high. Each SONACOTRA dormitory was managed by a director, and in 1972, 95 percent of resident directors had worked in the colonial administration or participated in military actions in Indochina or Africa. Residents often complained that the European residents received unmerited privileges and special treatment, and that those from North or sub-Saharan Africa experienced discrimination. These foyers thus illuminate the legacy of imperialism in their everyday management as well as in how they offered a certain idea of welfare decoupled from citizenship; Lyons, "Invisible Immigrants," 336. For a detailed description of life in the SONACOTRA foyers as well as discussion of the rent strikes of the 1970s, see Ginesy-Galano, *Les immigrés hors la cité*.

49. La migration algérienne et l'administration française by Michel Massenet, report, n. d. but circa 1964, CACF 19770391, art. 9, 6–9.

50. Ibid., 7–9.

51. Ibid.

52. Minutes of the meeting of the Groupe de synthèse régional de la promotion des migrants, November 17, 1965, CACF 19770391, art. 9, 4.

53. Ibid., 5.

54. Ginesy-Galano, *Les immigrés hors la cité*, 33.

55. For francophone literature on *les cités de transit*, see Vincent Viet, "La politique du logement des immigrés (1945–1990)," *Vingtième siècle* 64, no. 1 (1999): 91–103; Jean-Paul Tricart, "Genèse d'un dispositive d'assistance: Les 'cités de transit,'" *Revue française de sociologie* 18, no. 4 (October–December 1977): 601–624; Claude Liscia, "Miroir sans reflet: La famille dans les cités de transit," *Esprit* 5, no. 65 (Mai 1982): 43–60.

56. Letter from Mayor Gaston Defferre to Claude Pellat, President of the Comité interprofessionel du logement des Bouches-du-Rhône, May 5, 1966, AMM 483 W 245.

57. Ibid.

58. Memo from Ministère des Rapatriés: Service d'accueil et de reclassement des Français d'Indochine et des Français Musulmans, to all French departmental prefects, May 28, 1963, ADBR 12 O 1791, 2.

59. Sylvie Jarry, "La promotion et le logement des familles handicapées sociales," CLARB report, May 1976, AMM 748 W 7, 25.

60. Ibid.

61. Ibid.

62. Ibid.

63. Ibid., 26.

64. Ibid.

65. Ibid.

66. Ibid., 27–28.

67. Patrick Weil, "Racisme et discrimination dans la politique française de l'immigration 1938–1945/1974–1995," *Vingtième siècle* 47 (July–September 1995): 77–102, here 80; Patrick Weil, "Immigration and the Rise of Racism in France: The Contradictions in Mitterrand's Policies," *French Politics and Society* 9, no. 3/4 (Summer/Fall 1991): 82–100. See also Andrés Reggiani, "Procreating France: The Politics of Demography, 1919–1945," *French Historical Studies* 19, no. 3 (Spring 1996): 725–754; Alexis Spire, *Etrangers à la carte. L'administration de l'immigration en France (1945–1975)* (Paris: Grasset, 2005);

Paul-André Rosental, "Pour une histoire politique des populations," *Annales. Histoire, Sciences Sociales* 1 (January–February 2006): 7–29.

68. In Lyon, for example, LOGIREL worked closely with the local institution Notre Dame des sans abri. See, for example, CACF 19770391, art. 7.

69. Minutes, second meeting of the Groupe de synthèse régional de la promotion des migrants, January 28, 1966, CACF 19770391, art. 9.

70. See, for example, Lyons, *Civilizing Mission in the Metropole*.

71. See, for example, Hargreaves, *Immigration, 'Race' and Ethnicity in Contemporary France*.

72. Silverman, *Deconstructing the Nation*, 44–45.

73. Gary P. Freeman, *Immigrant Labor and Racial Conflict in Industrial Societies: The French and British Experience, 1945–1975* (Princeton, N.J.: Princeton University Press, 1979); Bernard Granotier, *Les travailleurs immigrés en France*, 3rd ed. (Paris: F. Maspero, 1976).

74. Lyons, "Invisible Familles," 301–304. See also Minutes of the meeting of the Groupe de synthèse régional de la promotion des migrants, November 17, 1965, CACF 19770391, art. 9, 2.

75. Lyons, "Invisible Families," 301–304.

76. Freeman, *Immigrant Labor and Racial Conflict in Industrial Societies*, 157–158.

77. *Le Provençal*, August 31, 1973.

78. Hargreaves, *Immigration, 'Race' and Ethnicity in Contemporary France*, 19.

79. Alain Girard, Yves Charbit, and Marie-Laurence Lamy, "Attitudes des français à l'égard de l'immigration étrangère. Nouvelle enquête d'opinion," *Population*, 29e année, no. 6 (November–December 1974): 1015–1069, esp. 1021.

80. Ibid., 1015–1069, esp. 1021.

81. Ibid., 1015–1069, esp. 1028.

82. In a 1971 study, Girard also addressed the problematic nature of referring to black Africans and North Africans as distinct nationalities, specifying that their choice to label these diverse groups as such was based on the fact that "the public does not distinguish or always clarify between Algerians, Moroccans and Tunisians, [or] between Senegalese and Malians." Alain Girard, "Attitudes des français a l'égard de l'immigration étrangère, Enquête d'opinion publique," *Population*, 26e année, no. 5 (September–October 1971): 827–875, esp. 836.

83. Alain Girard, Yves Charbit, and Marie-Laurence Lamy, "Attitudes des français à l'égard de l'immigration étrangère. Nouvelle enquête d'opinion," *Population*, 29e année, no. 6 (November–December 1974): 1015–1069, esp. 1032.

84. Ibid., 1015–1069, esp. 1031.

85. Ibid.

86. Alain Girard, "Attitudes des français a l'égard de l'immigration étrangère, Enquête d'opinion publique," *Population*, 26e année, no. 5 (September–October 1971): 827–875, esp. 851.

87. Freeman, *Immigrant Labor and Racial Conflict in Industrial Societies*, 157.

88. Massenet, quoted in Freeman, *Immigrant Labor and Racial Conflict in Industrial Societies*, 157.

89. Ibid.

90. Ibid.

91. Freeman, *Immigrant Labor and Racial Conflict in Industrial Societies*, 159.

92. Other academics, notably Hervé Le Bras, also participated in a sustained critique of the notion of France's so-called threshold of tolerance.

93. Alain Girard, *L'homme et le nombre des hommes: Essais sur les conséquences de la révolution démographique* (Paris: Presses Universitaires de France, 1984), 304–305.

94. Ibid., 304.

95. Centre interuniversitaire de recherche et de documentation sur les migrations, "Le seuil de tolérance aux étrangers," *Sociologie du sud-est*, numéro spécial, no. 5/6 (Juillet–Octobre 1975).

96. René Duchac, "Avant-propos," in Centre interuniversitaire de recherche et de documentation sur les migrations, "Le seuil de tolérance aux étrangers," 7–9, esp. 7; Carmel Camilleri, "Seuil de tolérance et perception de la différence," in Centre interuniversitaire de recherche et de documentation sur les migrations, "Le seuil de tolérance aux étrangers," 15–24, esp. 15.

97. Camilleri, "Seuil de tolérance et perception de la différence," 15–24, esp. 22.

98. René Duchac, "Le seuil de tolérance aux étrangers: Avatars d'un concept en situation de migration international," in Centre interuniversitaire de recherche et de documentation sur les migrations, "Le seuil de tolérance aux étrangers," *Sociologie du sud-est*, numéro spécial, no. 5/6 (Juillet–Octobre 1975): 25–39, esp. 27.

99. Camilleri, "Seuil de tolérance et perception de la différence," 15–24, esp. 23.

100. Duchac, "Le seuil de tolérance aux étrangers," 25–39, esp. 33–34.

101. While Germans were ranked least favorably in these immediate postwar studies, Italians and Spanish were ranked only somewhat favorably alongside North Africans. Only later, in studies from the 1970s, did Italians and Spanish rise dramatically in rankings to be considered the most favorable immigrants, while North Africans and black Africans fell to the least favorable ranking. Alain Girard, "Le problème démographique et l'évolution du sentiment public," *Population* (French Edition), 5e année, no. 2 (April–June 1950): 333–352, esp. 341.

102. Duchac, "Le seuil de tolérance aux étrangers: Avatars d'un concept en situation de migration international," in Centre interuniversitaire de recherche et de documentation sur les migrations, "Le seuil de tolérance aux étrangers," *Sociologie du sud-est*, numéro spécial, no. 5/6 (Juillet–Octobre 1975): 25–39, esp. 34.

103. Ibid., 25–39, esp. 35.

104. Girard, *L'homme et le nombre des hommes*, 306.

105. Ibid., 307.

106. Ibid.

107. See Patrick Weil, "Racisme et discrimination"; Hervé Le Bras, *Le sol et le sang* (La Tour d'Aigues: Editions de l'Aube, 1994).

108. For discussions of the paradoxes of and inherent tensions within the French model of republicanism, see Wilder, *Imperial-Nation State*, and Joan Scott, *Only Paradoxes to Offer: French Feminists and the Rights of Man* (Cambridge, Mass.: Harvard University Press, 1996).

109. For discussion of population analysis and immigration in twentieth-century France, see Sandrine Bertaux, "'Processus' et 'population' dans l'analyse démographique de l'immigration en France (1932–1996)," in *L'invention des populations: Biologique, idéologie et politique*, ed. Hervé Le Bras (Paris: Editions Odile Jacob, 2000).

110. Alain Drouard, "La création de l'INED," *Population*, 47e année, no. 6 (novembre–decembre 1992): 1453–1466, esp. 1455.

111. Alfred Sauvy, quoted in Drouard, "La création de l'INED," 1453–1466, esp. 1455–1456.

112. "Loi du 17 novembre 1941 créant la Fondation française pour l'études des problèmes humains," quoted in Andrés Horacio Reggiani, *God's Eugenicist: Alexis Carrel and the Sociobiology of Decline* (New York: Berghahn Books, 2007), 112.

113. "Carrel Foundation Maps Study of Man," *New York Times*, December 7, 1941, quoted in Reggiani, *God's Eugenicist*, 112.

114. See Joshua Cole, *The Power of Large Numbers: Population, Politics, and Gender in Nineteenth-Century France* (Ithaca, N.Y.: Cornell University Press, 2000).

115. Girard, *L'homme et le nombre des hommes*, 22.

5. NEIGHBORHOODS IN CRISIS

1. *Macro et Micro Frontières à Marseille*, n.d., circa 1978, ADBR 8 J 354.

2. "Study of Three Neighborhoods," n.d., ADBR Beta 745.

3. *Macro et Micro Frontières à Marseille*, n.d., circa 1978, ADBR 8 J 354.

4. For example, another Saint Marcel resident recalled tense relations between French residents and Italian migrants in the early twentieth century: "When the Italians first arrived, they lived in the part of the village known as Petit Piémont . . . Italians couldn't intermarry with French, and I can speak with knowledge because my father is originally Italian, and my mother is French, and it was a great problem when they married . . . it was a big problem." *Macro et Micro Frontières à Marseille*, n.d., circa 1978, ADBR 8 J 354.

5. Although Saint Marcel is in the eastern outskirts of the city, many residents equated so-called problems in their neighborhood with issues they believed epitomized Marseille's northern neighborhoods, or *quartiers nord*. Such concerns help to complicate the long-held consensus that Marseille's neighborhoods are best characterized by a north-south divide, with the city's affluent areas in the southern part of the city and the poorer areas to the north. Most important, Saint Marcel illustrates how such distinctions are themselves constructed and are part of a geographical but also imagined topography of city life.

6. "Les Banlieues de la Peur," *Le Nouvel Observateur*, June 18, 1973.

7. Interestingly, although Marseille's northern and eastern neighborhoods are distinct from the peripheral areas of other French cities—they are not suburbs but *part of* Marseille—public opinion nevertheless tended to conflate anxieties about Marseille's so-called *quartiers nords* with concerns about other French cities' *banlieues*.

8. See Timothy Smith, *France in Crisis: Welfare, Inequality and Globalization since 1980* (Cambridge: Cambridge University Press, 2004), esp. 6:149–175.

9. Smith, *France in Crisis*, 7:176–211.

10. For discussion of the New Left, see Eley, *Forging Democracy*; Robin Archer, *Out of Apathy: Voices of the New Left Thirty Years On* (London: Verso, 1989). For the French Left, see Tony Judt, *The Burden of Responsibility: Blum, Camus, Aron, and the French Twentieth Century* (Chicago: University of Chicago Press, 1998); Tony Judt, *Marxism and the French Left: Studies in Labour and Politics in France, 1830–1981* (Oxford: Oxford University Press, 1986); Tony Judt, *Past Imperfect: French Intellectuals, 1944–1956* (Berkeley: University of California Press, 1992).

11. Commission sociale sur le problème des migrants, Séance du 8 Juin 1977, Procès Verbal, ADBR 1447 W 2.

12. Memo from G. Lacroix, Inspecteur général des services techniques to Social Workers of La Cayolle, Cité provisoire de la Cayolle, January 3, 1978, AMM 753 W 60, 2.

13. Meeting minutes, Service de liaison et de promotion des migrants, Préfecture des Bouches-du-Rhône, January 7, 1976, AMM 753 W 60, 4.

14. Paul Chombart de Lauwe, *Famille et Habitation*, Centre National de la Recherche Scientifique, 1960.

15. Sarcelles was one of the largest *grands ensembles* constructed in France, with nearly 13,000 apartments in a vast complex located about ten miles north of the Paris city center. For discussion of "Sarcellite," see Loic Vadelorge, "Villes nouvelles et grands ensembles," *Histoire Urbaine* 17, no. 3 (2006): 67–84; Alain Vulbeau, "De la Sarcellite au malaise des banlieues: Trente ans de pathologie des grands ensembles," *Lumières de la ville* 5 (1992): 31–37.

16. Michael Mulvey, "Sheltering French Families: Parisian Suburbia and the Politics of Housing, 1939–1975" (PhD diss., University of North Carolina–Chapel Hill, 2011), 138–139.

17. For more extensive discussion of the Ministère de l'Equipement et du Logement and the shift toward constructing single-family homes, see Rudolph, *At Home in Postwar France*, esp. 6:186–222.

18. For Castells's classic work on social movements, see Manuel Castells, *The City and Grassroots: A Cross-Cultural Theory of Urban Social Movements* (Berkeley: University of California Press, 1983).

19. CERFISE was the Marseille-based center of CERFI, which was originally founded by Félix Guattari.

20. For a detailed discussion of the *Opération Million* project, see chapter 2.

21. Michel Anselme, *Du bruit à la parole: La scène politique des cités* (La Tour d'Aigues: Editions de l'Aube, 2000), 24.

22. Ibid., 35–36.

23. Ibid., 90.

24. Ibid., 33. For other studies of resident participation in Marseille's northern neighborhoods, see Michel Anselme, *Entrevues citadines: Les flamants, Marseille* (Marseille: Cerfise, 1988); Michel Anselme, "La formation des nouveaux territoires urbains et leur 'crise': Les quartiers nord de Marseille," *Peuples Méditerranéens*, no. 43 (April–June 1988): 121–130; Jean-Louis Parisis, *Office Public d'HLM de Marseille, Paroles de locataires 1919–1989* (Avignon: A. Barthélemy, 1989); Michel Peraldi, "Les noms du social dans l'urbain en crise," *Peuples Méditerranéens*, no. 43 (Avril–Juin 1988): 5–22.

25. Report, Ministère de l'équipement et du logement, December 15, 1971, CACF 19790367 art. 9. See also Report by André Trintignac, Administrateur civil chargé de mission, "Les dispositifs de concertation sur les problèmes de l'habitat," Groupe permanent de coordination "Habitat et vie sociale," February 1974. CACF, where he notes: "It is thus necessary to assess the opinion of these habitants, including facilitating dialogue between renter and management organisms (OPHLMs) and encouraging the participation of neighborhood associations."

26. See Dossier on the Développement sociale des Quartiers, ADBR 1451 W 111.

27. Circulaire du ministère de l'urbanisme et du logement, décret du 28 Octobre 1988. Quoted in Doytcheva, *Une discrimination positive à la française*, 44.

28. Circulaire du Premier Ministre du 22 mai 1989, quoted in Doytcheva, *Une discrimination positive à la française*, 49.

29. Doytcheva, *Une discrimination positive à la française*, 45.

30. Ibid., 41l.

31. Grand Saint Barthélemy refers to a cluster of *cités* in Marseille's 14th *arrondissement* including La Busserine, Saint Barthélémy 3, Picon, Le Mail, Les Flamants, Iris, Font-Vert, and Benausse. Saint Barthélémy is alternatively spelled Barthélemy, but the residents of the neighborhood utilize the former, which is how I've chosed to reproduce it here.

32. For discussion of the Saint Lazare collapse, see chapter 2.

33. For discussion of associational life in other *grands ensembles*, see Cupers, *The Social Project*, especially the chapter on participation and resident associations in Sarcelles, 137–166.

34. "Paroles de locataires," from the office archive of Comité Mam'ega in St. Barthélemy cité, Marseille 13004.

35. "Ega Panneau" from the office archive of Comité Mam'ega in St. Barthélemy cité, Marseille 13004.

36. Ega was especially committed to promoting literacy and was herself an accomplished writer although she had not completed degrees in higher education. In addition to working

with St. Barthélemy children on their reading and writing skills, Ega also helped migrant women who did not speak French as a first language with their administrative papers; http://www.vivreensemble.org/spip.php?article5.

37. "Panneau ses combats," from the office archive of Comité Mam'Ega, St. Barthélemy cité, Marseille 13004. Although Françoise Ega died prematurely in 1976, her contribution to St. Barthélemy life helped to encourage a legacy of resident participation and activism in local issues.

38. Jean-Louis Parisis, *La Logirem à 40 ans:1960–2000* (Marseille: Logirem, 2000), 30.

39. Ibid.

40. Another fight with LOGIREM centered on suspiciously high utility bills. As Jacques Marty recalled, "heating bills had become exorbitant, and when we investigated, we found several irregularities." To address the problem of the high heating charges, residents first met with LOGIREM. And when such meetings failed, many residents agreed to collectively stop paying their utility bills in protest of the high rates. Ultimately, residents were reimbursed for having been overcharged for heat in the amount of "12 or 13 million [francs]."

41. Plan de development d'un quartier: Le quartier de St. Barthélemy, by the Union Nationale des Federations d'Organismes d'Habitations à Loyer Moderé, Association Regionale de Provence-Alpes-Cotes d'Azur et de Corse, n.d., ADBR 1447 W 39, 1.

42. Plan de development d'un quartier: Le quartier de St. Barthélemy, by the Union nationale des fédérations d'organismes d'habitations à loyer moderé, Association Régionale de Provence-Alpes-Cotes d'Azur et de Corse, n.d., ADBR 1447 W 39, 3.

43. Ibid.

44. "Collectif expérimental de pré-attribution, compte-rendu de la réunion du 16/11/1983," ADBR 1447 W 39.

45. I have changed the names of these residents.

46. "Collectif de pré-attribution du 3 octobre 1984," ADBR 1447 W 39.

47. Collectif d'attribution Saint Barthélemy-Busserine-Picon, by Centre d'étude et de recherche sur les pratiques de l'espace (CERFISE), January 1–June 1, 1984, ADBR1447 W 39, 2.

48. Collectif de pre-attribution, Compte-rendu de la réunion 8 fevrier 1984, ADBR 1447 W 39.

49. Maitrise d'oeuvre social St. Barthélemy, by Centre d'étude et de recherche sur les pratiques de l'espace (CERFISE), February 1985, ADBR 1447 W 40, 4.

50. Collectif de pré-attribution, Compte-rendu de la réunion 8 février 1984, ADBR1447 W 39.

51. Ibid.

52. Collectif expérimental de pré-attribution compte-rendu de la réunion du 16/11/1983, ADBR 1447 W 39, 2.

53. Collectif de pré-attribution, Compte-rendu de la réunion 8 février 1984, ADBR1447 W 39.

54. Ibid.

55. Commission sociale sur le problème des Migrants, Séance du 8 Juin 1977, Procès Verbal, ADBR 1447 W 2.

56. Report: The Promotion and Housing of Socially Handicapped Families, Comité de liaison pour l'aide et resorption des bidonvilles, 1976, AMM 748 W 7.

57. Commission sociale sur le problème des Migrants, Séance du 8 Juin 1977, Procès Verbal, ADBR 1447 W 2.

58. Ibid.

59. See my discussion of the threshold of tolerance in chapter 5.

60. I have changed the names of the residents in this section. Collectif de pré-attribution, Procès-Verbal de la réunion du 8 février 1984, ADBR 1447 W 38.

61. Collectif de pré-attribution de Saint-Barthélemy, Procès verbal de la réunion du 4/7/1984, ADBR 1447 W 39, 2.

62. Ibid.

63. Collectif de pré-attribution de Saint-Barthélemy, Procès verbal de la réunion du 4/7/1984, ADBR 1447 W 39, 3.

64. Collectif de pré-attribution du 10 octobre 1984, ADBR 1447 W 39.

65. Letter from F. Deleuze, M. Candel, to the Collectif de Pré Attribution de Saint Barthélemy, 12 mai 1985, ADBR 1447 W 39.

66. Ibid.

67. Ibid.

68. Ibid.

69. Ibid.

70. Maitrise d'Oeuvre Social St. Barthélemy, by Centre d'étude et de recherche sur les pratiques de l'espace (CERFISE), February 1985, ADBR 1447 W 40, 34; italics in original.

71. Ibid., 36.

72. Ibid., 29.

73. Ibid., 4.

74. Ibid.; italics in original.

75. Ibid., 36.

76. For discussion of Habermas and alternative public spheres, see Calhoun, ed., *Habermas and the Public Sphere.*

77. Les Français Musulmans de la cité des Tilleuls à Marseille, report by Jacques Barou, Septembre 1984, ADBR 2137 W 108, 2 and 14.

78. *Le Monde*, January 24, 1975; *L'Union*, January 24, 1975; *Ouest France*, January 23, 1976; *Le Monde*, July 24, 1976.

79. Les Français Musulmans de la cité des Tilleuls à Marseille, report by Jacques Barou, Septembre 1984, ADBR 2137 W 108, 15.

80. Compte rendu, Meeting of January 15, 1985, with the Amicale des locataires de la cité des Tilleuls, ADBR 2137 W 108.

81. In recent studies scholars have examined how "*harki*" emerged as both a political and ethnic category during and after the Algerian war. For example, Todd Shepard and others have discussed how French officials distinguished *harkis* from *pieds noirs* and other Algerians. See, for example, Shepard, *The Invention of Decolonization.*

82. Les Français Musulmans de la cité des Tilleuls à Marseille, report by Jacques Barou, Septembre 1984, ADBR 2137 W 108, 25.

83. Les Français Musulmans de la cité des Tilleuls à Marseille, report by Jacques Barou, Septembre 1984, ADBR 2137 W 108, 11–13.

84. Letter from Michel Gagneux of SONACOTRA to Monsieur Santini, Secrétaire d'état aux rapatriés, September 10, 1986, ADBR 2137 W 108, 1.

85. See Patrcia Lorcin, *Imperial Identities: Stereotyping, Prejudice and Race in Colonial Algeria* (London: St. Martin's, 1995).

86. Les Français Musulmans de la cité des Tilleuls à Marseille, report by Jacques Barou, Septembre 1984, ADBR 2137 W 108, 7–8.

87. Ibid., 1.

88. Ibid., 22.

89. Composition des Familles de la Cité—Les Tilleuls de Marseille, n.d., ADBR 2137 W 108.

90. Letter from Michel Gagneux of SONACOTRA to Monsieur Santini, Secrétaire d'état aux rapatriés, September 10, 1986, ADBR 2137 W 108, 1.

91. Les Français Musulmans de la cité des Tilleuls à Marseille, report by Jacques Barou, Septembre 1984, ADBR 2137 W 108, 21–22.

92. Ibid., p. 22.

93. Ibid., p. 13.

94. Letter from Michel Gagneux of SONACOTRA to Monsieur Santini, Secrétaire d'état aux rapatriés, September 10, 1986, ADBR 2137 W 108, p. 1.

95. Ibid.

96. Les Français Musulmans de la cité des Tilleuls à Marseille, report by Jacques Barou, Septembre 1984, ADBR 2137 W 108, p. 22.

97. Letter from Bureau de l'action sociale française d'origine nord-africaine, Ministère du travail to Monsieur le Chef du Département 'Logement des Familles' SONACOTRA, September 29, 1976, ADBR 2137 W 108.

6. *BANLIEUE* YOUTH AND THE BODY POLITIC

1. "Ibrahim Ali. Retour sur un drame inoubliable," 00269 Le Média des Comoriens du Monde, http://www.00269.net/IBRAHIM-ALI-Retour-sur-un-drame-inoubliable_a261 .html.

2. Ibid.

3. Ibid.

4. Ibid.

5. *Le Provençal*, February 23, 1995.

6. Herman Lebovics, *True France: The Wars over Cultural Identity, 1900–1945* (Ithaca, N.Y.: Cornell University Press, 1994).

7. For discussion of the head-scarf affair and debates about "immigrant girls," see Trica Keaton, *Muslim Girls and the Other France: Race, Identity Politics and Social Exclusion* (Bloomington: University of Indiana Press, 2006); Saïd Bouamama, *L'affaire du foulard Islamique: La production d'un racisme respectable* (Roubaix: Geai bleu, 2004); John Richard Bowen, *Why the French Don't Like Headscarves: Islam, the State, and Public Space* (Princeton, N.J.: Princeton University Press, 2007); Françoise Gaspard and Farhad Khosrokhavar, *Le foulard et la république* (Paris: La Découverte, 1995); Joan Wallach Scott, *The Politics of the Veil* (Princeton, N.J.: Princeton University Press, 2007).

8. For discussion of 'immigrant youth,' juvenile delinquency, and the *banlieue*, see Joëlle Bordet, *Les "Jeunes de la cité"*, 1st ed. (Paris: Presses universitaires de France, 1998); Jean-Claude Boyer, *Les banlieues en France: Territoires et sociétés* (Paris: Armand Colin, 2000); Jacques Brun et al., *La segrégation dans la ville: Concepts et mesures* (Paris: L'Harmattan, 1994); Pierre Bruno, *Existe-t-il une culture adolescente?* (Paris: In press, 2000); Michel Kokoreff, *La force des quartiers: De la délinquance à l'engagement politique* (Paris: Payot, 2003); Jean-Marie Petitclerc, *Les nouvelles délinquances des jeunes: Violences urbaines et réponses éducatives* (Paris: Dunod, 2001).

9. "Les Banlieues de la Peur," *Le Nouvel Observateur*, June 18, 1973.

10. Report: The Promotion and Housing of Socially Handicapped Families, Comité de liaison pour l'Aide et Résorption des Bidonvilles, 1976, AMM 748 W 7.

11. Ibid.

12. Ibid., and Report: Juvenile Deliquency and Prevention, Ministry of Youth and Sports, April, 2, 1973, CACF 19790367 art. 13.

13. Report: Juvenile Deliquency and Prevention, Ministry of Youth and Sports, April, 2, 1973, CACF, 19790367 art. 13.

14. Report: The Promotion and Housing of Socially Handicapped Families, Comité de Liaison pour l'Aide et Resorption des Bidonvilles, 1976, AMM 748 W 7.

15. Ibid.

16. Minutes from Marseille City Council Meeting, March 28, 1975. AMM 599 W 217. See also AMM 599 W 219.

17. Susan J. Terrio, "You'll Get Your Day in Court: Judging Delinquent Youth at the Paris Palace of Justice," *Political and Legal Anthropology Review*, no. 26 (2003): 142.

18. Sarah Fishman, *The Battle for Children: World War II, Youth Crime, and Juvenile Justice in Twentieth-Century France* (Cambridge, Mass.: Harvard University Press, 2000), 20.

19. Some scholars have recently argued, however, that juvenile courts have begun to shift away from a rehabilitative to a more punitive approach in the last thirty years. With the spike of "immigrant" youth crimes beginning in the 1970s, some government officials recommended overturning the 1945 law and returning to a more punitive form of juvenile justice. Terrio argues that, since the 1970s, juvenile justice in France has shifted toward more punitive rather than rehabilitative measures including a greater tendency to try juveniles as adults and harsher punishments for offenses. Terrio, "You'll Get Your Day in Court."

20. Terrio, "You'll Get Your Day in Court," 137.

21. Ibid., 142.

22. François Dubet, *La Galère: Jeunes en survie* (Paris: Fayard, 1987).

23. Alain Touraine, Jon Clark, and Marco Diani, *Alain Touraine, Consensus and Controversy* (London: Falmer Press, 1996).

24. Ibid., 55.

25. Dubet, *La galère*.

26. One of the anonymous reviewers of the manuscript was immensely helpful in extrapolating the deeper history of the term *la galère*.

27. Dubet, *La galère*, 23.

28. In constructing *la galère* as a collective experience, Dubet conducted interviews with five sets of youths from five different *banlieues*. They were a mix of "immigrants and French" and between eighteen and twenty-five years of age: "The youth who came to our groups were really the image of the problem we wanted to study: they were most often unemployed, or following internships; four of them had achieved the baccalaureat; most had engaged in delinquent activities; some had done drugs or had been addicts, and several had been to prison" (ibid.). In other words, in defining his sample, Dubet chose youth who fit his image of *la galère*.

29. Ibid., 15.

30. Ibid., 23.

31. For discussion of the *banlieue rouge*, see Annie Fourcaut, *La banlieue en morceaux*; Annie Fourcaut, *Bobigny, Banlieue Rouge* (Paris: Editions ouvrières: Presses de la Fondation nationale des sciences politiques, 1986); Tyler Stovall, *The Rise of the Paris Red Belt*. For studies that integrate the late-twentieth-century *banlieue* into the longer history of the *banlieue* as an unruly, undisciplined space, see Frédéric Dufaux, Annie Fourcaut, and Rémi Skoutelsky, *Faire l'histoire des grands ensembles: Bibliographie, 1950–1980* (Lyon: ENS éditions, 2003); Annie Fourcaut, Emmanuel Bellanger, and Mathieu Flonneau, *Paris-Banlieues, conflits et solidarités: Historiographie, anthologie, chronologie, 1788–2006* (Paris: Creaphis, 2007); Annie Fourcaut and École normale supérieure de Fontenay-Saint-Cloud. Centre d'histoire urbaine, *La ville divisée: Les ségrégations urbaines en question: France XVIIIe–XXe siècles* (Grâne: Créaphis, 1996).

32. Dubet, *La galère*, 23.

33. For discussion of the relationship between social exclusion and post-industrialism, see Loïc Wacquant, "Urban Marginality in the Coming Millennium," *Urban Studies* 36, no. 10 (1999): 1639–1647.

34. Dubet, *La galère*, 24.

35. Ibid., 23–24.

36. Concerts were held in Vitry sur Seine, Marseille, Paris, and Lyon. Saïd Bouamama, *Dix ans de Marche des Beurs: Chronique d'un mouvement avorté* (Paris: Desclée de Brouwer, 1994), 36–37.

37. Between 1981 and 1983, youth from various neighborhoods around France organized a series of free concerts: "Rock against Police"; "the idea wasn't just to organize concerts as the single goal, but for the music we drew from the example of the experience of the British who organized large concerts: Rock against Racism. But with two differences: large concerts held on neutral ground, like Hyde Park, didn't serve to do anything: the people came as consumers. We always organized our concerts in our territory, where police battered our friends. We preferred Rock against Police to Rock against Racism, because everyone calls themselves antiracists"; quoted in Bouamama, *Dix ans de Marche des Beurs*, 36. From "Les Lascars s'organisent" Interview de Rock against Police, in *Questions clefs*, no. 2, 1982. Bouamama, *Dix ans de Marche des Beurs*, 53: "these actors defined themselves as immigrant youth and proletariats of the banlieues.... It was a movement expressing the rage of the *cités* through the common tool of rock." "[T]here was a discourse of radial critique of society, which reflected the lived experience of exclusion." Bouamama, *Dix ans de Marche des Beurs*, 37.

38. "Les Lascars s'organisent" Interview de Rock against Police, in *Questions clefs*, no. 2, 1982. Quoted in Bouamama, *Dix ans de Marche des Beurs*, 36.

39. Pamphlet, "Marche pour l'Egalité et contre le Racisme," ADBR, 1451 W 111.

40. Ibid.

41. La Cayolle was also the site of a recent bombing by the Comité Charles Martel, a far Right terrorist group that killed an eleven-year-old boy of Roma descent. The Charles Martel terrorist group took its name from Charles Martel, a Frankish military leader who successfully defended France from an invading force of Andalusian Muslims in 732. The Charles Martel Club, as it is also known, staged a series of terrorist attacks during and after the Algerian War of Independence, including a number of kidnappings and bombings. For references to the La Cayolle bombing in Marseille, see "Chemin de la Cayolle: Explosions Racistes," *L'Express*, http://www.lexpress.fr/informations/explosions-racistes _677755.html, and Mogniss H. Abdallah, "15 octobre 1983 à Marseille: Top depart de la March pour l'égalité et contre le racisme," http://www.med-in-marseille.info/spip.php ?article2153.

42. Abdallah, "15 octobre 1983 à Marseille."

43. Françoise Gaspard, *A Small City in France* (Cambridge, Mass.: Harvard University Press, 1995).

44. Bouamama, *Dix ans de Marche des Beurs*, 46 and 68.

45. *Le Monde*, July 25, 1980, also quoted in Catherine Wihtol de Wenden and Rémy Leveau, *La Beurgeoisie: Les trois âges de la vie associative issue de l'immigration* (Paris: CNRS, 2001), 26. Writings by Tahar Ben Jelloun include Tahar Ben Jelloun, *Hospitalité française: Racisme et immigration maghrébine* (Paris: Seuil, 1984); Tahar Ben Jelloun, *Le racisme expliqué à ma fille* (Paris: Seuil, 1998).

46. Catherine Wihtol de Wenden and Leveau, *La Beurgeoisie: Les trois âges de la vie associative issue de l'immigration*, 22.

47. Bouamama, *Dix ans de Marche des Beurs*, 46 and 68.

48. Ibid., 69.

49. Marilaure Mahé, "25 ans jour pour jour après l'arrivée de la March, une (authentique) Marcheuse pour l'égalité prend sa plume," http://www.med-in-marseille.info/spip .php?article305.

50. Bouamama, *Dix ans de Marche des Beurs*, 43.

51. Ibid.

52. For Désir's account of the early years and mission of SOS Racisme, see his memoir, Harlem Désir, *Touche pas à mon pôte* (Paris: B. Grasset, 1985).

53. Wihtol de Wenden and Leveau, *La Beurgeoisie*, 34.

54. For discussion of SOS Racisme's antiracist agenda, see Dominique Sopo, *S.O.S. Antiracisme* (Paris: Denoël, 2005).

55. See chapter 4.

56. The rise of the National Front (FN) and the decline of the French communist party (PCF) cannot be explained simply in terms of disillusioned blue-collar workers abandoning the Left. The decline of the PCF should be understood in a much broader context, particularly the decades-long post–World War II effort to marginalize the PCF in mainstream politics. Since 1947, when the communists were dismissed from high-level cabinet posts, center Right and moderate Left parties had actively worked to diminish PCF power in France. In 1958, a two-ballot voting system was initiated, which meant that unless a party could form a strong coalition, its candidate could not advance to the final round of elections. This meant that the PCF, which had been France's strongest party, became the country's weakest almost overnight, as the socialists rarely, if ever, consented to build coalitions with the PCF, preferring instead to strengthen their own base by allying themselves with center Right parties. This marginalization, along with the economic downturn of the 1970s and 1980s, made the PCF seem increasingly irrelevant and incapable of adequately responding to traditional working-class needs. For extended discussion of this subject, see James Shields, "The Front National since the 1970s: Electoral Impact and Party System Change," in *France since the 1970s: History, Politics and Memory in an Age of Uncertainty*, ed. Emile Chabal (London: Bloomsbury, 2015): 41–64; Pascal Perrineau, "The Great Upheaval: Left and Right in Contemporary French Politics," in *France since the 1970s: History, Politics and Memory in an Age of Uncertainty*, ed. Emile Chabal (London: Bloomsbury, 2015): 25–40; Nick Hewlett, "Class, Class Conflict and the Left: The Place of the People in French Politics," in *France since the 1970s: History, Politics and Memory in an Age of Uncertainty*, ed. Emile Chabal (London: Bloomsbury, 2015): 67–82; and Julian Mischi, *Le communisme désarmé: Le PCF et les classes populaires depuis les années 1970* (Marseille: Agone, 2014).

57. Françoise Gaspard, *A Small City in France.*

58. Bouamama, *Dix ans de Marche des Beurs*, 123.

59. SOS Racisme's debut event was a large concert at the Place de la Concorde in Paris on June 15, 1985 (http://www.sos-racisme.org/1985.html 5/30/09). Patterned after the Rock against Police concerts organized around France between 1981 and 1983 by local youth organizations like SOS Avenir Minguettes, the Concert de la Concorde drew a crowd of 300,000. The concert was covered by all the major television news stations, as well as the print media. Minister of Culture Jack Lang played a key role in the organization of the concert.

60. Kaissa Titous, *J'ai claqué la porte à SOS Racisme*, quoted in Bouamama, *Dix ans de Marche des Beurs*, 121.

61. Bouamama, *Dix ans de Marche des Beurs*, 211.

62. Wihtol de Wenden and Leveau, *La Beurgeoisie*, 51.

63. Ibid., 57.

64. For additional discussion of the new citizenship, particularly debates about local voting rights, see Etienne Balibar, *Droit de cité* (La Tour d'Aigues [Vaucluse]: Ed. de l'Aube, 1998); Richard Balme, *Les nouvelles politiques locales: Dynamiques de l'action publique* (Paris: Presses de Sciences Po, 1999); Azouz Begag, *Espace et exclusion: Mobilités dans les quartiers péripheriques d'Avignon* (Paris: L'Harmattan, 1995); Azouz Begag, *La ville des autres: La famille immigrée et l'espace urbain* (Lyon: Presses universitaires de Lyon, 1991); Catherine Neveu, *Citoyenneté et espace public: Habitants, jeunes et citoyens dans une ville du nord* (Villeneuve d'Ascq: Presses universitaires du Septentrion, 2003); Catherine Neveu, *Espace public et engagement politique: Enjeux et logiques de la citoyenneté locale* (Paris: L'Harmattan, 1999).

65. Saïd Bouamama quoted in Wihtol de Wenden and Leveau, *La Beurgeoisie*, 51.

66. Ibid., 57.

67. Saïd Bouamama, *Dix ans de Marche des* Beurs, 102.

68. Saïd Bouamama, *J'y suis, j'y vote: La lutte pour les droits politiques aux résidents étrangers* (Paris: Esprit frappeur, 2000), 60. For further discussion of multiculturalism and the right to difference, see Ian Shapiro et al., *Ethnicity and Group Rights* (New York: New York University Press, 1997); Will Kymlicka, *Multicultural Citizenship: A Liberal Theory of Minority Rights* (Oxford: Oxford University Press, 1995); Will Kymlicka, *Multicultural Odysseys: Navigating the New International Politics of Diversity* (Oxford: Oxford University Press, 2007); Will Kymlicka, *Politics in the Vernacular: Nationalism, Multiculturalism and Citizenship* (Oxford: Oxford University Press, 2001); Cécile Laborde, "The Culture(s) of the Republic: Nationalism and Multiculturalism in French Republican Thought," *Political Theory* 29, no. 5 (2001): 716–735; Danilo Martueccelli, "Les contradictions politiques du multiculturalisme," in *Une société fragmentée*, ed. Michel Wievorka (Paris: La Découverte, 1996), 61–82.

69. Miriam Felblum, *Reconstructing Citizenship: The Politics of Nationality Reform and Immigration in Contemporary France* (Albany: State University of New York Press, 1999), 49; Yasemin Soysal, *Limits of Citizenship: Migrants and Postnational Membership in Europe* (Chicago: University of Chicago Press, 1994), 107.

70. Saïd Bouamama, *Dix ans de Marche de Beurs*, 102–104.

71. http://www.truveo.com/F%C3%AAte-SOS-RACISME-%C3%A0-la-Concorde/id /3967468234.

72. http://www.truveo.com/F%C3%AAte-SOS-RACISME-%C3%A0-la-Concorde /id/3967468234.

73. Bouamama, *Dix ans de Marche des Beurs*, 186.

74. While the Ministry of Culture under André Malraux was dedicated to promoting "French high culture," Jack Lang's vision was to celebrate culture both "high" and popular. This opened up new recourses to funding for local artists not affiliated with the official national dance companies, opera houses, and theaters as well as groups seeking support for "cultural" celebrations.

75. Bouamama, *Dix ans de Marche des Beurs*, 156.

76. Ibid.

77. Ibid.

78. Ibid.

79. See Martin Barker, *The New Racism*; Gilroy, *"There Ain't No Black in the Union Jack."*

80. Bouamama, *Dix ans de Marche des Beurs*, 49. See also Dossiers Municipales Elections, 1977, 1979, 1989, in the ADBR 183 J.

81. For discussion of immigrant "assimilation," see Gérard Noiriel, *The French Melting Pot: Immigration, Citizenship, and National Identity* (Minneapolis: University of Minnesota Press, 1996). For discussion of Republican policies of assimilation during the Third Republic, see James R. Lehning, *Peasant and French: Cultural Contact in Rural France during the Nineteenth Century* (Cambridge: Cambridge University Press, 1995); Eugen Weber, *Peasants into Frenchmen: The Modernization of Rural France, 1870–1914* (Stanford, Calif.: Stanford University Press, 1976).

82. These studies also included reports from various special national committees, including the Comité national de liaison des clubs et équipes de preventions specialisée. See also, for example, Délinquance Juvéniles et Prévention, Direction de la jeunesse et des activités socio-éducative, Secrétariat d'état auprès du premier ministère charge de la jeunesse, des sports et des loisirs, 2 Avril 1973, CACF 19790367 art. 13; Réflexion sur la

spécificité de l'action de prévention spécialise, by the Comité national de liaison des clubs et équipes de prévention spécialisée, Février 1974, CACF 19790367 art. 13; Rapport du groupe: "Inadaptations et animation de la vie sociale," Commission Affaires Sociales Jeunesse, November 1976, CACF, 19790367 art. 13; and Rapport du groupe, Prévention-Police, Commission Affaires Sociales Jeunesse, Novembre 1976, CACF 19790367 art. 13.

83. Fiche Prévention, VIIe Plan, Ministre de la Qualité de la Vie: Jeunesse et Sports, March 12, 1975, CACF 19790367 art. 13, p. 1.

84. Rapport du Groupe, Inadaptations et Animation de la Vie Sociale, Commission Affaires Sociales Jeunesse, November 1976, CACF 19790367 art. 13, 3.

85. Délinquance Juvéniles et Prévention, Direction de la jeunesse et des activités socio-éducative, Secrétariat d'état auprès du premier ministère chargé de la jeunesse, des sports et des loisirs, 2 Avril 1973, CACF 19790367 art. 13, 1.

86. Ibid., 2.

87. Ibid.

88. Dominique Charrier, "Activités physiques et sportives et insertion des jeunes: Enjeux éducatifs et pratiques institutionnelles," report commissioned by the Ministère de la Jeunesse et des Sports, 1997, Bibliothèque Alcazar à Marseille, 35.

89. Ibid., 37.

90. Ibid., 5.

91. Ibid., 33–34.

92. Ibid.

93. For studies on state efforts to integrate youth through neighborhood programming and recreational activities, see Tissot, *L'état et les quartiers.*

94. Charrier, "Activités physiques et sportives et insertion des jeunes," 38, 90, and 129–133.

95. Ibid., 36.

96. Data from Josset, FAS, 1991.

97. Rapport Moral, MJC Corderie, Assemblée Générale pour 1988, February 23, 1989, AMM 895 W 8, 4.

98. Ibid.

99. Rapport Moral, MJC Corderie, Assemblée Générale pour 1988, February 23, 1989, AMM 895 W 8, 3.

100. Ibid., 5.

101. Ibid., 5.

102. Ibid., 1.

103. See also Kenny Cupers's discussion of *animation* in *The Social Project*, esp. chap. 3, 95–136.

104. *Dictionnaire de la langue française* (Paris: Larousse, 1994), 69.

105. Ibid.

106. Jean-Claude Gillet, *Animation et animateurs: Le sens de l'action* (Paris: L'Harmattan, 1995), 27.

107. Ibid., 29.

108. Ibid., 2.

109. Ibid., 22.

110. Ibid., 18.

111. Ibid., 22.

112. Ibid., 45–47.

113. Letter from the Youth of the Tilleuls Cité to Monsieur Fella, chef du groupe Sud de la SONCOTRA, September 30, 1977, ADBR 2137 W 108.

114. Saïd Regaoui, Abdelkader Ounnous, of the Association Culturelle et Sportive des Jeunes des Tilleuls, A l'attention des organismes intervenant en faveur des français-musulmans rapatriés, March 1, 1981, ADBR 2137 W 108.

115. Objet: Animation des Jeunes Français Musulmans de la Cité des Tilleuls à Marseille, October 19, 1977, ADBR 2137 W 108.

116. For details on Abdelkader Ounnous's activities in the Tilleuls Cité, see Bruno Pufal and Bernand Quartino, Region Provence ZFC Les Tilleuls, Rapport d'activities, November 14–19, 1983, ADBR 2137 W 108; Letter from Bruno Pufal and Bernard Quartino to parents regarding stolen ping-pong rackets, November 1983, ADBR 2137 W 108; and Abdelkader Ounnous, Assistant socio-administratif Tilleuls, Rapport d'activities, January 3–7, 1983, ADBR 2137 W 108.

117. Saïd Regaoui, Moniteur Centre Socio-Culturel et Sportif "Les Tilleuls," Rapport d'activités, July 1978, ADBR 2137 W 108.

118. Ibid.

119. Bilan: Emplois-Habitat, Cité des Tilleuls de Marseille, by Thierry Vandecasteele in collaboration with Ahmed Ounnous, July–August 1986, ADBR 2137 W 108.

120. Ibid., p. 1.

121. Ibid., p. 18.

122. Abdelkader Ounnous, Assistant socio-administratif Tilleuls, Rapport d'activités, January 14–21, 1983, ADBR 2137 W 108.

123. Bilan: Emplois-Habitat, Cité des Tilleuls de Marseille, by Thierry Vandecasteele in collaboration with Ahmed Ounnous, July–August 1986, ADBR 2137 W 108, p. 18.

124. Abdelkader Ounnous, Assistant socio-administratif Tilleuls, Rapport d'activités, January 3–7, 1983, ADBR 2137 W 108.

125. Saïd Regaoui, Abdelkader Ounnous, of the Association Culturelle et Sportive des Jeunes des Tilleules, A l'attention des organismes intervenant en faveur des français-musulmans rapatriés, March 1, 1981, ADBR 2137 W 108.

126. Scholarship in the then emerging field of gender studies also helped call into question the older male breadwinner models of welfare. See, for example, Carole Pateman, "The Patriarchal Welfare State," in *Democracy and the Welfare State*, ed. Amy Gutman (Princeton, N.J.: Princeton University Press, 1988), 231–260.

127. Meeting of the Ad Hoc Group, Objet: Animation des Jeunes Français Musulmans de la Cité des Tilleuls à Marseille, October 19, 1977, ADBR 2137 W 108, p. 2.

128. Ibid.

129. Efforts to reach out to and empower immigrant women formed part of the mandate of the new Ministry of the Rights of Woman, which was created in 1981 as part of the socialists' efforts to promote sweeping social change. The ministry was concerned broadly with promoting the "autonomy" of women. They wanted to rework women's place within the social contract definitively by retooling welfare institutions, guaranteeing equality and fundamentally changing gendered attitudes in France. As part of this broader goal, the ministry began to fund a series of local programs—sometimes partnering with older institutions such as ATOM and the FAS—to address issues particular to "immigrant" women. For discussion of the historical tensions concerning French women's movements, the particularities of women's bodies, and the universalism of French republicanism, see Joan Wallach Scott, *Only Paradoxes to Offer*. For discussion of key themes within French feminism and the women's liberation movement, see Nancy Fraser and Sandra Lee Bartky, *Revaluing French Feminism: Critical Essays on Difference, Agency, and Culture* (Bloomington: Indiana University Press, 1992); Françoise Gaspard, Claude Servan-Schreiber, and Anne Le Gall, *Au pouvoir, citoyennes: Liberté, égalité, parité* (Paris: Editions du Seuil, 1992).

130. Laura Lee Downs, *Childhood in the Promised Land: Working-Class Movements and the Colonies de Vacances in France, 1180–1960* (Durham, N.C.: Duke University Press, 2002), 9.

131. Pierre Arnaud, "Introduction," in *Les athlètes de la république: Gymnastique, sport et idéologie républicaine 1870–1914*, ed. Pierre Arnaud (Paris: L'Harmattan, 1987), 19–24, here 20–22.

132. See Judith Surkis, *Sexing the Citizen: Morality and Masculinity in France, 1870–1920* (Ithaca, N.Y.: Cornell University Press, 2006).

133. For studies on early hip-hop in the United States, see Johan Kugelberg, Joe Conzo, and Afrika Bambaataa, *Born in the Bronx: A Visual Record of the Early Days of Hip-hop* (New York: Rizzoli, 2007); Joseph Glenn Schloss, *Foundation: B-Boys, B-Girls, and Hip-Hop Culture in New York* (Oxford: Oxford University Press, 2009); Carla Stalling Huntington, *Hip-hop Dance: Meanings and Messages* (Jefferson, N.C.: McFarland & Co., 2007).

134. Claudine Moïse, "Dire la danse hip-hop: Questions de création et de transmission," *Histoires de corps: A propos de la formation du danseur* (1998), 119.

135. For the burgeoning literature on hip-hop in France, see Hugues Bazin, *La culture hip-hop* (Paris: Desclée de Brouwer, 1995); Steve Cannon, "Paname City Rapping: B-boys in the Banlieues and Beyond," in *Post-Colonial Cultures in France*, ed. Alec G. Hargreaves and Mark McKinney (New York: Routledge, 1997), 150–166; Felicia McCarren, "Monsieur Hip-Hop," in *Blackening Europe: The African American Presence*, ed. Heike Raphael-Hernandez (New York: Routledge, 2004), 157–170; Tony Mitchell, *Global Noise: Rap and Hip-Hop Outside the USA* (Middletown, Conn.: Wesleyan University Press, 2001).

136. Radio Star and Radio Spring were Marseille radio stations that started playing American hip-hop as well as the music of emerging local hip-hop groups. Beatrice Sberna, *Une sociologie du rap à Marseille: Identité marginale et immigrée* (Paris: L'Harmattan, 2001), 150 and 156.

137. Marseille City Breakers began to dance and perform by the Hotel de Ville, Opera, and next to the Vieux Port in the 1980s. Sberna, *Une sociologie du rap à Marseille*, 156.

138. One of Marseille's oldest and best-known groups, IAM, was originally formed in late 1985 under the name Lively Crew. The group's original members, MC Akhenaton (Philippe Fragione) and DJ Kheops (Eric Mazel), both grew up in the northern neighborhoods of Marseille. Fragione's family was originally from Italy, and Mazel's mother was Spanish. In 1988 the group changed its name to B Boys Stance and several new members joined the group, including Freeman (Malek Brahimi), who was born in Algiers but grew up in Marseille; Imhotep (Pascal Perez), also born in Algiers; Shurik'n (Geoffroy Mussard), born in Réunion; and Kephren, born in Paris to Senegalese parents.

139. Several French hip-hop sites featuring music and dance have become important forums for live chat, blogging, and discussion. See, for example, www.style2ouf.fr and www.streetlive.fr.

140. "La Sound Musical School/B.Vice" website: http://www.infapaca.com/~feuillet /sms-site/historiquebvice.html.

141. According to MT Soly, when the Comoros voted for independence his father exclaimed: "I fought for France [in World War II] . . . I thus have no intention of renouncing my nationality today. I fought to have it . . . and my children will go to French schools just like all other French children." *Note intention artistique*, from the personal archive of Mbaé Tahamida "Soly" Mohamed.

142. Ali Ibrahima interview in Caroline Fontana, *De Grande Comore: Six histoires de vie à Marseille* (Le Lilas: Khiasma Editions, 2004), 59–77.

143. Histoire SMS, from the personal archive of Mbaé Tahamida "Soly" Mohamed.

144. "La Sound Musical School/B.Vice," http://www.infapaca.com/~feuillet/sms-site/historiquebvice.html.

145. Histoire SMS, from personal archive of Mbaé Tahamida "Soly" Mohamed.

146. Sberna, *Une sociologie du rap à Marseille*, 176. Moreover, as Philip Nord has shown, this commitment to cultivating culture and the arts was an important part of the French notions of welfare. See Nord, *France's New Deal*.

147. Extrait de la "Présentation du Bilan de l'année 1994 à Marseille" du conseil regional. Quoted in Sberna, *Une sociologie du rap à Marseille*, 174.

148. Ibid., 175.

149. Ibid., 176.

150. http://www.infapaca.com/~feuillet/sms-site/lequipe.html.

151. "La Sound Musical School/B. Vice," http://www.infapaca.com/~feuillet/sms-site/historiquesms.html. See also Ali Ibrahima interview in Caroline Fontana, *De Grande Comore*, 59–77.

152. Histoire SMS from personal archive of Mbaé Tahamida "Soly" Mohamed.

153. http://www.infapaca.com/~feuillet/sms-site/lequipe2.html.

154. Ibid.

155. Ibid.

156. MT Soly CV, from the personal archive of Mbaé Tahamida "Soly" Mohamed, 3.

157. http://www.infapaca.com/~feuillet/sms-site/lequipe3.html.

158. Histoire SMS, from personal archive of Mbaé Tahamida "Soly" Mohamed.

159. Paul Silverstein, "'Why Are We Waiting to Start the Fire?': French Gangsta Rap and the Critique of State Capitalism," in *Black, Blanc, Beur: Rap Music and Hip-Hop Culture in the Francophone World*, ed. Alain-Philippe Durand (Lanham, Md.: Scarecrow Press, 2002), 45–46. "Nique la police" is likely an allusion to the 1998 protest song "Fuck Tha Police," by the American hip-hop group, N.W.A.

160. Silverstein, "'Why Are We Waiting to Start the Fire?'," 46.

161. On gender and hip-hop in *animation*, see Sylvia Faure, "Filles et garçons en danse hip-hop: La production institutionnelle de pratiques sexuées," *Sociétés contemporaines*, no. 55 (2004/3): 5–20. On hip-hop and *animation*, see Sylvia Faure and Marie-Carmen Garcia, *Culture hip-hop, jeunes de cités et politiques publiques* (Paris: La Dispute, 2005); Loïc Lafargue de Grangeneuve, *Politique de hip-hop: Action publique et cultures urbains* (Toulouse: Presses Universitaires du Mirail, 2008).

162. Bruno Mégret press statement, broadcast on Television 3 on February 22, 1995; original video accessed through http://www.00269.net/PARLONS-d-IBRAHIM-ALI_a399.html.

163. "Ibrahim Ali. Retour sur un drame inoubliable," 00269 Le Média des Comoriens du Monde, http://www.00269.net/IBRAHIM-ALI-Retour-sur-un-drame-inoubliable_a261.html.

164. "Devoir de mémoire," http://www.00269.net/DEVOIR-DE-MEMOIRE_a401.html.

165. "Ibrahim Ali. Retour sur un drame inoubliable," 00269 Le Média des Comoriens du Monde, http://www.00269.net/IBRAHIM-ALI-Retour-sur-un-drame-inoubliable_a261.html.

166. Ibid.

167. "Qui était Ibrahim Ali?," interview on Le Média des Comoriens du Monde, http://www.00269.net/Qui-etait-IBRAHIM-ALI_a400.html.

168. *Le Provençal*, February 26, 1995.

169. Ibid.

170. Ibid.

171. Ibid.

EPILOGUE

1. http://www.centrevillepourtous.asso.fr/rubrique.php?id_rubrique=40.

2. Charter of un centre ville pour tous, http://www.centrevillepourtous.asso.fr/rubrique.php?id_rubrique=40.

3. Recherche-Action, Renouvellement Urbain à Marseille: Centralité Populaire et Mobilisation Collective le Cas de la Rue de la République, Final Report, 2007, Jean-Stéphane Borja, Martine Derain, Véronique Manry, Association Transvercité, 41 rue Jobin, 13003 Marseille, 2007, p. 176. See also Charter of Un Centre Ville Pour Tous, http://www.centrevillepourtous.asso.fr/rubrique.php?id_rubrique=40.

4. http://www.marseille-tourisme.com/en/discover-marseille/discover/marseille-the-new-projects.

5. Ibid.

Bibliography

ARCHIVES, LIBRARIES, AND COLLECTIONS CONSULTED

Archives départementals des Bouches-du-Rhône
Archives municipales de Marseille
Archives nationales (Paris)
Bibliothèque Alcazar (Marseille)
Bibliothèque nationale (Paris)
Centre des archives contemporaines (Fontainebleau)
Centre des archives d'outre-mer (Aix-en-Provence)
Centre d'urbanisme (Paris)
Collection from the offices of Comité Mam'Ega (Saint Barthélemy 13014 Marseille)
Fonds d'action et de soutien pour l'intégration et la lutte contre les discriminations (Paris)
Le Musée Social (Paris)
Private Collection of Mbaé Tahamida (Soly) Mohamed (Marseille)

SERIAL PUBLICATIONS CONSULTED OR CITED

Hommes et Migrations
La Marseillaise
La Provençe
Le Figaro
Le Méridional
Le Monde
Le Monde Ouvrier
Le Nouvel Observateur
Le Provençal
Les Cahiers Nords Africains
L'Express
L'Humanité
L'Union
Ouest France
Population
Revue de la chambre de commerce et d'industrie de Marseille
Urbanisme

INTERVIEWS AND ORAL HISTORIES

E. L. Panier resident, November 2007
A. V. Marseille resident and elementary schoolteacher, December 2007
J. S. Panier resident, December 2007
R. L. Panier resident, March 2008

Collection of interviews of friends and family members of Ibrahim Ali Abdallah

Le Média des Comoriens du Monde, http://www.00269.net/IBRAHIM-ALI-Retour-sur-un
-drame-inoubliable_a261.html

SELECTED PUBLISHED PRIMARY AND SECONDARY SOURCES

Abitbol, Michel, and Alan Astro. "The Integration of North African Jews in France." *Yale French Studies* 85 (1994): 248–261.

Accampo, Elinor A., Rachel G. Fuchs, and Mary Lynn Stewart, eds. *Gender and the Politics of Social Reform in France, 1870–1914.* Baltimore: Johns Hopkins University Press, 1995.

Adereth, M. *The French Communist Party: A Critical History (1920–1984), from Comintern to "the Colours of France."* Manchester: Manchester University Press, 1984.

Aisenberg, Andrew Robert. *Contagion: Disease, Government, and the "Social Question" in Nineteenth-Century France.* Stanford, Calif.: Stanford University Press, 1999.

Alexander, Claire. "Making Bengali Brick Lane: Claiming and Contesting Space in East London." *British Journal of Sociology* 62, no. 2 (June 2011): 201–220.

Aly, Götz, Peter Chroust, and Christian Pross. *Cleansing the Fatherland: Nazi Medicine and Racial Hygiene.* Baltimore: Johns Hopkins University Press, 1994.

Ancelin, Jacqueline. *L'action sociale familiale et les caisses d'allocations familiales: Un siècle d'histoire.* Paris: Association pour l'étude de l'histoire de la sécurité sociale, 1997.

Anderson, Benedict R. *Imagined Communities: Reflections on the Origin and Spread of Nationalism.* London: Verso, 2006.

Anselme, Michel. *Du bruit à la parole: La scène politique des cités.* La Tour d'Aigues: Editions de l'Aube, 2000.

———. *Entrevues citadines: Les flamants, Marseille.* Marseille: Cerfise, 1988.

———. "La formation des nouveaux territoires urbains et leur 'crise': Les quartiers nord de Marseille." *Peuples Méditerranéens,* no. 43 (avril-juin 1988): 121–130.

Anthias, Floya, and Gabriella Lazaridis. *Gender and Migration in Southern Europe: Women on the Move.* Oxford: Berg, 2000.

———. *Into the Margins: Migration and Exclusion in Southern Europe.* Aldershot: Ashgate, 1999.

Archer, Robin, ed. *Out of Apathy: Voices of the New Left Thirty Years On.* London: Verso, 1989.

Arendt, Hannah. *The Origins of Totalitarianism.* New York: Harcourt Brace, 2004.

Arnaud, Pierre, ed. *Les athlètes de la république: Gymnastique, sport et idéologie républicaine 1870–1914.* Paris: L'Harmattan, 1987.

Ascaride, Gilles, and Salvatore Condro. *La ville précaire: Les isolés du centre-ville de Marseille.* Paris: L'Harmattan, 2001.

Auzelle, Robert. "Vers une généralisation des enquêtes sur l'habitat." *Urbanisme* 7–8 (1951).

Bailkin, Jordanna. *The Afterlife of Empire.* Berkeley: University of California Press, 2012.

Baker, Keith Michael. *Inventing the French Revolution.* Cambridge: Cambridge University Press, 1990.

Baldwin, Peter. *The Politics of Social Solidarity: Class Bases of the European Welfare State, 1875–1975.* Cambridge: Cambridge University Press, 1990.

Balibar, Etienne. *Droit de cité.* La Tour d'Aigues: Ed. de l'Aube, 1998.

———. *Les frontières de la démocratie.* Paris: La Découverte, 1992.

———. *Nous, citoyens d'Europe: Les frontières, l'état, le peuple.* Paris: La Découverte, 2001.

Balibar, Etienne, and Immanuel Maurice Wallerstein. *Race, Nation, Class: Ambiguous Identities.* London: Verso, 1991.

Balme, Richard. *Les nouvelles politiques locales: Dynamiques de l'action publique.* Paris: Presses de Sciences Po, 1999.

Barker, Martin. *The New Racism: Conservatives and the Ideology of the Tribe.* Frederick, Md.: Aletheia Books, 1982.

Barnes, David S. *The Making of a Social Disease: Tuberculosis in Nineteenth-Century France.* Berkeley: University of California Press, 1995.

Bauböck, Rainer. *Citizenship Policies in the New Europe.* Amsterdam: Amsterdam University Press, 2007.

Bauer, Alain, and Xavier Raufer. *Violences et insécurité urbaines.* Paris: Presses universitaires de France, 1999.

Bazin, Hugues. *La culture hip-hop.* Paris: Desclée de Brouwer, 1995.

Begag, Azouz. *Espace et exclusion: Mobilités dans les quartiers périphériques d'Avignon.* Logiques Sociales. Paris: L'Harmattan, 1995.

———. *Ethnicity and Equality: France in the Balance.* Lincoln: University of Nebraska Press, 2007.

———. *La ville des autres: La famille immigrée et l'espace urbain.* Lyon: Presses universitaires de Lyon, 1991.

———. *Un mouton dans la baignoire.* Paris: Fayard, 2007.

Bell, David Scott, and Byron Criddle. *The French Communist Party in the Fifth Republic.* Oxford: Oxford University Press, 1994.

Ben Jelloun, Tahar. *Hospitalité française: Racisme et immigration maghrébine.* Paris: Seuil, 1984.

———. *Le racisme expliqué à ma fille.* Paris: Seuil, 1998.

Bernadot, Marc. "Une politique du logement: Sonacotra (1956–1992)." PhD diss., Sorbonne, 1997.

Bertaux, Sandrine. "'Processus' et 'population' dans l'analyse démographique de l'immigration en France (1932–1996)." In *L'invention des populations: Biologique, idéologie et politique,* edited by Hervé Le Bras and Sandrine Bertaux, 214–254. Paris: Editions Odile Jacob, 2000.

Bertrand, Claude. *Illusions et réalités de la vie politique à Marseille.* Paris: Editions Payot & Rivages, 1998.

Bonillo, Jean. *La reconstruction à Marseille: Architectures et projets urbains, 1940–1960.* Marseille: Imbemon, 2008.

———. *Marseille, ville et port.* Marseille: Parenthèses, 1992.

Bonin, Hubert, Sylvie Guillaume, and Bernard Lachaise. *Bordeaux et la Gironde pendant la Reconstruction, 1945–1954: Actes du colloque de Talence tenu du 16 au 18 Novembre 1995.* Talence: Editions de la Maison des sciences de l'homme d'Aquitaine, 1997.

Bordet, Joëlle. *Les "Jeunes de la cité."* Paris: Presses universitaires de France, 1998.

Bouamama, Saïd. *Dix ans de marche des Beurs: Chronique d'un mouvement avorté.* Paris: Desclée de Brouwer, 1994.

———. *J'y suis, j'y vote: La lutte pour les droits politiques aux résidents étrangers.* Paris: Esprit frappeur, 2000.

———. *L'affaire du foulard Islamique: La production d'un racisme respectable.* Roubaix: Geai bleu, 2004.

Bowen, John Richard. *Why the French Don't Like Headscarves: Islam, the State, and Public Space.* Princeton, N.J.: Princeton University Press, 2007.

Boyer, Jean-Claude. *Les banlieues en France: Territoires et sociétés.* Paris: Armand Colin, 2000.

Branche, Raphaëlle. *La guerre d'indépendance des Algériens: 1954–1962.* Paris: Perrin, 2009.

Branche, Raphaëlle, Sylvie Thénault, and Marie-Claude Albert. *La France en guerre, 1954–1962: Expériences métropolitaines de la guerre d'indépendance algérienne.* Paris: Autrement, 2008.

Branson, Noreen. *History of the Communist Party of Great Britain 1941–1951.* London: Lawrence and Wishart, 1997.

Brodiez-Dolino, Axelle. *Emmaüs et l'Abbé Pierre.* Paris: Presses des Sciences Po, 2009.

Brubaker, Rogers. *Citizenship and Nationhood in France and Germany.* Cambridge, Mass.: Harvard University Press, 1992.

——. *Ethnicity without Groups.* Cambridge, Mass.: Harvard University Press, 2004.

Brun, Jacques, et al. *La ségrégation dans la ville: Concepts et mesures.* Paris: L'Harmattan, 1994.

Bruno, Pierre. *Existe-t-il une culture adolescente?* Paris: In-press, 2000.

Buchanan, Tom, and Martin Conway, eds. *Political Catholicism in Europe, 1918–1965.* Oxford: Oxford University Press, 1996.

Bullock, Nicholas. *Building the Post-War World: Modern Architecture in Britain.* New York: Routledge, 2002.

Burke, Roland. *The Politics of Decolonization and the Evolution of International Human Rights.* Philadelphia: University of Pennsylvania Press, 2010.

Burleigh, Michael. *Death and Deliverance: "Euthanasia" in Germany c. 1900–1945.* Cambridge: Cambridge University Press, 1994.

Burton, Antoinette M. *After the Imperial Turn: Thinking with and through the Nation.* Durham, N.C.: Duke University Press, 2003.

——. *At the Heart of the Empire: Indians and the Colonial Encounter in Late-Victorian Britain.* Berkeley: University of California Press, 1998.

——. *Burdens of History: British Feminists, Indian Women, and Imperial Culture, 1865–1915.* Chapel Hill: University of North Carolina Press, 1994.

Butler, Rémy, and Patrice Noisette. *Le logement social en France, 1815–1981: De la cité ouvrière au grand ensemble.* Paris: La Découverte/Maspero, 1983.

Byrnes, Melissa. "French Like Us? Municipal Policies and North African Migrants in the Parisian Banlieues 1945–1975." PhD diss., Georgetown University, 2008.

Calhoun, Craig, ed. *Habermas and the Public Sphere.* Cambridge, Mass.: MIT Press, 1992.

Camiscioli, Elisa. *Reproducing the French Race: Immigration, Intimacy, and Embodiment in the Early Twentieth Century.* Durham, N.C.: Duke University Press, 2009.

Campt, Tina. *Other Germans: Black Germans and the Politics of Race, Gender, and Memory in the Third Reich.* Ann Arbor: University of Michigan Press, 2004.

Canfora-Argandoña, Elsie, and Roger-Henri Guerrand. *La répartition de la population: Les conditions de logement des classes ouvrières à Paris au 19e siècle.* Paris: Centre de sociologie urbaine, 1976.

Canning, Kathleen. *Gender History in Practice: Historical Perspectives on Bodies, Class and Citizenship.* Ithaca, N.Y.: Cornell University Press, 2005.

Cannon, Steve. "Paname City Rapping: B-Boys in the Banlieues and Beyond." In *Post-Colonial Cultures in France,* edited by Alec G. Hargreaves and Mark McKinney, 150–166. New York: Routledge, 1997.

Castells, Manuel. *The City and Grassroots: A Cross-Cultural Theory of Urban Social Movements.* Berkeley: University of California Press, 1983.

Celik, Zeynep. *Urban Forms and Colonial Confrontations: Algiers under French Rule.* Berkeley: University of California Press, 1997.

Centre for Contemporary Cultural Studies. *The Empire Strikes Back: Race and Racism in 70s Britain.* London: Hutchinson; in association with the Centre for Contemporary Cultural Studies, University of Birmingham, 1982.

Centre interuniversitaire de recherche et de documentation sur les migrations. "Le seuil de tolérance aux étrangers." *Sociologie du sud-est,* no. 5/6 (juillet–octobre 1975).

Certeau, Michel de. *The Practice of Everyday Life*. Berkeley: University of California Press, 1984.

Cesari, Jocelyne. *Être musulman en France*. Paris: Kathala, 1994.

———. "L'intégration des femmes Maghrébines dans la ville: L'exemple de Marseille." In *Marseillaises: Les femmes et la ville (des origines à nos jours)*, edited by Yvonne Knibiehler, 359–368. Paris: Côte-Femmes, 1993.

———. *Musulmans et républicains: Les jeunes, l'Islam et la France*. Brussels: Editions Complexe, 1998.

Chabal, Emile, ed. *France since the 1970s: History, Politics and Memory in an Age of Uncertainty*. London: Bloomsbury, 2015.

Chapman, Herrick. "Review: Modernity and National Identity in Postwar France." *French Historical Studies* 22, no. 2 (1999): 291–314.

———. *State Capitalism and Working-Class Radicalism in the French Aircraft Industry*. Berkeley: University of California Press, 1991.

Chapman, Herrick, and Laura Levine Frader. *Race in France: Interdisciplinary Perspectives on the Politics of Difference*. New York: Berghahn Books, 2004.

Charrier, Dominique. *Activités physiques et sportives et insertion des jeunes: Enjeux éducatifs et pratiques institutionnelles*. Report commissioned by the Ministère de la jeunesse et des sports. Paris: La documentation française, 1997.

Chartier, Roger. *The Cultural Origins of the French Revolution*. Durham, N.C.: Duke University Press, 1991.

Chatterjee, Partha. *The Politics of the Governed: Reflections on Popular Politics in Most of the World*. New York: Columbia University Press, 2004.

Chevalier, Louis. *Classes laborieuses et classes dangereuses à Paris pendant la première moitié du XIXe siècle*. Paris: Plon, 1958.

Childers, Kristen Stromberg. *Fathers, Families and the State in France, 1914–1945*. Ithaca, N.Y.: Cornell University Press, 2003.

Chin, Rita C. K., ed. *After the Nazi Racial State: Difference and Democracy in Germany and Europe*. Ann Arbor: University of Michigan Press, 2009.

———. *The Guest Worker Question in Postwar Germany*. Cambridge: Cambridge University Press, 2007.

Chombart de Lauwe, Paul. *Famille et habitation*. Paris: Centre National de la Recherche Scientifique, 1960.

Clancy-Smith, Julia. *Mediterraneans: North Africa and Europe in an Age of Migration, c. 1800–1900*. Berkeley: University of California Press, 2011.

Clancy-Smith, Julia, and Frances Gouda, eds. *Domesticating the Empire: Race, Gender and Family Life in French and Dutch Colonialism*. Charlottesville: University Press of Virginia, 1998.

Clarke, Paula. *The Soderini and the Medici: Power and Patronage in Fifteenth-Century Florentine Society*. Oxford: Oxford University Press, 1991.

Cole, Joshua. *The Power of Large Numbers: Population, Politics, and Gender in Nineteenth-Century France*. Ithaca, N.Y.: Cornell University Press, 2000.

Conklin, Alice L. "Colonialism and Human Rights: A Contradiction in Terms? The Case of France and West Africa, 1895–1914." *The American Historical Review* 103, no. 2 (1998): 419–442.

———. *In the Museum of Man: Race, Anthropology, and Empire in France, 1850–1950*. Ithaca, N.Y.: Cornell University Press, 2013.

———. *A Mission to Civilize: The Republican Idea of Empire in France and West Africa, 1895–1930*. Stanford, Calif.: Stanford University Press, 1997.

Connelly, Matthew James. *A Diplomatic Revolution: Algeria's Fight for Independence and the Origins of the Post-Cold War Era*. Oxford: Oxford University Press, 2002.

Connolly, James J. *The Triumph of Ethnic Progressivism: Urban Political Culture in Boston, 1900–1925.* Cambridge, Mass.: Harvard University Press, 1998.

Cooper, Frederick. *Africa since 1940: The Past of the Present.* Cambridge: Cambridge University Press, 2002.

———. *Colonialism in Question: Theory, Knowledge, History.* Berkeley: University of California Press, 2005.

———. *Decolonization and African Society: The Labor Question in French and British Africa.* Cambridge: Cambridge University Press, 1996.

Cooper, Frederick, and Ann Laura Stoler, eds. *Tensions of Empire: Colonial Cultures in a Bourgeois World.* Berkeley: University of California Press, 1997.

Coppolani, Jean. *Toulouse au XXe siècle.* Toulouse: Privat, 1963.

Cornuel, Didier, and Bruno Duriez. *Le mirage urbain: Histoire du logement à Roubaix.* Paris: Anthropos, 1983.

Crane, Sheila. *Mediterranean Crossroads: Marseille and Modern Architecture.* Minneapolis: University of Minnesota Press, 2011.

Cristofol, Jacqueline, and Alain Dugrand. *Batailles pour Marseille: Jean Cristofol, Gaston Defferre, Raymond Aubrac.* Paris: Flammarion, 1997.

Cupers, Kenny. *The Social Project: Housing Postwar France.* Minneapolis: University of Minnesota Press, 2014.

Davidson, Naomi. *Only Muslim: Embodying Islam in Twentieth-Century France.* Ithaca, N.Y.: Cornell University Press, 2012.

Davis, Belinda J. *Home Fires Burning: Food, Politics and Everyday Life in World War I Berlin.* Chapel Hill: University of North Carolina Press, 2000.

Debord, Guy. *The Society of the Spectacle.* New York: Zone Books, 1994.

De Grazia, Victoria. *Irresistible Empire: America's Advance through Twentieth-Century Europe.* Cambridge, Mass.: Belknap Press of Harvard University Press, 2005.

Dermenjian, Geneviève, ed. *Femmes, familles et action ouvrière: Pratiques et responsabilités féminines dans les mouvements familiaux populaires 1935–1958.* Villeneuve d'Asq: Groupement pour la recherche sur les mouvements familiaux, 1991.

Désir, Harlem. *Touche pas à mon pôte.* Paris: B. Grasset, 1985.

Dikec, Mustafa. *Badlands of the Republic: Space, Politics and Urban Policy.* Malden, Mass.: Blackwell, 2007.

Donzel, André. *Marseille: L'expérience de la cité.* Paris: Anthropos, 1998.

———. *Métropolisation, gouvernance et citoyenneté dans la région urbaine Marseillaise.* Paris: Maisonneuve et Larose, 2001.

———. *Le nouvel esprit de Marseille.* Paris: L'Harmattan, 2014.

Donzelot, Jacques. *The Policing of Families.* New York: Pantheon Books, 1979.

———. *L'état animateur: Essai sur la politique de la ville.* Paris: Editions Esprit, Seuil, 1994.

Downs, Laura Lee. *Childhood in the Promised Land: Working-Class Movements and the Colonies de Vacances in France, 1180–1960.* Durham, N.C.: Duke University Press, 2002.

Doytcheva, Milena. *Une discrimination positive á la française: Ethnicité et territoire dans les politiques de la ville.* Paris: La Découverte, 2007.

Drouard, Alain. "La création de l'INED." *Population,* 47e année, no. 6, Hommage à Alfred Sauvy (novembre–décembre 1992): 1453–1466.

Dubet, François. *La Galère: Jeunes en survie.* Paris: Fayard, 1987.

Dubet, François, and Didier Lapeyronnie. *Les quartiers d'exil.* Paris: Seuil, 1992.

Dubois, Laurent. *A Colony of Citizens: Revolution and Slave Emancipation in the French Caribbean, 1787–1804.* Chapel Hill: University of North Carolina Press, 2004.

Duquesne, Jacques. *Les Catholiques sous l'occupation.* Paris: B. Grasset, 1966.

Durand, Alain-Philippe, ed. *Black, Blanc, Beur: Rap Music and Hip-Hop Culture in the Fran-cophone World*. Lanham, Md.: Scarecrow Press, 2002.

Durbach, Nadja. "London, Capital of Exotic Exhibitions from 1830 to 1860." In *Human Zoos: Science and Spectacle in the Age of Colonial Empires*, edited by Pascal Blanchard, 81–88. Liverpool: Liverpool University Press, 2008.

——, ed. *Les catholiques dans la république, 1905–2005*. Paris: Editions de l'Atelier, 2005.

Duriez, Bruno, and Michel Chauvière, eds. *La bataille des squatters et l'invention du droit au logement, 1945–1955*. Villeneuve d'Ascq: Groupement pour la recherche sur les mouvements familiaux, 1992.

Dutton, Paul V. *Origins of the French Welfare State: The Struggle for Social Reform in France, 1914–1947*. Cambridge: Cambridge University Press, 2002.

Effosse, Sabine. *L'invention du logement aidé en France: L'immobilier au temps des trente glorieuses*. Paris: Comité pour l'histoire économique et financière de la France, 2003.

Eley, Geoff. *Forging Democracy: The History of the Left in Europe, 1850–2000*. Oxford: Oxford University Press, 2002.

Eley, Geoff, and Atina Grossmann. "Maternalism and Citizenship in Weimar Germany: The Gendered Politics of Welfare." *Central European History* 30, no. 1 (1997): 67–75.

Eley, Geoff, and Keith Nield. *The Future of Class in History: What's Left of the Social?* Ann Arbor: University of Michigan Press, 2007.

Eley, Geoff, and Ronald Grigor Suny. *Becoming National: A Reader*. New York: Oxford University Press, 1996.

Esping-Andersen, Gøsta. *The Three Worlds of Welfare Capitalism*. Cambridge: Polity, 1990.

Ewald, François. *L'état providence*. Paris: B. Grasset, 1986.

Ezra, Elizabeth. *The Colonial Unconscious: Race and Culture in Interwar France*. Ithaca, N.Y.: Cornell University Press, 2000.

Fanon, Frantz. *Les damnées de la terre*. Paris: François Maspero, 1961.

——. *Peau noire, masques blancs*. Paris: Seuil, 1952.

Fassin, Dider, and Eric Fassin, eds. *De la question sociale à la question raciale: Représenter la société française*. Paris: La Découverte, 2006.

Faure, Sylvia. "Filles et garçons en danse hip-hop: La production institutionnelle de pra-tiques sexuées." *Sociétés contemporaines*, no. 55 (2004): 5–20.

Faure, Sylvia, and Marie-Carmen Garcia. *Culture hip-hop, jeunes de cités et politiques pub-liques*. Paris: La Dispute, 2005.

Fehrenbach, Heide. *Race after Hitler: Black Occupation Children in Postwar Germany and America*. Princeton, N.J.: Princeton University Press, 2005.

Feldblum, Miriam. *Reconstructing Citizenship: The Politics of Nationality Reform and Im-migration in Contemporary France*. Albany: State University of New York Press, 1999.

Fijalkow, Yankel, and Marcel Roncayolo. *La construction des îlots insalubres: Paris 1850–1945*. Paris: L'Harmattan, 1998.

Finkielkraut, Alain. *La défaite de la pensée: Essai*. Paris: Gallimard, 1987.

Finlayson, Geoffrey. *Citizen, State, and Social Welfare in Britain 1830–1990*. Oxford: Oxford University Press, 1994.

Fischer, Brodwyn. *A Poverty of Rights: Citizenship and Inequality in Twentieth-Century Rio de Janeiro*. Stanford, Calif.: Stanford University Press, 2008.

Fishman, Sarah. *The Battle for Children: World War II, Youth Crime, and Juvenile Justice in Twentieth-Century France*. Cambridge, Mass.: Harvard University Press, 2002.

Flamand, Jean-Paul, and Roger-Henri Guerrand. *Loger le peuple: Essai sur l'histoire du loge-ment social en France*. Paris: La Découverte, 1989.

Fletcher, Yael Simpson. "Capital of the Colonies: Real and Imagined Boundaries between Metropole and Empire in 1920s Marseille." In *Imperial Cities: Landscape, Display and Identity*, edited by Felix Driver and David Gilbert, 134–151, Manchester: Manchester University Press, 1999.

———. "Catholics, Communists and Colonial Subjects: Working-Class Militance and Racial Difference in Postwar Marseille." In *The Color of Liberty: Histories of Race in France*, edited by Sue Peabody and Tyler Edward Stovall, 338–350. Durham, N.C.: Duke University Press, 2003.

———. "City, Nation and Empire in Marseilles." PhD diss., Emory University, 1999.

Fogg, Shannon Lee. *The Politics of Everyday Life in Vichy, France: Foreigners, Undesirables, and Strangers*. Cambridge: Cambridge University Press, 2009.

Fontana, Caroline. *De Grande Comore: Six histoires de vie à Marseille*. Les Lilas: Khiasma Editions, 2004.

Foucault, Michel, Graham Burchill, Colin Gordon, and Peter M. Miller. *The Foucault Effect: Studies in Governmentality: With Two Lectures by and an Interview with Michel Foucault*. London: Harvester Wheatsheaf, 1991.

Fourastié, Jean. *Les trente glorieuses: Ou, la révolution invisible de 1946 à 1975*. Paris: Fayard, 1979.

Fourcaut, Annie. *Bobigny, Banlieue Rouge*. Paris: Editions ouvrières, Presses de la Fondation nationale des sciences politiques, 1986.

———. *La banlieue en morceaux: La crise des lotissements défectueux en France dans l'entre-deux-guerres*. Grâne: Créaphis, 2000.

———. "Les premiers grands ensembles en région parisienne: Ne pas refaire la banlieue?" *French Historical Studies* 27, no. 1 (Winter 2004): 295–218.

———. *Un siècle de banlieue parisienne: 1859–1964*. Paris: L'Harmattan, 1988.

Fourcaut, Annie, Emmanuel Bellanger, and Mathieu Flonneau. *Paris-Banlieues, conflits et solidarités: Historiographie, anthologie, chronologie, 1788–2006*. Paris: Créaphis, 2007.

Fourcaut, Annie, Frédéric Dufaux, Paul Chemetov. *Le monde des grands ensembles*. Paris: Créaphis, 2004.

Fourcaut, Annie, and École normale supérieure de Fontenay-Saint-Cloud. Centre d'histoire urbaine, *La ville divisée: Les ségrégations urbaines en question: France XVIIIe–XXe siècles*. Grâne: Créaphis, 1996.

Fournier, Pierre, and Sylvie Mazzella. *Marseille, entre ville et ports: Les destins de la rue de la République*. Paris: La Découverte, 2004.

Frader, Laura Levine. *Breadwinners and Citizens: Gender in the Making of the French Social Model*. Durham, N.C.: Duke University Press, 2008.

Fraser, Nancy, and Sandra Lee Bartky. *Revaluing French Feminism: Critical Essays on Difference, Agency, and Culture*. Bloomington: Indiana University Press, 1992.

Freeman, Gary P. *Immigrant Labor and Racial Conflict in Industrial Societies: The French and British Experience, 1945–1975*. Princeton, N.J.: Princeton University Press, 1979.

Fuchs, Rachel G. *Contested Paternity: Constructing Families in Modern France*. Baltimore: Johns Hopkins University Press, 2008.

———. *Poor and Pregnant in Paris: Strategies for Survival in the Nineteenth Century*. New Brunswick, N.J.: Rutgers University Press, 1992.

Gallie, Duncan, and Serge Paugam. *Welfare Regimes and the Experience of Unemployment in Europe*. Oxford: Oxford University Press, 2000.

Gaspard, Françoise. *A Small City in France*. Cambridge, Mass.: Harvard University Press, 1995.

Gaspard, Françoise, Claude Servan-Schreiber, and Anne Le Gall. *Au pouvoir, citoyennes: Liberté, égalité, parité*. Paris: Seuil, 1992.

Gaspard, Françoise, and Farhad Khosrokhavar. *Le foulard et la république*. Paris: La Découverte, 1995.

Gillet, Jean-Claude. *Animation et Animateurs: Le sens de l'action*. Paris: L'Harmattan, 1995.

Gilroy, Paul. *"There Ain't No Black in the Union Jack"*: *The Cultural Politics of Race and Nation*. Chicago: University of Chicago Press, 1991.

Ginesy-Galano, Mireille. *Les immigrés hors la cité: Le système d'encadrement dans les foyers, 1973–1982*. Paris: L'Harmattan/CIEM, 1984.

Ginsborg, Paul. "The Politics of the Family in Twentieth-Century Europe." *Contemporary European History* 9, no. 3 (November 2000): 411–444.

Girard, Alain. "Attitudes des français à l'égard de'immigration étrangère. Enquête d'opinion publique." *Population*, 26e année, no. 5 (September–October 1971): 827–875.

———. "Le problème démographique et l'évolution du sentiment public." *Population*, 5e année, no. 2 (April–June 1950): 333–352.

———. *L'homme et le nombre des hommes: Essais sur les conséquences de la révolution démographique*. Paris: Presses universitaires de France, 1984.

Girard, Alain, Yves Charbit, and Marie-Laurence Lamy. "Attitudes des français à l'égard de l'immigration étrangère. Nouvelle enquête d'opinion." *Population*, 29e année, no. 6 (November–December 1974): 1015–1069.

Goodman, Dena. "Public Sphere and Private Life: Toward a Synthesis of Current Historiographical Approaches to the Old Regime." *History and Theory* 31 (1992): 1–20.

Gouda, Frances. *Poverty and Political Culture: The Rhetoric of Social Welfare in the Netherlands and France, 1815–1854*. Lanham, Md.: Rowman and Littlefield, 1995.

Gramsci, Antonio. *Prison Notebooks*. New York: Columbia University Press, 1991.

Granotier, Bernard. *Les travailleurs immigrés en France*. Paris: F. Maspero, 1976.

Green, Elna C. *Before the New Deal: Social Welfare in the South, 1830–1930*. Athens: University of Georgia Press, 1999.

Gregor, Neil. *Haunted City: Nuremberg and the Nazi Past*. New Haven, Conn.: Yale University Press, 2008.

Gruber, Helmut. *Red Vienna: Experiment in Working-Class Culture, 1919–1934*. New York: Oxford University Press, 1991.

Guerrand, Roger-Henri. *Les origines du logement social en France*. Paris: Editions ouvrières, 1966.

Guicheteau, Gérard. *Marseille, 1943: La fin du Vieux-Port*. Paris: Editions Daniel, 1973.

Gutman, Amy, ed. *Democracy and the Welfare State*. Princeton, N.J.: Princeton University Press, 1988.

Haber, Carole, and Brian Gratton. *Old Age and the Search for Security: An American Social History*. Bloomington: University of Indiana Press, 1994.

Haffner, Jeanne. *The View from Above: The Science of Social Space*. Cambridge, Mass.: MIT Press, 2014.

Hall, Catherine, and Sonya O. Rose. *At Home with the Empire: Metropolitan Culture and the Imperial World*. Cambridge: Cambridge University Press, 2006.

Hall, Stuart, and Paul du Gay. *Questions of Cultural Identity*. London: Sage, 1996.

Hall, Stuart, and Tony Jefferson. *Resistance through Rituals: Youth Subcultures in Post-War Britain*. London: Unwin Hyman, 1989.

Harding, Robert. *Anatomy of a Power Elite: The Provincial Governors of Early Modern France*. New Haven, Conn.: Yale University Press, 1978.

Hargreaves, Alec G. *Immigration, "Race" and Ethnicity in Contemporary France*. London: Routledge, 1995.

Hargreaves, Alec G., and Mark McKinney. *Post-Colonial Cultures in France*. London: Routledge, 1997.

Harootunian, Harry. *History's Disquiet: Modernity, Cultural Practice, and the Question of Everyday Life*. New York: Columbia University Press, 2000.

Harris, Ruth. *Murders and Madness: Medicine, Law, and Society in the Fin de Siècle*. Oxford: Oxford University Press, 1989.

Harvey, David. *Paris, Capital of Modernity*. New York: Routledge, 2003.
——. *Social Justice and the City*. Baltimore: Johns Hopkins University Press, 1977.
——. *Spaces of Capital: Towards a Critical Geography*. New York: Routledge, 2001.
Hauw, David. "Les opérations de relogement en habitat collectif à Casablanca, de la vision des aménageurs aux pratiques des habitants." PhD diss., Université François Rabelais, Tours, 2004.
Healy, Maureen. *Vienna and the Fall of the Habsburg Empire: Total War and Everyday Life in World War I*. Cambridge: Cambridge University Press, 2004.
Hecht, Gabrielle. *The Radiance of France: Nuclear Power and National Identity after World War II*. Cambridge, Mass.: MIT Press, 1998.
Hellman, John. *Emmanuel Mounier and the New Catholic Left, 1930–1950*. Toronto: University of Toronto Press, 1981.
Hennock, E. P. *The Origin of the Welfare State in England and Germany, 1850–1914*. Cambridge: Cambridge University Press, 2007.
Hervo, Monique. *Chroniques du Bidonville: Nanterre en guerre d'Algérie, 1959–1962*. Paris: Seuil, 2001.
Hewlett, Nick. "Class, Class Conflict and the Left: The Place of the People in French Politics." In *France since the 1970s: History, Politics and Memory in an Age of Uncertainty*, edited by Emile Chabal, 67–82. London: Bloomsbury, 2015.
Hifi, Belkacem. *L'immigration algérienne en France: Origines et perspectives de non-retour*. Paris: L'Harmattan, 1985.
Highmore, Ben. *Everyday Life and Cultural Theory: An Introduction*. London: Routledge, 2002.
——. *The Everyday Life Reader*. London: Routledge, 2002.
Hill, Dianna Murray. "Who Are the Squatters?" *Pilot Papers* 1, no. 4 (November 1946): 11–27.
Hinton, James. "Self-Help and Socialism, the Squatters' Movement of 1946." *History Workshop*, no. 25 (Spring 1988): 100–126.
Hoffmann, Stefan-Ludwig, ed. *Human Rights in the Twentieth Century*. Cambridge: Cambridge University Press, 2011.
Holt, Thomas C. "Marking: Race, Race-Making and the Writing of History." *American Historical Review* 100, no. 1 (1995): 1–17.
——. *The Problem of Freedom: Race, Labor, and Politics in Jamaica and Britain, 1832–1938*. Baltimore: Johns Hopkins University Press, 1992.
Horne, Alistair. *A Savage War of Peace: Algeria 1954–1962*. London: MacMillan, 1977.
Horne, Janet R. *A Social Laboratory for Modern France: The Musée Social and the Rise of the Welfare State*. Durham, N.C.: Duke University Press, 2002.
House, Jim, and Neil MacMaster. *Paris 1961: Algerians, State Terror, and Memory*. Oxford: Oxford University Press, 2006.
Hull, Isabel. *Absolute Destruction: Military Culture and the Practices of War in Imperial Germany*. Ithaca, N.Y.: Cornell University Press, 2005.
Huntington, Carla Stalling. *Hip Hop Dance: Meanings and Messages*. Jefferson, N.C.: McFarland & Co., 2007.
Huston, James A. *Across the Face of France: Liberation and Recovery, 1944–63*. West Lafayette, Ind.: Purdue University Studies, 1963.
Jackson, Patrick Thaddeus. *Civilizing the Enemy: German Reconstruction and the Invention of the West*. Ann Arbor: University of Michigan Press, 2006.
Jacob, Margaret C. "The Mental Landscape of the Public Sphere: A European Perspective." *Eighteenth-Century Studies* 28 (1994): 95–113.

Jankowski, Paul. *Communism and Collaboration: Simon Sabiani and Politics in Marseille, 1919–1944*. New Haven, Conn.: Yale University Press, 1989.

Jennings, Jeremy. "Citizenship, Republicanism, and Multiculturalism in Contemporary France." *British Journal of Political Science* 30, no. 4 (2000): 575–598.

Jones, Gareth Stedman. *Outcast London: A Study in the Relationship between Classes in Victorian Society*. Oxford: Clarendon Press, 1971.

Jones, Kathleen. *The Making of Social Policy in Britain, 1830–1990*. London: Athlone Press, 1994.

Jordi, Jean-Jacques. *De l'exode à l'exil: Rapatriés et pieds-noirs en France: L'exemple marseillais, 1954–1992*. Paris: L'Harmattan, 1993.

———. *1962, l'arrivée des pieds-noirs*. Paris: Editions Autrement, 1995.

Jordi, Jean-Jacques, Emile Témime, and Abdelmalek Sayad. *Marseille et le choc des décolonisations: Les Rapatriements, 1954–1964*. Aix-en-Provence: Edisud, 1991.

Josset, Sohpie. *Le FAS:1958–1998*. Internal report commissioned by the Fonds d'action et de soutien pour l'intégration et la lutte contre les discriminations, 1998.

Judt, Tony. *The Burden of Responsibility: Blum, Camus, Aron, and the French Twentieth Century*. Chicago: University of Chicago Press, 1998.

———. *Marxism and the French Left: Studies in Labour and Politics in France, 1830–1981*. Oxford: Oxford University Press, 1986.

———. *Past Imperfect: French Intellectuals, 1944–1956*. Berkeley: University of California Press, 1992.

Katz, Michael B. *In the Shadow of the Poorhouse: A Social History of Welfare in America*. New York: Basic Books, 1996.

Keaton, Trica. *Muslim Girls and the Other France: Race, Identity Politics and Social Exclusion*. Bloomington: University of Indiana Press, 2006.

Kedward, H. R., and Nancy Wood. *The Liberation of France: Image and Event*. Washington, D.C.: Berg, 1995.

Kent, F. W., Patricia Simons, and J. C. Eade, eds. *Patronage, Art, and Society in Renaissance Italy*. Oxford: Oxford University Press, 1987.

Kettering, Sharon. *Patrons, Brokers and Clients in Seventeenth-Century France*. Oxford: Oxford University Press, 1986.

King, Anthony D. *Buildings and Society: Essays on the Social Development of the Built Environment*. London; Boston: Routledge & Kegan Paul, 1980.

King, Ross. *Emancipating Space: Geography, Architecture, and Urban Design*. New York: Guilford Press, 1996.

Kitson, Simon. "French Police, German Troops and the Destruction of the Old Districts of Marseille, 1943." In *Policing and War in Europe*, edited by Louis Knafla, 133–144. Westport, Conn.: Greenwood Press, 2002.

———. "The Police and the Deportation of Jews from the Bouches-du-Rhône in August and September 1942." *Modern and Contemporary France* 5, no. 3 (August 1997): 309–319.

Kleinman, Mark. *Housing, Welfare, and the State in Europe: A Comparative Analysis of Britain, France, and Germany*. Cheltenham, U.K.: E. Elgar, 1996.

Klemek, Christopher. *The Transatlantic Collapse of Urban Renewal Postwar Urbanisms from New York to Berlin*. Chicago: University of Chicago Press, 2011.

Kokoreff, Michel. *La force des quartiers: De la délinquance à l'engagement politique*. Paris: Payot, 2003.

Koven, Seth, and Sonya Michel. "Womanly Duties: Maternalist Politics and the Origins of Welfare States in France, Germany, Great Britain, and the United States, 1880–1920." *The American Historical Review* 95, no. 4 (October 1990): 1076–1108.

Kugelberg, Johan, Joe Conzo, and Afrika Bambaataa. *Born in the Bronx: A Visual Record of the Early Days of Hip Hop*. New York: Rizzoli, 2007.

Kühl, Stefan. *The Nazi Connection: Eugenics, American Racism, and German National Socialism*. Oxford: Oxford University Press, 1994.

Kuisel, Richard F. *Capitalism and the State in Modern France: Renovation and Economic Management in the Twentieth Century*. Cambridge: Cambridge University Press, 1981.

——. *Ernest Mercier: French Technocrat*. Berkeley: University of California Press, 1967.

——. *Seducing the French: The Dilemma of Americanization*. Berkeley: University of California Press, 1993.

Kymlicka, Will. *Multicultural Citizenship: A Liberal Theory of Minority Rights*. Oxford: Oxford University Press, 1995.

——. *Multicultural Odysseys: Navigating the New International Politics of Diversity*. Oxford: Oxford University Press, 2007.

——. *Politics in the Vernacular: Nationalism, Multiculturalism and Citizenship*. Oxford: Oxford University Press, 2001.

Laborde, Cécile. "The Culture(s) of the Republic: Nationalism and Multiculturalism in French Republican Thought." *Political Theory* 29, no. 5 (2001): 716–735.

Ladd, Brian. *The Ghosts of Berlin: Confronting German History in the Urban Landscape*. Chicago: University of Chicago Press, 1998.

Ladd-Taylor, Molly. *Mother-Work: Women, Child Welfare, and the State, 1890–1930*. Urbana: University of Illinois Press, 1994.

Lafargue de Grangeneuve, Loïc. *Politique du hip-hop: Action publique et cultures urbaines*. Toulouse: Presses universitaires du Mirail, 2008.

Lagayette, Pierre, ed. *Géopolitique et mondialisation*. Paris: Sorbonne, 2003.

Lebovics, Herman. *Bringing the Empire Back Home: France in the Global Age*. Durham, N.C.: Duke University Press, 2004.

——. *Mona Lisa's Escort: André Malraux and the Reinvention of French Culture*. Ithaca, N.Y.: Cornell University Press, 1999.

——. *True France: The Wars over Cultural Identity, 1900–1945*. Ithaca, N.Y.: Cornell University Press, 1994.

Le Bras, Hervé. *Le sol et le sang*. La Tour d'Aigues: Editions de l'Aube, 1994.

Lefebvre, Henri. *Critique of Everyday Life*. London: Verso, 2008.

——. *The Production of Space*. Oxford: Blackwell, 1991.

Lehning, James R. *Peasant and French: Cultural Contact in Rural France during the Nineteenth Century*. Cambridge: Cambridge University Press, 1995.

Lequin, Yves. *Histoire des étrangers et de l'immigration en France*. Paris: Larousse, 1992.

——. *La Mosaïque, France: Histoire des étrangers et de l'immigration*. Paris: Larousse, 1988.

Le Sueur, James D. *The Decolonization Reader*. New York: Routledge, 2003.

——. *Uncivil War: Intellectuals and Identity Politics during the Decolonization of Algeria*. 2nd ed. Lincoln: University of Nebraska Press, 2005.

Levine, Philippa. *Gender and Empire*. New York: Oxford University Press, 2004.

——. *Prostitution, Race, and Politics: Policing Venereal Disease in the British Empire*. New York: Routledge, 2003.

Lewis, Jane. *The Politics of Motherhood: Child and Maternal Welfare in England, 1990–1939*. Montreal: McGill-Queen's University Press, 1980.

Lewis, Mary Dewhurst. *The Boundaries of the Republic: Migrant Rights and the Limits of Universalism in France, 1918–1940*. Stanford, Calif.: Stanford University Press, 2007.

——. "The Strangeness of Foreigners: Policing Migration and Nation in Interwar Marseille." *French Politics, Culture & Society* 20, no. 3 (Fall 2002): 65–96.

Liscia, Claude. "Miroir sans reflet: La famille dans les cités de transit." *Esprit* 5, no. 65 (Mai 1982): 43–60.

Loew, Jacques. *Mission to the Poorest*. New York: Sheed &Ward, 1950.

Lombroso, Cesare, Mary Gibson, and Nicole Hahn Rafter. *Criminal Man*. Durham, N.C.: Duke University Press, 2006.

Londres, Albert. *Oeuvres complètes*. Paris: Arléa, 2007.

Lopez, Renée, and Emile Témime. *Histoire des migrations à Marseille. 2, L'expansion marseillaise et l'invasion italienne*. Aix-en-Provence: Edisud, 1990.

Lorcin, Patricia M. E. *Algeria and France, 1800–2000: Identity, Memory, Nostalgia*. Syracuse, N.Y.: Syracuse University Press, 2006.

———. *Imperial Identities: Stereotyping, Prejudice and Race in Colonial Algeria*. London: I. B. Tauris, 1995.

Lüdtke, Alf, ed. *The History of Everyday Life: Reconstructing Historical Experiences and Ways of Life*. Princeton, N.J.: Princeton University Press, 1995.

Lyons, Amelia. *The Civilizing Mission in the Metropole: Algerian Families and the French Welfare State during Decolonization*. Stanford, Calif.: Stanford University Press, 2013.

———. "Invisible Immigrants: Algerian Families and the French Welfare State, 1947–1974." PhD diss., University of California–Irvine, 2004.

MacMaster, Neil. *Colonial Migrants and Racism. Algerians in France, 1900–1962*. New York: St. Martin's Press, 1997.

Mann, Gregory. *Native Sons: West African Veterans and France in the Twentieth Century*. Durham, N.C.: Duke University Press, 2006.

Marcus, Jonathan. *The National Front and French Politics: The Resistible Rise of Jean-Marie Le Pen*. New York: New York University Press, 1995.

Marcuse, Harold. *Legacies of Dachau: The Uses and Abuses of a Concentration Camp, 1933–2001*. Cambridge: Cambridge University Press, 2001.

Marion, Georges. *Gaston Defferre*. Paris: Albin Michel, 1989.

Marshall, T. H. *Citizenship and Social Class, and Other Essays*. Cambridge: Cambridge University Press, 1950.

Massenet, Michel. *Sauvage immigration*. Monaco: Editions du Rocher, 1994.

Massey, Doreen. *For Space*. London: SAGE, 2005.

Mattsson, Helena, and Sven-Olov Wallenstein, eds. *Swedish Modernism: Architecture, Consumption and the Welfare State*. London: Black Dog Publishing, 2010.

Maury, Yan. *Les HLM: L'état providence vu d'en bas*. Paris: L'Harmattan, 2001.

Mazower, Mark. *Dark Continent: Europe's Twentieth Century*. New York: Knopf, 1999.

———. *No Enchanted Palace: The End of Empire and the Ideological Origins of the United Nations*. Princeton, N.J.: Princeton University Press, 2008.

Mazur, Amy. *Gender Bias and the State: Symbolic Reform at Work in Fifth Republic France*. Pittsburgh, Pa.: University of Pittsburgh Press, 1995.

McCaffery, Peter. *When Bosses Ruled Philadelphia: The Emergence of the Republican Machine, 1867–1933*. University Park: Pennsylvania State University Press, 1993.

McCarren, Felicia. "Monsieur Hip-Hop." In *Blackening Europe: The African American Presence*, edited by Heike Raphael-Hernandez, 157–170. New York: Routledge, 2004.

McCoy, Alfred W. *The Politics of Heroin: CIA Complicity in the Global Drug Trade*. Brooklyn, N.Y.: Lawrence Hill Books, 1991.

McKay, Claude. *Banjo*. London: X Press, 2000.

Memmi, Albert, and Robert Bononno. *Decolonization and the Decolonized*. Minneapolis: University of Minnesota Press, 2006.

Mencherini, Robert. *La libération et les entreprises sous gestion ouvrière Marseille, 1944–1948*. Paris: L'Harmattan, 1994.

———. *Ici-même: Marseille 1940–1944: De la défaite à la libération.* Marseille: J. Laffitte, 2013.

Mencherini, Robert, and Yves Jeanmougin. *Mémoire du camp des Milles, 1939–1942.* Marseille: Métamorphoses-ben en l'air, 2013.

Merriman, John. *The Margins of City Life: Explorations on the French Urban Frontier.* New York: Oxford University Press, 1991.

Milza, Pierre, and Denis Peschanski, eds. *Exils et migration: Italiens et espagnols en France, 1938–1946.* Paris: L'Harmattan, 1994.

Mischi, Julian. *Le communisme désarmé: Le PCF et les classes populaires depuis les années 1970.* Marseille: Agone, 2014.

Mitchell, Tony. *Global Noise: Rap and Hip-Hop Outside the USA.* Middletown, Conn.: Wesleyan University Press, 2001.

Moch, Leslie Page. *Moving Europeans: Migration in Western Europe since 1650.* Bloomington: Indiana University Press, 1992.

———. *Paths to the City: Regional Migration in Nineteenth-century France.* Beverly Hills, Calif.: Sage Publications, 1983.

Moïse, Claudine. "Dire la danse hip-hop, questions de transmission et de création." In *Histoires de corps: A propos de la formation du danseur,* edited by Centre de ressources musique et danse, 119–132. Paris: Cité de la musique, 1998.

Moore, Damian. *Ethnicité et politique de la ville en France et en Grande Bretagne.* Paris: L'Harmattan, 2001.

Mosse, George L. *Nationalism and Sexuality: Respectability and Abnormal Sexuality in Modern Europe.* 1st ed. New York: H. Fertig, 1985.

Mousnier, Rouland. *Les institutions de la France sous la monarchie absolue.* Vol. 1: *Société et état.* Paris: Presses universitaires de France, 1974.

Moyn, Samuel. *The Last Utopia: Human Rights in History.* Cambridge, Mass.: Harvard University Press, 2010.

Mulvey, Michael. "Sheltering French Families: Parisian Suburbia and the Politics of Housing, 1939–1975." PhD diss., University of North Carolina–Chapel Hill, 2011.

Nasiali, Minayo. "Citizens, Squatters and Asocials: The Right to Housing and the Politics of Difference in Post-Liberation France." *The American Historical Review,* 119, no. 2 (April 2014): 434–459.

———. "Ordering the Disorderly Slum: 'Standardizing' Quality of Life in Marseille Tenements and Bidonvilles, 1953–1962." *Journal of Urban History* 38, no. 6 (November 2012): 1021–1035.

Naylor, Ed, ed. "The Politics of a Presence: Algerians in Marseille from Independence to 'Immigration Sauvage' (1962–1974)." PhD diss., Queen Mary University of London, 2011.

N'Diaye, Pap. "Pour une histoire des populations noires en France: Préalables théoriques." *Le Mouvement Social,* no. 213 (2005): 91–108.

Neveu, Catherine. *Citoyenneté et espace public: Habitants, jeunes et citoyens dans une ville du nord.* Villeneuve d'Ascq: Presses universitaires du Septentrion, 2003.

———. *Espace public et engagement politique: Enjeux et logiques de la citoyenneté locale.* Paris: L'Harmattan, 1999.

Newsome, Brian. "The 'Apartment Referendum' of 1959: Toward Participatory Architectural and Urban Planning in Postwar France." *French Historical Studies* 28, no. 2 (2005): 329–358.

———. *French Urban Planning, 1940–1968: The Construction and Deconstruction of an Authoritarian System.* New York: Peter Lang, 2009.

———. "The Rise of the Grands Ensembles: Government, Business and Housing in Postwar France." *The Historian* 66, no. 4 (2004): 793–816.

Niehuss, Merith. "French and German Family Policy 1945–60." *Contemporary European History* 4, no. 3 (November 1995): 293–313.

Noiriel, Gérard. *Etat, nation et immigration: Vers une histoire du pouvoir*. Paris: Belin, 2001.

——. *Immigration, antisémitisme et racisme en France, XIXe–XXe siècles: Discours publics, humiliations privées*. Paris: Fayard, 2007.

——. *Le creuset français: Histoire de l'immigration XIXe–XXe siècles*. Paris: Seuil, 1988.

Noiriel, Gérard, and FASILD. *Atlas de l'immigration en France: Exclusion, intégration*. Paris: Autrement, 2002.

Noiriel, Gérard, and Bertrand Richard. *Racisme, la responsabilité des élites*. Paris: Textuel, 2007.

Nora, Pierre. *Les lieux de mémoire*. Paris: Gallimard, 1984.

Nord, Philip. *France's New Deal: From the Thirties to the Postwar Era*. Princeton, N.J.: Princeton University Press, 2010.

——. *The Republican Moment: The Struggle for Democracy in Nineteenth-Century France*. Cambridge, Mass.: Harvard University Press, 1995.

——. "The Welfare State in France, 1870–1914." *French Historical Studies* 18, no. 3 (1994): 821–838.

Nye, Robert A. "The Bio-Medical Origins of Urban Sociology." *Journal of Contemporary History* 20, no. 4 (October 1985): 659–675.

——. *Crime, Madness, and Politics in Modern France: The Medical Concept of National Decline*. Princeton, N.J.: Princeton University Press, 1984.

Organisation for Economic Co-operation and Development. "The Welfare State in Crisis: An Account of the Conference on Social Policies in the 1980s, OECD, Paris, 20–23 October 1981." OECD Publications and Information Center, 1983.

Pacini, Alfred, and Dominque Pons. *Docker à Marseille*. Paris: Payot/Rivages, 1996.

Parisis, Jean-Louis. *La logirem à 40 ans: 1960–2000*. Marseille: Logirem, 2000.

——. *Office Public d'HLM de Marseille, Paroles de locataires 1919–1989*. Avignon: A. Barthélemy, 1989.

Pateman, Carole. "The Patriarchal Welfare State." In *Democracy and the Welfare State*, edited by Amy Gutman, 231–260. Princeton, N.J.: Princeton University Press, 1988.

Pattieu, Sylvain. "Souteneurs noirs à Marseille, 1918–1921: Contribution à l'histoire de la minorité noire en France." *Annales Histoire, Sciences Sociales*, no. 6 (novembre–décembre 2009): 1361–1386.

Paugam, Serge. *La société française et ses pauvres: L'expérience du revenu minimum d'insertion*. Paris: Presses universitaires de France, 2002.

——. *Le salarié de la précarité: Les nouvelles formes de l'intégration professionnelle*. Paris: Presses universitaires de France, 2000.

——. *Les formes élémentaires de la pauvreté*. Paris: Presses universitaires de France, 2005.

Paul, Kathleen. *Whitewashing Britain: Race and Citizenship in the Postwar Era*. Ithaca, N.Y.: Cornell University Press, 1997.

Paxton, Robert O. *Vichy France: Old Guard and New Order, 1940–1944*. New York: Knopf, 2001.

Peabody, Sue, and Tyler Edward Stovall. *The Color of Liberty: Histories of Race in France*. Durham, N.C.: Duke University Press, 2003.

Péchu, Cécile. *Droit au logement: Genèse et sociologie d'une mobilisation*. Paris: Dalloz, 2006.

Pedersen, Susan. *Family, Dependence, and the Origins of the Welfare State: Britain and France, 1914–1945*. Cambridge: Cambridge University Press, 1993.

Peraldi, Michel, "Les noms du social dans l'urbain en crise." *Peuples Méditerranéens*, no. 43 (avril–juin 1988): 5–22.

Peraldi, Michel, and Michel Samson. *Gouverner Marseille: Enquête sur les mondes politiques Marseillais*. Paris: La Découverte, 2006.

Peraldi, Michel, Claire Duport, and Michel Samson. *Sociologie de Marseille*. Paris: La Découverte, 2015.

Perrineau, Pascal. "The Great Upheaval: Left and Right in Contemporary French Politics" In *France since the 1970s: History, Politics and Memory in an Age of Uncertainty*, edited by Emile Chabal, 25–40. London: Bloomsbury, 2015.

Petit, Jacques G., and Christine Bard. *Intégration et exclusion sociale: D'hier à aujourd'hui*. Paris: Anthropos, 1999.

Petitclerc, Jean-Marie. *Les nouvelles délinquances des jeunes: Violences urbaines et réponses éducatives*. Paris: Dunod, 2001.

Pick, Daniel. *Faces of Degeneration: A European Disorder, c.1848–c.1918*. Cambridge: Cambridge University Press, 1989.

Pinto, Pedro Ramos. "Housing and Citizenship: Building Social Rights in Twentieth-Century Portugal." *Contemporary European History* 18, no. 2 (May 2009): 199–215.

Qualls, Karl D. *From Ruins to Reconstruction: Urban Identity in Soviet Sevastopol after World War II*. Ithaca, N.Y.: Cornell University Press, 2009.

Quintana, Isabela Seong-Leong. "National Borders, Neighborhood Boundaries: Gender, Space and Border Formation in Chinese and Mexican Los Angeles, 1871–1938." PhD diss., University of Michigan, 2010.

Rabinow, Paul. *French Modern: Norms and Forms of the Social Environment*. Chicago: University of Chicago Press, 1995.

Radford, Gail. *Modern Housing for America: Policy Struggles in the New Deal Era*. Chicago: University of Chicago Press, 1996.

Ravetz, Alison. *Council Housing and Culture: The History of a Social Experiment*. London: Routledge, 2001.

Reddy, William. "Postmodernism and the Public Sphere: Implications for an Historical Ethnography." *Cultural Anthropology* 7 (1992): 135–169.

Reeve, Kesia. "Squatting since 1945." In *Housing and Social Policy: Contemporary Themes and Critical Perspectives*, edited by Peter Somerville and Nigel Sprigings, 197–216. New York: Routledge, 2005.

Reggiani, Andrés Horacio. *God's Eugenicist: Alexis Carrel and the Sociobiology of Decline*. New York: Berghahn Books, 2007.

——. "Procreating France: The Politics of Demongraphy, 1919–1945." *French Historical Studies* 19, no. 3 (Spring 1996): 725–754.

Robcis, Camille. *The Law of Kinship: Anthropology, Psychoanalysis, and the Family in Twentieth-Century France*. Ithaca, N.Y.: Cornell University Press, 2013.

Roberts, John. *Philosophizing the Everyday: Revolutionary Praxis and the Fate of Cultural Theory*. London: Pluto Press, 2006.

Roman, Joel. "Pour un multiculturalisme temperé." *Hommes et Migrations* 1197 (1996): 18–22.

——. "Un multiculturalisme à la française." *Esprit* 212 (1995): 145–160.

Roncayolo, Marcel. *Les grammaires d'une ville: Essai sur la genèse des structures urbaines à Marseille*. Paris: Ecole des hautes études en sciences sociales, 1996.

——. *L'imaginaire de Marseille: Port, ville, pôle*. Marseille: Chambre de commerce et d'industrie de Marseille, 1990.

——. *Marseille: Les territoires du temps*. Paris: Editions locales de France, 1996.

Rosanvallon, Pierre. *La crise de l'Etat providence*. Paris: Seuil, 1981.

——. *La nouvelle question sociale: Repenser l'état-providence*. Paris: Seuil, 1995.

——. *The New Social Question: Rethinking the Welfare State*. Princeton, N.J.: Princeton University Press, 2000.

Rosenberg, Clifford D. *Policing Paris: The Origins of Modern Immigration Control between the Wars.* Ithaca, N.Y.: Cornell University Press, 2006.

Rosenfeld, Gavriel D., and Paul B. Jaskot, eds. *Beyond Berlin: Twelve German Cities Confront the Nazi Past.* Ann Arbor: University of Michigan Press, 2008.

Rosental, Paul-André. *L'intelligence démographique: Sciences et politiques des populations en France, 1930–1960.* Paris: O. Jacob, 2003.

———. "Pour une histoire politique des populations." *Annales. Histoire, Sciences Sociales* 1 (January–February 2006): 7–29.

Rose, Sonya. *Which People's War?: National Identity and Citizenship in Britain, 1939–1945.* New York: Oxford University Press, 2003.

Ross, Kristin. *Fast Cars, Clean Bodies: Decolonization and the Reordering of French Culture.* Cambridge, Mass.: MIT Press, 1995.

———. *May '68 and Its Afterlives.* Chicago: University of Chicago Press, 2002.

Rudolph, Nicole. *At Home in Postwar France: Modern Mass Housing and the Right to Comfort.* New York, Berghahn, 2015.

Ryan, Diana F. *The Holocaust and the Jews of Marseille: The Enforcement of Anti-Semitic Politics in Vichy France.* Champaign: University of Illinois Press, 1996.

Saada, Emmanuelle. *Empire's Children: Race, Filiation, and Citizenship in the French Colonies.* Chicago: University of Chicago Press, 2012.

Sadler, Simon. *The Situationist City.* Cambridge, Mass.: MIT Press, 1998.

Sanchez, George J. *Becoming Mexican American: Ethnicity, Culture and Identity in Chicano Los Angeles, 1900–1945.* New York: Oxford University Press, 1993.

Sanmarco, Philippe. "Le clientélisme, comment ça marche? Clientélisme et politique en région Provence Alpes Côte D'azur." In *Démocratie et territoires,* Université d'Aix-Marseille: Centre d'études en sciences sociales appliquées et appuis, recherche, éducation pour la négociation locale sur les environnements, 2003.

Sberna, Beatrice. *Une sociologie du rap à Marseille: Identité marginale et immigrée.* Paris: L'Harmattan, 2001.

Sbriglio, Jacques. *Le Corbusier: L'unité d'habitation de Marseille et les autres unités d'habitation à Rezé-Les-Nantes, Berlin, Briey en Forêt et Firminy.* Paris: Fondation Le Corbusier, 2004.

Schloss, Joseph Glenn. *Foundation: B-Boys, B-Girls, and Hip-Hop Culture in New York.* Oxford: Oxford University Press, 2009.

Schnapper, Dominique. *Exclusions au coeur de la cité.* Paris: Anthropos, 2001.

———. *Le communauté des citoyens: Sur l'idée moderne de nation.* Paris: Gallimard, 1994.

Schneider, William. *Quality and Quantity: The Quest for Biological Regeneration in Twentieth-Century France.* Cambridge: Cambridge University Press, 1990.

Schor, Ralph. *L'opinion française et les étrangers, 1919–1939.* Paris: Publications de la Sorbonne, 1985.

Scioldo-Zürcher, Yann. *Devenir métropolitain: Politique d'intégration et parcours de rapatriés d'Algérie en métropole (1954–2005).* Paris: Editions de l'Ecole des hautes études en sciences sociales, 2010.

Scott, Joan Wallach. *Only Paradoxes to Offer: French Feminists and the Rights of Man.* Cambridge, Mass.: Harvard University Press, 1996.

———. *Parité! Sexual Equality and the Crisis of French Universalism.* Chicago: University of Chicago Press, 2005.

———. *The Politics of the Veil.* Princeton, N.J.: Princeton University Press, 2007.

Scullion, Rosemarie. "On the Waterfront: Class Action and Anti-Colonial Engagements in Paul Carpita's *Le Rendez-vous des quais.*" *South Central Review* 17, no. 3 (Autumn 2000): 35–49.

Sengel, Marie. "Nana-Benz de Noailles." *Hommes et Migrations* 1224 (Mars–Avril 2000): 71–78.

Sewell, Sara Ann. "Bolshevizing Communist Women: The Red Women and Girls' League in Weimar Germany." *Central European History* 45, no. 2 (June 2012): 268–305.

Sewell, William H., Jr. *Structure and Mobility: The Men and Women of Marseille, 1820–1870.* Cambridge: Cambridge University Press, 1985.

Shapiro, Ann-Louise. *Housing the Poor of Paris, 1850–1902.* Madison: University of Wisconsin Press, 1985.

Shapiro, Ian, and Will Kymlicka. *Ethnicity and Group Rights.* New York: New York University Press, 1997.

Shapiro, Roberta. "The Aesthetics of Institutionalization: Breakdancing in France." *Journal of Arts Managements, Law, and Society* 33, no. 4 (2004): 316–335.

Shennan, Andrew. *Rethinking France: Plans for Renewal, 1940–1946.* Oxford: Oxford University Press, 1989.

Shepard, Todd. *The Invention of Decolonization: The Algerian War and the Remaking of France.* Ithaca, N.Y.: Cornell University Press, 2006.

Shields, James. "The Front National since the 1970s: Electoral Impact and Party System Change." In *France since the 1970s: History, Politics and Memory in an Age of Uncertainty,* edited by Emile Chabal, 41–64. London: Bloomsbury, 2015.

Silverman, Maxim. *Deconstructing the Nation: Immigration, Racism, and Citizenship in Modern France.* New York: Routledge, 1992.

——. *Race, Discourse, and Power in France.* Aldershot: Avebury, 1991.

Simpson, A. W. B. *Human Rights and the End of Empire: Britain and the Genesis of the European Convention.* Oxford: Oxford University Press, 2001.

Smith, Cecil O., Jr. "The Longest Run: Public Engineers and Planning in France." *The American Historical Review* 95, no. 3 (1990): 657–692.

Smith, Mark B. *Property of Communists: The Urban Housing Program from Stalin to Khrushchev.* DeKalb: Northern Illinois University Press, 2010.

Smith, Timothy B. *Creating the Welfare State in France, 1880–1940.* Montreal: McGill-Queen's University Press, 2003.

——. *France in Crisis: Welfare, Inequality, and Globalization since 1980.* Cambridge: Cambridge University Press, 2004.

Somers, Margaret. "Let Them Eat Social Capital." *Thesis Eleven* 81 (May 2005): 5–19.

Sonn, Richard. "Your Body Is Yours: Anarchism, Birth Control, and Eugenics in Interwar France." *Journal of the History of Sexuality* 14, no. 4 (2005): 415–432.

Sopo, Dominique. *S.O.S. Antiracisme.* Paris: Denoël, 2005.

Soysal, Levent. "Rap, Hip hop, Kreuzberg: Scripts of/for Migrant Youth Culture in the World City Berlin." *New German Critique* 92 (Spring–Summer 2004): 62–81.

Soysal, Yasemin. *Limits of Citizenship: Migrants and Postnational Membership in Europe.* Chicago: University of Chicago Press, 1994.

Spencer, Ian R. G. *British Immigration Policy since 1939: The Making of Multi-Racial Britain.* New York: Routledge, 1997.

Spire, Alexis. *Etrangers à la carte: L'administration de l'immigration en France, 1945–1975.* Paris: Grasset, 2005.

Stébé, Jean-Marc. *Le logement social en France: 1789 à nos jours.* Paris: Presses universitaires de France, 2002.

Steedman, Carolyn. *Landscape for a Good Woman: A Story of Two Lives.* New Brunswick, N.J.: Rutgers University Press, 1987.

——. *The Tidy House: Little Girls Writing.* London: Virago, 1982.

Steege, Paul, Andrew Stuart Bergerson, Maureen Healy, and Pamela E. Swett. "The History of Everyday Life: A Second Chapter," *Journal of Modern History* 80 (June 2008): 358–378.

Steinhouse, Adam. *Workers' Participation in Post-Liberation France*. Lanham, Md.: Lexington Books, 2001.

Steinmetz, George. *Regulating the Social: The Welfare State and Local Politics in Imperial Germany*. Princeton, N.J.: Princeton University Press, 1993.

Sternhell, Steev. *Neither Right nor Left: Fascist Ideology in France*. Princeton, N.J.: Princeton University Press, 1996.

Stewart, Mary Lynn. *Women, Work and the French State: Labour Protection and Social Patriarchy, 1879–1919*. Kingston, Ont.: McGill-Queen's University Press, 1989.

Stieber, Nancy. *Housing Design and Society in Amsterdam: Reconfiguring Urban Order and Identity, 1990–1920*. Chicago: University of Chicago Press, 1998.

Stoler, Ann Laura. *Carnal Knowledge and Imperial Power: Race and the Intimate in Colonial Rule*. Berkeley: University of California Press, 2002.

Stora, Benjamin. *Histoire de la guerre d'Algérie (1954–1962)*. 4th ed. Paris: La Découverte, 2004.

——. *La gangrène et l'oubli: La mémoire de la guerre D'Algérie*. Paris: La Découverte, 1991.

Stora, Benjamin, and Emile Témime. *Immigrances: L'immigration en France au XXe siècle*. Paris: Hachette, 2007.

Stovall, Tyler Edward. "The Color Line behind the Lines: Racial Violence in France during the Great War." *The American Historical Review* 103, no. 3 (1998): 737–769.

——. *Paris and the Spirit of 1919: Consumer Struggles, Transnationalism, and Revolution*. Cambridge: Cambridge University Press, 2012.

——. *The Rise of the Paris Red Belt*. Berkeley: University of California Press, 1990.

Stovall, Tyler Edward, and Georges van den Abbeele. *French Civilization and Its Discontents: Nationalism, Colonialism, Race*. Lanham, Md.: Lexington Books, 2003.

Surkis, Judith. *Sexing the Citizen: Morality and Masculinity in France, 1870–1920*. Ithaca, N.Y.: Cornell University Press, 2006.

Swett, Pamela E. *Neighbors and Enemies: The Culture of Radicalism in Berlin, 1929–1933*. Cambridge: Cambridge University Press, 2004.

Tabili, Laura. *We Ask for British Justice: Workers and Racial Difference in Late Imperial Britain*. Ithaca, N.Y.: Cornell University Press, 1994.

Taguieff, Pierre-André. *La force du préjugé: Essai sur la racisme et ses doubles*. Paris: La Découverte, 1987.

Taguieff, Pierre-André, and Michèle Tribalat. *Face au Front national: Arguments pour une contre-offensive*. Paris: La Découverte, 1998.

Takeda, Junko. *Between Crown and Commerce: Marseille and the Early Modern Mediterranean*. Baltimore: Johns Hopkins University Press, 2011.

Témime, Emile. *Histoire de Marseille: De la révolution à nos jours*. Paris: Perrin, 1999.

——. *Le camp du Grand Arénas, Marseille 1944–1966*. Paris: Autrement, 2001.

——. *Marseille transit: Les passagers de Belsunce*. Paris: Autrement, 1995.

Témime, Emile, and Pierre Echinard. *Migrance: Histoire des migrations à Marseille*. Aix-en-Provence: Edisud, 1989.

Terrio, Susan J. "You'll Get Your Day in Court: Judging Delinquent Youth at the Paris Palace of Justice." *Political and Legal Anthropology Review*, no. 26 (2003): 136–164.

Thoenig, Jean-Claude. *L'ère des technocrats: Le cas des ponts et chaussées*. Paris: L'Harmattan, 1987.

Thompson, Elizabeth. *Colonial Citizens: Republican Rights, Paternal Privilege, and Gender in French Syria and Lebanon*. New York: Columbia University Press, 2000.

Thompson, E. P. *The Making of the English Working Class*. New York: Pantheon Books, 1964.

Tissot, Sylvie. *L'état et les quartiers: Genèse d'une catégorie de l'action publique.* Paris: Seuil, 2007.

Todd, Emmanuel. *The Making of Modern France: Ideology, Politics and Culture.* Oxford: Blackwell, 1991.

Topalov, Christian. *Le logement en France: Histoire d'une merchandise impossible.* Paris: Presses de la Fondation nationale des sciences politiques, 1987.

Touraine, Alain, Jon Clark, and Marco Diani. *Alain Touraine.* London: Falmer Press, 1996.

Tribalat, Michèle. *Faire France: Une grande enquête sur les immigrés et leurs enfants.* Paris: La Découverte, 1995.

Tricart, Jean-Paul. "Genèse d'un dispositive d'assistance: Les 'cités de transit.'" *Revue française de sociologie* 18, no. 4 (October–December 1977): 601–624.

Vadelorge, Loic. "Villes nouvelles et grands ensembles." *Histoire Urbaine* 17, no. 3 (2006): 67–84.

Viard, Jean. *Marseille, une ville impossible.* Paris: Payot & Rivages, 1995.

Viet, Vincent. "La politique du logement des immigrés (1945–1990)." *Vingtième siècle* 64, no. 1 (1999): 91–103.

Voldman, Danièle. "Aménager la région parisienne (février 1950–août 1960)." *Cahiers de l'Institut d'histoire du temps présent,* no. 17 (1990): 49–54.

——. *Fernand Pouillon.* Paris: Payot, 2006.

——. *Images, discours et enjeux de la reconstruction des villes françaises après 1945.* Paris: Centre national de la recherche scientifique, 1987.

——. *La Reconstruction des villes françaises de 1940 à 1954: Histoire d'une politique.* Paris: L'Harmattan, 1997.

Voldman, Danèle, ed. *Désirs de toit: Le logement entre désire et contrainte depuis la fin du XIXe siècle.* Grâne: Créaphis éditions, 2010.

Vulbeau, Alain. "De la sarcellite au malaise des banlieues: Trente ans de pathologie des grands ensembles." *Lumières de la ville* 5 (1992): 31–37.

Wacquant, Loïc. "Urban Marginality in the Coming Millennium." *Urban Studies* 36, no. 10 (1999): 1639–1647.

Wakeman, Rosemary. *The Heroic City: Paris, 1945–1958.* Chicago: University of Chicago Press, 2009.

——. *Modernizing the Provincial City: Toulouse, 1945–1975.* Cambridge, Mass.: Harvard University Press, 1997.

——. "Reconstruction and the Self-Help Housing Movement: The French Experience." *Housing Studies* 14, no. 3 (1999): 355–366.

Wall, Richard. *The Upheaval of War: Family, Work and Welfare in Europe, 1914–1918.* Cambridge: Cambridge University Press, 1988.

Weber, Eugen. *Peasants into Frenchmen: The Modernization of Rural France, 1870–1914.* Stanford, Calif.: Stanford University Press, 1976.

Weil, Patrick. "Immigration and the Rise of Racism in France: The Contradictions in Mitterrand's Policies." *French Politics and Society* 9, no. 3/4 (Summer/Fall 1991): 82–100.

——. *La France et ses étrangers: L'aventure d'une politique de l'immigration de 1938 à nos jours.* Paris: Gallimard, 2005.

——. *La république et sa diversité: Immigration, intégration, discrimination.* Paris: Seuil, 2005.

——. "Racisme et discrimination dans la politique française de l'immigration 1938–1945/1974–1995." *Vingtième siècle* 47 (July–September 1995): 77–102.

Weil, Patrick, and Randall Hansen. *Nationalité et citoyenneté en Europe.* Paris: La Découverte, 1999.

Weil, Patrick, and Catherine Porter. *How to Be French: Nationality in the Making since 1789.* Durham, N.C.: Duke University Press, 2008.

Whitney, Susan B. *Mobilizing Youth: Communists and Catholics in Interwar France.* Durham, N.C.: Duke University Press, 2009.

Wievorka, Michel. *Commenter La France.* Paris: Editions de l'aube, 1997.

———. "Is Multiculturalism the Solution?" *Ethnic and Racial Studies* 21, no. 5 (1998): 881–910.

———. "Le multiculturalisme, est-il la réponse?" *Cahiers internationaux de sociologie* 105 (1998): 233–260.

———, ed. *Une société fragmentée.* Paris: La Découverte, 1996.

Wihtol de Wenden, Catherine. *Citoyenneté, nationalité et immigration.* Paris: Arcantère, 1987.

———. *La citoyenneté européenne.* Paris: Presses de Sciences Po, 1997.

———. *Les immigrés dans la cité: La représentation des immigrés dans la vie publique en Europe.* Paris: Documentation française, 1978.

———. *Les immigrés et la politique: Cent cinquante ans d'évolution.* Paris: Presses de la Fondation nationale des sciences politiques avec le concours du Centre national de la recherche scientifique, 1988.

Wihtol de Wenden, Catherine, and Rémy Leveau. *La Beurgeoisie: Les trois âges de la vie associative issue de l'immigration.* Paris: CNRS, 2001.

Wild, Mark. *Street Meeting: Multiethnic Neighborhoods in Early Twentieth-Century Los Angeles.* Berkeley: University of California Press, 2005.

Wildenthal, Lora. *German Women for Empire, 1884–1945.* Durham, N.C.: Duke University Press, 2001.

Wilder, Gary. *The French Imperial Nation-State: Negritude and Colonial Humanism between the Two World Wars.* Chicago: University of Chicago Press, 2005.

Wood, Nancy. "Remembering the Jews of Algeria." In *French Civilization and Its Discontents,* edited by Tyler Stovall and Georges van den Abbeele, 251–270. Lanham, Md.: Lexington Books, 2003.

Wood, Simon. *From the Cradle to the Grave, Social Welfare in Britain, 1890s.* London: Hodder & Stoughton Educational, 2002.

Wright, Gwendolyn. *The Politics of Design in French Colonial Urbanism.* Chicago: University of Chicago Press, 1991.

Wright, Patrick. *On Living in an Old Country: The National Past in Contemporary Britain.* London: Verso, 1985.

Ysmal, Colette. *La carrière politique de Gaston Defferre.* Paris: Fondation nationale des sciences politiques, 1965.

Zahra, Tara. *The Lost Children: Reconstructing Europe's Families after World War II.* Cambridge, Mass.: Harvard University Press, 2011.

Zarecor, Kimberly Elman. *Manufacturing a Socialist Modernity: Housing in Czechoslovakia, 1945–1960.* Pittsburgh, Pa.: University of Pittsburgh Press, 2011.

Index

Note: Page numbers in italics refer to figures.

CPSIA information can be obtained
at www.ICGtesting.com
Printed in the USA
LVOW11*1914030517

533129LV00006B/56/P